RECONCILING INTERNATIONAL HUMAN RIGHTS AND CULTURE

RECONCILING INTERNATIONAL HUMAN RIGHTS AND CULTURE

MK Prasad

MD PUBLICATIONS PVT LTD
NEW DELHI
www.mdppl.com

Published by:

MD Publications Pvt Ltd
"MD House", 11, Darya Ganj,
New Delhi - 110 002
Phone : +91-11-45355555
E-mail : contact@mdppl.com
website : www.mdppl.com

ISBN: 978-81-7533-306-2

Published and Printed by Mr. Pranav Gupta on behalf of **MD Publications Pvt Ltd** at JJ offset Printers, Delhi.

PREFACE

The United Nations, as is the case with so many organisations today, is preparing itself for the challenges and promises of the twenty-first century. Its founders recognized over 50 years ago that, in order for the United Nations to reach its goals of peace and security, development and human rights for all people, each goal would need to be pursued with equal vigour and understood as inextricably linked with the others.

The promise which the Universal Declaration of Human Rights symbolized at the time of its adoption today seems more possible than ever. The international community has made substantial progress over the past 50 years in the implementation of human rights concepts through the passage of nearly 50 human rights treaties and the establishment of international human rights machinery. Yet, the Universal Declaration still serves as the example by which we measure not only our successes and shortcomings, but also the foundation upon which we continue our efforts to make all human rights a reality. As this century quickly passes away, we should not only be proud of the advances made in the protection of human rights in the past 50 years, but also be increasingly aware of what still must be done to ensure that the rights many of us now take for granted are enjoyed by all people.

Human rights are an ever-present, ongoing challenge which must be met again and again. No one can be absolutely sure of their protection from one generation to the next. Even in those places where human rights may seem most secure, the message must continue to be heard. It must not be forgotten, however, that the primary responsibility for the promotion and protection of human rights remains with Governments. United Nations agencies or NGOs, important as they are, could never replace Governments in the difficult task of ensuring the enjoyment of human rights for all the people of a given State or territory. Support should be offered to Governments to assist in efforts such as developing national programmes related to ratification of treaties, adopting human rights legislation and strengthening capacities for addressing the rights of vulnerable groups.

Universal human rights are further established by the two international covenants on human rights (International Covenant on Economic, Social and Cultural Rights, and International Covenant on Civil and Political Rights), and the other international standard-setting instruments which address numerous concerns, including genocide, slavery, torture, racial discrimination, discrimination against women, rights of the child, minorities and religious tolerance.

These achievements in human rights standard-setting span nearly five decades of work by the United Nations General Assembly and other parts of the United Nations system. As an assembly of nearly every State in the international community, the General Assembly is a uniquely representative body authorized to address and advance the protection and promotion of human rights. As such, it serves as an excellent indicator of international consensus on human rights.

I am very grateful to Mr. Pranav Gupta, Director of MD Publications Pvt Ltd, New Delhi, for his kind cooperation and support for this book.

MK Prasad

Contents

1

Culture and Human Rights

The devastating human atrocities of World War II produced a major international commitment to the concept and practice of "universal human rights." This commitment was demonstrated in 1948, with the United Nations' adoption of the "Universal Declaration on Human Rights" and the "Convention on the Prevention and Punishment of the Crime of Genocide." Although these documents were negotiated among most of the then-existing states, from all regions of the world, the following decades were characterized by conflictual approaches to rights, with Western states supporting civic, political, and individual rights, and Socialist states championing socioeconomic and collective rights. Since the end of the Cold War, there has been a sharpening international conflict among governments over human rights.

While many formerly communist Eastern European nations have adopted a position sympathetic to civic and political rights of individuals, many governments in the developing world remain uneasy with, and on occasion even resentful of, what they perceive as Western triumphalism, interventionism, and cultural imperialism in the area of rights. While the question of universal human rights is embroiled in power politics, it has also given rise to renewed intellectual debate over longstanding issues of cultural relativism and universalism. Because the relativist side of the argument has been articulated most forcefully in this latest round of debate by some Asian governments, the discussion has been labelled the "Asian values debate." The debate has been at its best intense, multicultural, and intellectually substantial, developing arguments of significance within the areas of ethics, international law, and comparative politics.

In 1997, as part of its series of Summer Seminars for College Teachers, the National Endowment for the Humanities sponsored an eight-week seminar at Columbia University, led by Andrew J. Nathan, on "The Asian Values Debate: Human Rights and the Study of Culture as Problems for Area Studies." Fifteen college and university teachers gathered to discuss a series of issues related to the Asian values debate. Our members included two historians of modern China; five experts in comparative politics, with specialities in Chinese, Israeli, and Islamic (especially Pakistani) affairs; a moral philosopher, with interest and expertise in both Western and Buddhist thought; two lawyers, one of whom has a strong background in Chinese legal affairs and the other also having an advanced degree in ethics (and a strong interest in Buddhism); a communications specialist, with a focus on the Palestinian and Israeli presses; an anthropologist with a China focus, interested in issues of language and culture; a sociologist with a strong interest in communitarian thought; a historian of modern Russia; and two literature specialists.

We also had visiting participants who were experts of one kind or another on human rights issues. Three among the core group of fifteen had a very strong interest in feminist issues related to the Asian values debate, and encouraged the group as a whole to integrate feminist thinking and approaches into our discussions. From the start, we were uncomfortable with the rigid dichotomy embedded in the Asian values debate, between an arrogant universalism that seemed to force its values on others, and a morally vacuous relativism that seemed to flee from hard judgments and to justify non-democratic practices.

Through group debate and personal struggle we found common ground by the end of the summer in a chastened universalism which would seek to reconstitute the debate as a respectful, yet still assertive dialogue across cultures, in search not so much for pre-existing common values, but for ways to create them. This book articulates this position and its complexities, from a variety of disciplinary points of view. In so doing, it offers a new synthesis between uncritical (and even imperialistic) universalism and unquestioning (and sometimes aggressive) relativism.

UNIVERSALISM VS. RELATIVISM IN THOUGHT AND POLITICS

In the world of international affairs among governments and citizenries attempting to define and live within a framework of mutually-agreed-upon rights, those taking the universalist position usually have maintained that human rights are derived from the essence of humanity itself. Every person has (or should have) comprehensive and equal rights, as an individual living within human society. Although under international law some rights are derogable (that is, they can be restricted), derogation is permitted only for specific purposes of the highest urgency, and certain rights are not derogable under any circumstances. To the extent that individual rights might sometimes be curtailed by the state, this could be done only under severe stress (war, for example) or to protect other rights, and for limited duration.

Moreover, rights are absolute in the sense that they cannot be taken away or given away, and they are seen by Universalists as constituting the highest purpose of the political order. Rights are either "sacred" in origin (that is, God-given), or "inalienable" and "self-evident" (to use Thomas Jefferson's more secular language). While Universalists do not deny that "cultures" are different, they argue (in effect) that individual sameness, or similarity, among human beings should prevail over cultural difference when it comes to human rights. Those taking a relativist position on the question of human rights reject the above notions of universal human rights as naive, lacking empirical validity, ahistorical, and (worst of all) culturally imperialistic.

The relativists begin by asserting the empirical fact that historically, different societies have had different (or no) notions of rights. They also claim that individual rights are not God-given or self-evident; rather, they are a historical construct. They began in Europe, and were given particularly clear and forceful articulation in the writings of the eighteenth-century British thinker John Locke. They then spread to the American colonies (reflected especially in the Virginia and Massachusetts constitutions), and were eventually enshrined in two documents-the American Declaration of Independence (1776) and the French Declaration on the Rights of Man (1791).

Thus, argue the relativists, individual human rights are not universal, but rather, particularistic Western values masquerading as universal concepts. Today's relativists in Asia, the Middle East, and elsewhere, see the Universalists as imperialistic-dictating Anglo-American values to everyone else. In the parlance of modern political science, this is a form of coercion by intellectual means, the use of "soft power" par excellence. These conflicting political positions on human rights developed side-by side with an expanding intellectual debate on universalism and relativism, as well as institutional substructures through which the debate was advanced.

In the post World War II period, American universities carved out new territories for intellectual inquiry into the nature of other societies, or "cultures." Supported by a governmental desire to better understand both our potential friends and enemies, huge sums of government funding were poured into the creation of "area studies" centres, dedicated to studying "areas" of the world about which Americans knew little, and located at some of the most prestigious institutions of higher learning in the nation. Subsequently, the foreign policy approaches of several U.S. presidents-Jimmy Carter's emphasis on human rights, Ronald Reagan's anti-Soviet thrust, and Bill Clinton's return to a human-rights-centred approach, with a critique of Asian governments that do not seem to share U.S. goals-have kept citizens and academics alike pondering the "correct" cross-cultural approach to human rights.

As Richard Haass points out, U.S. foreign policy often has been argued from a moral perspective, emphasizing democracy, civil society, and human rights, a line of argument that has characterized both the left and the right in American politics. And yet, many "cultural experts," trained to a large extent in government-supported area studies centres, were not always sure that they shared the universalistic position on human rights. They countered with their own, and varied, brands of cultural relativism, often arguing for the uniqueness of "cultures" around the globe. In various ways, by the 1990s, the strains long inherent in debates over universalism and relativism had reached a newly heightened point of tension. The fall of the Soviet Union and the Western victory in the Persian Gulf War brought a note of triumphalism to Western public discourse and foreign policy.

Francis Fukuyama, former Deputy Director the U.S. State Department's policy planning staff, argued that we had reached "the end of history" with the victory of democracy, free markets, and Western ideals. Playing on another potential outcome of the collapse of the Soviet Union as the main "counterpoint" to the democratic West, the influential Harvard-based scholar, Samuel Huntington, argued that the world was facing an impending "clash of civilizations," which in effect described the contemporary world as an arena for continuous conflict between a West claiming to possess universalistic values and a series of rival civilizations each proud of its uniqueness.

Whether the previous era's struggles between "communism and democracy" meant the end of global struggles altogether (a' la Fukuyama), or their shifting to new axes of conflict (a' la Huntington), it was clear that the traditional forms and expectations of area studies, as we had once known them, were now over. Funding for area studies centres as they had existed in the Cold War era began to evaporate, and defining the study of global "cultures" was now up for grabs. It is in this context that some intellectuals and several governments in East Asia, Russia, and the Middle East began to subscribe to cultural relativism.

THE ASIAN VALUES DEBATE

In the American frame of reference, one of the most graphic demonstrations of what could go wrong when Western values were ignored is the Tiananmen Square incident in the People's Republic of China in the spring of 1989. Although accounts of what happened in the early morning hours of June 4 in Tiananmen vary widely, one thing is clear- there was a brutal government crackdown on demonstrators, most of whom were young students advocating democratic reforms. Many died that night, although exactly where, when, and how is a matter of dispute. Nonetheless, for our purposes, these events are critical because of the degree to which they captured the American imagination about the nature of the Chinese government, and its apparent total disregard for Western notions of universal human rights.

In response to Western sanctions placed on China in the aftermath of this incident, many Third World countries began to counter what they saw as an American-led Western trend toward intervention in the affairs of weaker countries and to assert the validity of different national approaches to political questions. The Foreign Ministry of Singapore played an especially active role in this process, concerned lest the force of American cultural self-confidence collide with Chinese defensiveness and lead to dangerous polarization in Asia and a threat to the security of smaller countries there.

In many ways, Singapore's UN Ambassador Bilahari Kausikan, a former official of the Singaporean Foreign Ministry trained in the U.S. at Columbia University, has become a bellwether for this debate, articulating the Singaporean government's particular "take" on Asian values along with several of his colleagues. As a seminar group, we had a chance to meet with Ambassador Kausikan, to hear his rationales for Asian governments to define and defend Asian values in opposition to Western notions of universal human rights, and to implement them in their own countries.

The position Ambassador Kausikan ascribes to in terms of Asian values is a strongly cultural relativist one, adhered to not only by the government of Singapore, but also by the Chinese, Indonesian, and Malaysian governments, and also democratic India. The view expressed by these governments is that human rights have a different meaning in group-oriented Asian cultures from their meaning in the individualistic West. They argue that Asian cultures value family over the individual, harmony over conflict, discipline and deference to authority over self-assertion, and welfare over freedom. A set of related arguments cites state sovereignty, economic development, and political stability as current Third-World goals to which Western-style human rights policies are inimical.

Within the West, human rights diplomacy has attracted criticism from those who argue that rights conceptions vary across cultures or by levels of economic development; from specialists who stress the importance of strategic considerations in foreign policy; and from constituencies who believe that business ties and economic growth will solve human rights problems more effectively than political pressure. Lively debates over most-favoured nation trading privileges for China have mobilized both the human rights constituency and business and other groups. Human rights issues have also entered into domestic discussion of American policy in Haiti, Rwanda, Bosnia, and elsewhere, and into American dialogue with allies like Japan and France over foreign policy cooperation.

Such claims have prompted counter moves against the Asian values position. To cite some of the most prominent examples, the UN's 1993 Vienna Conference on Human Rights affirmed the universality of concepts embodied in the original 1948 UN Universal Declaration on Human Rights and subsequent conventions. At the same time, the political declaration of the 1993 Tokyo Summit of the G-7 countries emphasized the industrialized nations' commitment to the principles of human rights. The American administration, backed by Canada, Australia, and New Zealand, argued for the universality and indivisibility of human rights, and gave the issue prominence in its foreign policy declarations. The

American position found support from the growing movement of dissident Asian human rights nongovernmental organizations (NGOs).

Within Asia, governments taking the Asian values position face challenges by increasingly vocal human rights activists and movements. Debates have occurred in China, Korea, Taiwan, and Singapore, among other countries, over the relationships among human rights, economic development, and political stability. Voices for the rule of law and political liberalization in China are persistent and seem to be growing stronger. In Thailand and China, population planning and the AIDS crisis have forced issues of women's rights onto the domestic and foreign policy agendas. Democratization in the Republic of Korea led to a new foreign policy that included the appointment of a special Ambassador for Human Rights Affairs.

Japan asserted the universality of human rights at the 1993 Bangkok preparatory conference on human rights, but Japanese human rights politics remain cautious in light of Japan's wartime history, its concern with Asian regional stability, and its commitment to economic growth as the key to improvement in the conditions of life. Outside the political sphere, the Asian values debate has revived and sharpened a series of classic questions regarding universal human rights and cultural differences. These issues reach in many disciplinary directions, involving the humanities, social sciences, and law, and they are being discussed in a growing scholarly literature. The debate involves two broad issues that involve several disciplines.

The first is how to justify human rights, which is usually discussed as part of political philosophy; the second is the nature of culture and how cultures differ, which is studied in the context of area studies, but also as part of anthropology, sociology, political science, and the growing interdisciplinary field of "cultural studies." Triangulating these issues raises the central question of whether justifications for human rights are, or should be, culturally specific or universalistic. It is a question dealt with uneasily by several disciplines and successfully by none alone.

RECRAFTING THE STUDY OF CULTURE

It was with these realizations about the centrality of assessing cultural differences in the context of the Asian values debate that our seminar group began its discussions. We were all aware, to varying degrees, of the large role played by area studies in major U.S. universities in the study of cultures in the non-Western world, including Asia. There were certain strengths that we recognized in the past history of area studies (indeed, several of us were trained as area studies specialists). Area studies scholars learned to confront problems of culture central to the modern humanities and social sciences, but which usually had been overlooked by those who investigate the same culture they occupy.

A twentieth-century American student of nineteenth century American literature may have to translate from one cultural context to another, but does not have to notice that she is doing so (although some do). By contrast, scholars in area studies, by definition, have been trained to operate from within one cultural context in seeking to understand another. Thus, some of the central concerns of area studies scholars are exactly what we as a seminar group were interested in confronting: What do we mean by culture when we compare cultures? How can a culture's distinctiveness be conceptualized? What is required to demonstrate that such distinctiveness exists, what it consists of, and what influence it has on the performance of societies?

And how does, or should, the difference of cultures matter to the value judgments we make, and to the political actions that flow from these judgments? At this intersection between knowledge and values the issues are both epistemological and ethical. Area studies scholars have traditionally responded to these issues by acknowledging-or asserting-a fundamental difference in the value commitments of cultures and then by disclaiming any right to make value judgments in the face of such differences. This position has been criticized on several grounds: that it essentializes cultures and ignores differences within cultures; that the value differences across cultures are more often assumed than demonstrated; and that it creates a moral equivalence between good and bad values.

On the other hand, the Universalist alternative is counter-criticized for its impatient attack on others' values without an understanding of the contexts in which they have become the preferences of large groups of people around the world. But area studies' dilemmas have been only a special, and perhaps in some respect especially clear, case of problems that underlie all studies of culture. Understanding people across the world is not categorically different from understanding people across the street. These considerations pushed us to explore more deeply new ways of studying culture. At this point, insights from current developments in the realm of "cultural studies" came into play, and we discussed and debated these for several days in the seminar setting and for the next several months as we prepared.

We do not claim that as a group we have arrived at a unified definition of "culture"; what we do have is a shared realization of the importance of debating the meaning of culture, including the practical and political ways in which the exploration of cultural difference should inform our position on the question of human rights. Scholars who have been active in the field commonly called "cultural studies" in American and European academia see their enterprise as both ethical and political. Like many of the contributors, they are self-consciously opposed to rigid disciplinary boundaries as they are currently constituted in Western academic life.

Accordingly, practitioners of cultural studies eclectically borrow analytical and critical methods, and the propensity to theorize findings, from across many disciplinary perspectives. Feminism, race consciousness, and the study of sexual identity have all played a role in crafting recent trends in cultural studies. One of the central commitments among many practitioners of cultural studies is that "difference" should not be obliterated in the study of culture; rather, it should be understood as an ongoing tension in all human interaction, something to be recognized, understood, and lived with. Sometimes people with different perspectives, arising from their culture, their gender or some other aspect of their identity, if they are to coexist and work together productively, must simply "agree to disagree."

The development of cultural studies has, among many things, generated new understandings of the meaning of culture itself. An earlier notion of culture was that it constituted a core set of values, psychological dispositions, and behaviours (both individual and social) that gave a group of people a common identity and way of life. Thus, to give an example, in the earlier way of thinking, often developed within the context of area studies, most people believed that the Chinese had a core "culture" the characteristics of which could be discovered, itemized, analyzed, and understood, as a way to predict individual and social behaviour and outcomes of that behaviour. Within the context of cultural studies, however, this "positivistic" view of culture has waned considerably; culture is now more likely to be viewed as unstable, "processual," or "discursive," as a repertoire of ways of thinking and acting that are constantly in the process of becoming.

Moreover, culture is usually viewed by the new cultural theorists as contested-a social context in which power struggles are constantly waged over the meaning and control of what Pierre Bourdieu has called "symbolic capital" as well as over more overtly material forms of wealth and power. In short, culture is not a given, but rather a congeries of ways of thinking, believing, and acting that are constantly in the state of being produced; it is contingent and always unstable, especially as the forces of "modernity" have barrelled down upon most people throughout the world over the course of the twentieth century.

Explaining the ways in which these cultural battles are played out, therefore, has become one of the primary goals of cultural studies, with the more theoretically minded inclined to be seeking comparative insights across newly evolving cultural formations. The recognition that culture is not a unitary, stable formation, but rather something constantly contested and in flux gave the contributors to this opportunity to analyze and critique the Asian values debate in new and, we believe, profitable ways.

It allowed us to see that even within a single culture, values and their meaning are subject to different interpretations. In this book we work toward varied strategies, developed through different disciplinary approaches, to determine when and how human rights claims might be agreed upon across treacherous philosophical, ethical, political, and sexual divides. Cultural difference is not erased in the process; rather, it is negotiated, as part of an effort to create a world in which all people should be free to deliberate, develop, and choose values to help them live more equitable and fulfilling lives.

As individuals, we have oscillated over the course of working together between "more universalist" versus "more relativist" positions. In the final versions of our individual chapters, we have ended up with variations on what we believe is a thoughtful, informed universalism that is tenable both intellectually and ethically. The chapters can be read independently, or in sequence, as a progressive dialogue. They are synthetic, approaching and discussing a wide variety of pertinent previous literature, and written in a way that, we hope, makes them accessible not only to specialists, but also to college and university students and other interested readers with no prior background or specialized knowledge of Asia. Each chapter is oriented to contemporary issues, yet places them in a perspective of long-standing intellectual concerns.

Following this introduction, introduces and critiques the Asian values debate in light of discursive notions of culture, demonstrating that arguments on both sides of the debate are designed by states to enhance their dominance in world affairs. As an ethnographically minded historian of modern China, Bell also uses interview data to ferret out diverse understandings of "rights" and "identities" (as opposed to a single set of Asian values or a single Asian "identity"). She discovers a high degree of consensus on the issue of equality for women among those she interviewed in one Chinese village, and thus argues that the primary difficulty in attaining the goal of "equal pay for equal work" is not one of cultural difference, but rather of gender difference.

In this matter, Bell worries that human rights legal instruments may not help since gender discrimination laws in all cultures have had a chequered past in actual implementation. Thus, Bell observes a high degree of universal moral consciousness about women's rights, but remains cautious about the prospects of using international legal strategies and western-derived human rights' instruments to better Third World women's lives. It is common to make the leap from cultural difference to value relativism, but Barnhart questions this. He presents a surprising, counterintuitive, yet in the end eloquently convincing argument that cultural difference does not matter for moral reasoning.

His reason is apparently simple, yet full of complexities: it is that moral reasoning is autonomous. But Barnhart does not conclude with a doctrinaire absolutism. He argues for intercultural dialogue toward a value consensus, converging on this point with Charles Taylor in a paper that influenced many of the seminar participants. Kenneth Morris tacitly accepts Barnhart's premise that moral reasoning is autonomous, but he reminds us that this does not settle the question of the universality of human rights. The human rights idea has been subjected to devastating critiques not just from Asia, but from within the Western philosophical tradition as well, so even on the pure ground of moral reasoning it may not be all that easy to defend.

The strongest criticisms were voiced by the classic conservative authors and have been revived in recent years especially by feminists and communitarians. Taking all these criticisms into consideration, the strongest case that can be made for rights is a fairly weak one, says Morris; indeed, he thinks this is why rights proponents often modulate or qualify their claims for universality in such a way that the gap between them and the Asian values proponents narrows to a matter of rhetorical style. But like Barnhart, Morris ends with a final twist that modifies his argument. He critiques the critics (both Western and Asian) and shows that the human rights idea survives much of their fire. He believes that this idea holds promise of universal appeal if it can be reconstructed on the basis of communitarian ideology.

The next contribution, by Steven Hood, rotates the perspective on these issues yet another few degrees. For him, as for Barnhart and Morris, the human rights idea is universally valid, but he disagrees with those who might argue that it is a Rome that can be reached by many roads. For Hood, human rights are a concept of Western origin that can only be grounded in Western ideas. Among these, he stresses the Western conception of nature (as differentiated from the human realm of morality and religion) and the Western belief in the equal status of each person. The search for alternative roots, he believes, is fated to fail.

Yet cultures may converge, he suggests, on another set of related values, which he labels virtues. He illustrates his arguments with sympathetic yet critical interpretations of classical Confucianism and Islam. Although all great traditions are equally deserving of respect, he concludes, this does not mean that they converge on common values. If the rights idea is to spread, it will have to do so through the acceptance of the distinctively Western values that underlie it, by civilizations where these values are not indigenous. The three philosophically informed perspectives share a commitment to universalism of values as well as a chastened awareness of the reality of value diversity.

Yet on the details of this common position they differ more than they agree. Many in the West, including the most influential NGOs in the human rights field, respond to this problem by shifting the debate to the ground of international law. According to this viewpoint, whatever their origins and philosophical basis, fundamental rights have now become legal obligations under the law of nations, as embodied in such declarations, treaties, and conventions as the Universal Declaration of Human Rights, the International Covenant on Civil and Political Rights, the International Covenant on Social, Economic, and Cultural Rights, and the Convention on the Elimination of All Forms of Discrimination against Women (CEDAW).

States are obligated by these instruments regardless of the degree to which, or the ways in which, their cultures support the human rights idea. The essays in part II contribute some original and surprising perspectives to this part of the debate. All three of the authors in this section are lawyers, and they provide expert knowledge of, and analytical insights into, the legal dimension of the Asian values debate. Michael W. Dowdle argues that rights cannot be merely a matter of law, because they are commands to justice which involve an intrinsic appeal to an overarching standard of morality.

It is precisely because they are moral rules that rights prescriptions are neither universal nor absolute, since moral prescriptions always involve tradeoffs along various other dimensions of moral concern. To construe human rights law as nothing but positive law is to deprive it both of the moral force that makes it special, and of the room to grow. Dowdle makes these points through an analysis of the 1993 Bangkok Declaration, a statement of the Asian values viewpoint which was widely dismissed in the West as a propaganda statement by authoritarian Asian regimes. To accept the Declaration's views of the cultural conditionality of rights, Dowdle suggests, is actually to acknowledge rather than threaten rights' moral standing.

Lucinda Joy Peach exposes the limits of a legal approach to redressing one of the most pervasive categories of rights violations, those against women. This issue is crucial for understanding the relationship between culture and values precisely because the status of women is so central to the self-definition of every culture. Peach grounds her analysis in a review of the status of women's rights in international law and of the criticisms that have been offered from several perspectives of a rights-based approach to the rights of women. If in the West women are "human" in the sense of being rights-bearers equivalent to men, in some other cultures women, however highly valued, and are considered to be too different from men to be treated as legally equivalent.

To illustrate this problem, Peach presents the case of Buddhist Thailand and its attitudes toward women engaged in sex work. In such a culture, women themselves are among the people least sympathetic to a rights-based approach to their problems and international and even domestic law offer few resources of practical benefit to improving women's lot. To grapple with this issue Peach suggests what she calls a feminist pragmatist approach to women's rights which aims to achieve the universalistic ends of improvement of the status of women by particularistic means, designed to function effectively within-and even by taking advantage of-the constraints of particular cultural situations. Such a fine-grained analysis suggests ways in which the universalism-particularism opposition dissolves when one moves from the realm of human rights theory to that of praxis.

Sharon Hom, although not a member of the seminar, visited with us as a guest speaker for a lively session on human rights issues in the People's Republic of China, with special emphasis on her own experiences at the UN's 1995 International Forum on Women, which met in Beijing, and also on NGO activities, in China and elsewhere, concerning the status of women. The paper we include here is reprinted from an American law school's legal journal. In this piece, Hom eloquently argues the position that states have intervened far too much in human rights issues on both sides of the Asian values debate. She notes the difficulties inherent in practical human rights work that involve translation-not only of words (from English to Chinese and vice versa), but also of ideas.

As a result, she advocates an activist role for women such as herself, who are not just bilingual but bicultural, in the processes of "cultural translation" that must take place in order to cooperate across cultures to advance human rights. This is especially important in the treacherous territory in which a variety of NGOs seek legal redress for human rights violations, when expectations are so different across cultural divides as to what law might be capable of achieving. Peach and Hom thus have suggested how different the human rights idea looks when seen from the trenches of struggle.

Human rights are not just a matter of philosophy and law. From the beginning the human rights idea has been a political tool, used by various governments and social forces to increase their influence. And in the current period, they have also become part of international politics. But, given the context of the earlier essays in the volume, we do not present these case studies to reach the familiar, facile conclusion that because human rights are political, they are also meaningless and not worth striving for. Just the opposite is true: the contextualizing of the human rights idea in time and space reveals its persistence and importance.

Xiaoqun Xu sets forth the general position that the "discourse on universality"-the claim to be in possession of a universally valid concept-is always put forward by historical actors pursuing particular purposes. Rhetorically and politically, universalism is a form of seizing the discursive high ground that is repeated over and over in historically situated struggles. Xu illustrates this point with three such power struggles among contending groups in modern Chinese history-Christian missionaries and their opponents, proponents of Western-style versus native-style medicine, and proponents of judicial independence and those who resisted their policies. But to say that universalism is a power claim is not to say that it is wrong: in fact, it is often both right and successful.

Applying his insight to the contemporary debate over human rights, Xu suggests that the idea has become widely accepted in principle and that the struggle has shifted from legitimizing human rights to identifying the balance among different kinds of rights. Farhat Haq takes us into the important realm of Islamic fundamentalism in the context of the Asian values debate. Some Islamicists have seen the Western human rights movement as a kind of cultural jihad against Islam, and many Westerners see Muslim resistance to the human rights idea as part of a jihad against the West. Yet, Haq points out, the Islamic concept of jihad, or holy war, is itself subject to varied interpretations from within and outside the Islamic tradition. Her opening discussion of jihad functions as a metaphor for her central point-that within the apparently conservative, authoritarian traditions of Islam, there has been room for several modernist intellectuals to construct new rights-seeking strategies.

Islam cannot be seen as a unitary, closed cultural system inimical to all forms of rights-seeking, as many believe, but rather as a fluid, evolving bundle of ideas, beliefs, and social practices within which some of its members might construct strategies for improving personal and group rights. On the important question of women's rights, however, Haq is pessimistic, arguing that the issue of women's none quality with men in Islam is so politically charged that to evoke human rights law in the name of Muslim women is a highly problematic strategy at present.

The human rights idea is not the only one in world history that has made a claim to universal validity. Some other examples that come easily to mind are Islam, Confucianism, Buddhism, and Catholicism, which all claim to be universally valid systems of belief. But most commentators view these traditions as more or less compatible in theory or practice with much if not all of the human rights agenda. Less commonly noted are competing universalisms that are entirely antagonistic to the human rights idea. Dmitry Shlapentokh explores in detail one such stream of thought: nineteenth century Slavicist nationalism, which posited as a universal value the active rejection of the human rights idea. Indeed, what was universal for the late nineteenth-century Slavicists in Russia, he shows, was not the sameness but rather the uniqueness of each nation and the superiority of the Russian soul above those of other nations.

Although the position sounds paradoxical, it only seems so when we view it from the perspective of Western rights-based individualism. Shlapentokh's vivid account of an entirely different cast of mind reminds us that messianic, all-encompassing value systems are not limited to those which purport to apply equally to everybody. Seen in Shlapentokh's historical retrospective, the Slavophiles were almost endearingly eccentric, but their ideas carried forward to exert great influence in the Soviet regime and still have strong echoes not only in Russia but in the various nationalisms of other parts of the post-Soviet empire as well. His analysis underscores the fragility and, in a sense, the parochialism inherent in the very universalism of the human rights idea, and the way in which both the Western liberal value system and that of various messianic nationalisms grow out of power relations specifically located in time and place.

Ilan Peleg explores the intense conflict between the "communal agenda" and the "rights agenda" that often explodes in countries where several ethnic or religious communities coexist, as indeed they do in most parts of the world. It is precisely when such a country becomes democratic that the dilemma of communal versus individual rights is likely to become most challenging. If the equal political rights of individuals are juridically guaranteed, the largest ethnic group is likely to use these rights to dominate the minority group or groups.

In that sense, a rights-based system may, through democracy, be used for oppressive purposes. Peleg cites several such cases, focusing his analysis on the example of Israel. But he sees an internal evolution in the Israeli system away from the ethnically oppressive uses of democracy to a more liberal view that protects the rights of the minority as effectively as those of the majority. This process, too, is political, Peleg argues: it is primarily the struggle of the Israeli Arabs themselves, as well as international pressure, that have moved elements of the Israeli political system and public opinion toward more protection for the civil rights of Arab citizens.

Tomas Santos shifts the locus of discussion from the power struggle of groups to the striving of individuals for integrity and insight. He offers a writer's appreciation for three Chinese short stories read in translation. His reading illuminates both the authors' struggle for freedom of expression within political constraints, and the fictional protagonists' struggles for personal integrity under conditions of powerlessness and turmoil. Santos implies that the actual struggle for human rights is carried on in millions of specific venues, and that it matters little whether or not the language of rights is used since the values at stake are intensely personal at the same time that they are universally human.

The first, by Andrew J. Nathan, interrogates the concept of the universal which underlies so much of the discussion in the book. Nathan asks what there is about the contemporary version of this concept that creates so much difficulty over cross-cultural values. He suggests that contemporary intellectual life is strongly shaped by the opposition and symbiosis between area studies and the disciplines. This structure of knowledge depends on a conceptual division between universal forms of rationality and culturally particular values which make it difficult to ascribe universality to whatever is conceived of as culturally situated. In short, our present notions set the universal against culture, creating the fallacy that whatever is culturally valued cannot be conceived of as universal.

The recognition that all social facts and all values are culturally situated would dissolve this dilemma and might open new prospects not only for the human rights debate but for the study of culture more generally. Finally, Jennifer Goodman takes a long historical and comparative view of the Asian values debate, reminding us that the dualisms underlying it have been rejected by sages East and West in centuries past.

Universal and relative, self and other, freedom and constraint, man and nature and for that matter East and West themselves are oppositions that may mislead us. Arguing for the value of harmony rather than conflict in human affairs, she suggests we may find our rights best guaranteed not in opposition to others but in cooperation with them. Hers is not intended as a practical program, but as a reminder that our cultural resources, and those of others, offer alternative ways to conceive of the problems which bother us today. The Asian values debate, we believe, is a constructive one, but it need not be resolved entirely within its current terms of reference.

A COMMUNITARIAN ALTERNATIVE

If the response of the human rights community to the "Asian values" debate is a reliable indicator, human rights are in more trouble than is generally recognized. For striking about this response was its failure to make a positive case for rights. "Liberal critics ... devoted their efforts to refuting Asian states' claims," notes Joseph Chan, instead of "substantiating and determining the scope of international human rights law." So, for example, Sharon Hom's rebuttal to Singapore apologist Bilahari Kausikan fails to mention that a positive case for rights might also be made.

Or Charles Taylor urges rights proponents to make their case by seeking values similar to their own in other cultural traditions because he concedes that a universal claim for rights cannot be made across cultures. Even Chan, although obviously sensitive to the problem of a human rights community cornered into a defensive position, adopts a similar stance in his work. Calling for a "search for a political morality" that can promote "human rights norms in Asia," he does not say why rights are good in the first place. That good is simply presupposed.

The mushrooming numbers of NGOs and human rights activists who have been quick to reassert their position in response to the Asian challenge suggest that Chan overstates the defensiveness of the human rights community. Yet, busy activism may not signal rational assurance. As one critic of rights charged more than a century ago, many rights proponents seem to hold their beliefs "as a religious faith" and "truths...to do battle for" rather than as rational convictions. Nor does the activists' affirmative of rights under the guise of the "positive law" of international document signal rational certainty. Proponents of "Asian values" were not challenging the existence of international human rights law or even its binding character, but its moral and philosophical foundation. Responses in terms of "positive law" dodge this challenge.

Recent philosophical justifications of rights also typically fail to support the absolute positions many activists promote. Ronald Dworkin's (1978) work may come the closest, but even it is replete with qualifications. John Rawls's work-at least since A Theory of Justice-is however less useful. Rawls now asks to avoid "claims to universal truth, or claims about the essential nature and identity of persons" in favour of a more modest "moral conception worked out for a specific subject, namely, the basic structure of a constitutional democratic regime".

This conception of justice obviously cannot be transposed to other "subjects" in Asia. Even Jack Donnelly, who takes up the challenge of defending rights across cultures, abdicates at the outset. In the same introductory paragraph in which he declares that human rights are the "highest moral rights" and "hold 'universally' against all other persons and institutions," he concedes that this only applies "in ordinary circumstances." Since the gist of the "Asian values" challenge has been the claim that rights are relative to cultural circumstances, it is difficult to understand how this kind of immediately qualified case for rights answers the challenge.

The reticence of rights proponents when confronted by the "Asian values" challenge, coupled with the weak contemporary philosophical defence of rights, suggests that something is seriously amiss in the rights agenda. This is the conjecture to explore in the initial portions of this chapter. Specifically, to remind rights advocates that long before the "Asian values" debate erupted Western intellectual traditions had themselves levelled similar criticisms of human rights. These criticisms have yet to be adequately answered by the proponents of rights and therefore continue to resurface, particularly in contemporary communitarianism.

THE WESTERN CRITIQUE OF RIGHTS

In an essay on "The Permanent Structure of Antiliberal Thought," Stephen Holmes identifies fully twenty major recurring Western objections to liberalism, and so to human rights. The objections, while often substantively similar, come from a wide array of philosophical traditions. Thus, while Jeremy Bentham's notion of human rights as "nonsense upon stilts" is perhaps the most cited of all Western anti-rights aphorisms, objections to rights arise from within conservatism and Marxism as well as Bentham's utilitarianism, and were of course a cornerstone of fascist ideology too.

Despite this array of criticisms (and at some risk of oversimplification), the major criticisms can be grouped into two main categories, the ontological and the teleological. Further, while diverse thinkers have advanced ontological criticisms of rights, the conservative tradition can perhaps best serve as a template for the teleological criticism. This is so because conservative critics have generally been more articulate and forceful in their criticisms than others. Michael Freeman even concludes that "almost all of the values said to be 'Asian,' are similar to conservative Western values." Although this may be an overstatement, any summary of the teleological critique of rights should probably emphasize the conservative tradition-which of course also advances the ontological critique.

THE ONTOLOGICAL CRITIQUE

The ontological critique states that rights do not actually exist except by social convention. Most serious critics of rights embrace this critique and assert that there is neither evidence of persons possessing these rights in nature nor any plausible reason for imagining them this way. Consider what the champions of human rights believe them to be. Human rights are a "special class of rights" that an individual possesses simply because they are "human."

They are "extralegal" in that they exist prior to and even in defiance of the state and other social institutions. They are derived from the fundamental equality of persons. Indeed, society (including the state) is understood to be at least an implicit contract among rights-bearing persons legitimated primarily on the grounds that is the insurer of rights.

The case against this notion of rights was first and most famously made by David Hume. To the advocates of rights, Hume simply asked: Where is the evidence? For him John Locke's notion "that government in its earliest infancy arose from consent or rather the voluntary acquiescence of the people" is at most a plausible conjecture. But Locke's further insistence that "even at present" government "rests on no other foundation" is contradicted by all available evidence.

"Almost all governments, which exist at present, or of which there remains any record in story," observed Hume, "have been founded originally, either on usurpation or conquest, or both, without any pretence of fair consent, or voluntary subjection of the people." Hume adds that "when a new government is established, by whatever means, the people are commonly dissatisfied with it, and pay obedience more from fear and necessity, than from any idea of allegiance or of moral obligation." Nevertheless, "everywhere" one finds "princes, who claim their subjects as their property," and "subjects, who acknowledge this right in their prince." To have thought otherwise in most societies would have been to run the risk of having "your friends ... shut you up as delirious."

Hume's critique of rights thus rests upon empirical evidence. Since the record of human history reveals little or no evidence of natural human rights, the original equality from which they are thought to spring, or the contractual society and state, Hume dismisses these notions as pure fancy. "So refined and philosophical a system," he writes, "corresponds" to "nothing" in "the world."

From Hume there stretches an almost unbroken line of thought-generally regarded as conservative-which repeats his arguments. Edmund Burke was perhaps the most famous of these challengers. His Reflections on the Revolution in France, often considered the classic work of the conservative tradition, was at base a strident attack on the notion of universal human rights founded in nature. Everywhere Burke looked he saw people not as possessors of abstract rights but as embedded in particular traditions, enmeshed in concrete attachments, obligated to others in reciprocal relationships. To conceive of persons as endowed with abstract rights of the sort that supersede their social attachments and obligations struck him as absurd and dangerous.

Complementing these conservative criticisms of rights ontology are the similar criticisms levelled by Jeremy Bentham and Karl Marx. For Bentham, rights as expressed in the French Declaration of the Rights of Man were literally nonsense. His point-for-point critique of that document was not so much a moral polemic as it was a logical and ontological critique of the rhetoric of rights. The basis for Marx's criticism was similar. The "so-called rights of man," he writes, "are nothing but the rights of the member of civil society." This "egoistic man," or "man separated from other from other men and the community," derived not from any universal ontology but "from the relationship of the political state to civil society" in the bourgeois era.

Rights proponents have generally been willing to concede the empirical case against rights. But they consider the lack of evidence for rights to be beside the point. For them the truth of rights is ascertained not by appealing to the evidence of history but to the evidence of conscience. This conscience is-in good Kantian fashion-a priori, that is, it exists prior to experience and shapes experience. For many proponents of rights this moral logic is written into human hearts from the beginning.

Ask rational human beings how they might ideally conceive of justice, the proponents say, and the answer given will correspond at least roughly to a notion of human rights. From this standpoint, the affirmation of rights is a normative posture that, by corresponding to a moral imperative embedded in the psyche, need not correspond to anything in the empirical world.

Of course, this defence of rights does not effectively counter the critics who deny it-since it amounts to simply positing an alternative epistemology and metaphysics. Perhaps for this reason, it is increasingly avoided even by many rights advocates who, like Rawls, advance it not as a universal moral position but merely as one consistent with the "intuitive ideas ... latent in the public political culture of a democratic society". But such consistency is a far cry from the rationalist defence of rights, as Rawls acknowledges. It also opens the door to other, equally "intuitive" moral ideas, like those communitarians claim to discover by appealing to a "final position".

In contrast to Rawls's "original position" in which autonomous individuals behind a "veil of ignorance" arrive at moral ideas, the "final position" asks that the reflections of persons on their deathbeds be considered the paradigmatic basis for morality. Since these reflections do not generally include the affirmation of any universal morality-much less of rights-but rather focus on the continuity of the particular communal traditions with which people have been associated, this exercise casts doubt on the value of even a heuristic rationalist defence of rights. A rationalist case for the ontology of rights of course remains available to those who wish to embrace one. But in the face of historic criticisms and contemporary doubts, the strategy is increasingly implausible.

THE TELEOLOGICAL CRITIQUE

The teleological critique of rights criticizes the ends to which rights based morality leads. The paradigmatic expression of this critique may have been James Fitzjames Stephen's rebuttal to John Stuart Mill's On Liberty, now regarded as one of the classics of conservative thought. A contemporary and admirer of Mill, Stephen read On Liberty sympathetically. "I am not the advocate of Slavery, Caste, and Hatred," Stephen writes, "nor do I deny that ... Liberty...maybe regarded as good." But sympathy gave way to criticism as Mill's "theories" of liberty struck Stephen as logically "unsound."

Stephen's principal objection was that rights ("liberties" in Mill) cannot be "ends in themselves" since the ends to which they lead "do not typify, however vaguely, any state of society which a reasonable man ought to regard with enthusiasm or devotion." "All morality" and "all religion" operate not by respecting rights but by restricting them. It follows that "Mr. Mill's system is violated not only by every system of theology which concerns itself with morals" but also "by every known system of morality."

Since "there is hardly a habit which men in general regard as good which is not acquired by a series of more or less painful and laborious acts," Stephen is compelled to ask, "Why, then, is liberty, defined as Mr. Mill defines it, to be regarded as so precious?" This teleological criticism of rights has often been implied by those who decry the alleged licentiousness and social chaos of the societies that enshrine them. Lee Kuan Yew and Amitai Etzioni are two recent instances of this type of critic. But it is important not to confuse practical criticisms of rights-based societies with the theoretical rebuff.

Practical criticisms are more easily countered by the proponents of rights who say, first, that the descriptions are vastly exaggerated and, second, that the cost of occasional excess is a price worth paying for liberty. The more serious criticism is that any philosophy which elevates rights to a supreme principle (i.e., as "trumps") confuses means with ends, and insofar as any society enacts this confusion it must necessarily become licentious and chaotic. Much of the fame accorded to Edmund Burke's condemnation of the French Revolution came from his prediction of the chaos and tyranny that would follow the attempt to implement rights. He foresaw what Stephen also detected: the elevation of rights to moral ends can only destroy the moral and social fabric of a society.

The force of the teleological critique of rights is thus different from the ontological critique-and perhaps more devastating. For as Stephen shows with respect to Mill, if his moral system were to be realized it would deprive people of every system of meaning or morality beyond that of rights. But since people do desire to inhabit a social world in which meanings are at least in part hierarchically arranged and socially maintained, a society in which rights really were the highest moral good would be one in which inhabitants could lead only purposeless, anomic lives. To this criticism the proponent of rights has no effective rebuttal. After all, it merely casts a critical gaze on liberalism's affirmative case.

The rationale for a liberal rights regime is that it is the best practical solution to a situation of moral pluralism. Because people disagree in their conceptions of the good (and following a century of religious warfare over such disagreements), liberalism arose as an alternative to authoritarian attempts to impose a moral scheme on dissenters. But by this very rationale the liberal must concede that rights are not the highest end, only a provisional means for reducing discord. Indeed, Mill himself does not claim that liberty is the highest good, only that it creates the conditions necessary for discovering those goods. But if this is true it amounts to conceding that rights are not in fact the highest good and can be "trumped" by even higher goods. The rights advocate is therefore caught in the awkward position of promoting a social ethic that, if successful, is ideally superseded. How then can this ethic be posited as the highest good?

Both Bentham and Marx reveal their essential sympathy with this teleological critique of rights indirectly by attempting to unmask what they propose to be the real ends lurking beneath the rhetoric of liberty. The "cry of rights," notes Bentham, arises when "a man has a political caprice to gratify but can give no reason why it should be gratified." For Marx, the interpretation is a little more complex. "The freedom in question is that of a man treated as an isolated monad and withdrawn into himself". In other words it is the "freedom" of alienated, bourgeois man suffering the effects of a society with a deeply distorted moral aim.

None of which is to say that proponents of rights in liberal regimes have no arguments to advance. They do. It is that in the absence of consensus about social goods rights-based liberalism may be the most peaceful arrangement possible. Even so, this case for rights concedes the teleological case against them: those rights of themselves are inadequate moral ends.

Historically, therefore, this case has been most convincingly made only in very limited arenas, such as in certain restrictions on state interference with religion. But these instances do not show rights to be goods in themselves, only to be a plausible means for enabling people who disagree about goods to coexist in relative tranquillity. A glance at most contemporary liberal political theory as well as many recent human rights documents (e.g. CEDAW) reveals that the impulse to promulgate rights has expanded well beyond these modest and pragmatic beginning compromises. Rights are no longer promoted as the means to other goods but as the highest goods themselves. In this way they are subject to the teleological critique.

ECHOES OF THE CRITIQUE

Although many of the foregoing criticisms of rights have reappeared in the "Asian values" debate, it is worth noting that they have resurfaced in contemporary Western guises as well. (They have also generally been abandoned by conservatism, which has for the most part allied itself with a rights based economic liberalism.) The two most important areas of this resurgence may be feminism and communitarianism. Feminism arose in the West more or less in tandem with human rights and may be thought of as an instance of them.

Nevertheless, some recent feminists have begun to question the appropriateness of a rights-based agenda for women. A main feminist critique is, as it has been historically, ontological and epistemological. Since Carol Gilligan's study of female moral development many have come to question the existence of an innate rationalist moral sense. They argue that the principled type of moral reasoning that underlies the assumption of universal human rights is typical of male morality but atypical of female moral reasoning. For women moral values like caring, sympathy, and relatedness take precedence over values like rights.

Although the bulk of this literature focuses on substantive issues at a considerable remove from human rights, it does parallel ontological criticisms of rights by asserting that the same morality is not available to all persons simply by virtue of their humanity but is a constructed feature of social-psychological experience.

Whether based upon this epistemology or not, some contemporary feminists proceed to echo the teleological criticism of rights. These feminists, sometimes called "difference theorists", assert that the differences between women and men are such that the application of the same rights to both is inappropriate. To some the application of supposedly universal rights to women has the effect of undermining a specifically feminine way of being, while to others it is the impossibility of the sexes ever relating as equals that prohibits the indiscriminate application of the same moral principals to both. Either way, the conclusion is the same. Women are conceived of as different from men and therefore entitled to different treatment; context-in this case gender-dictates morality.

If this branch of feminist thinking suggests the Asian argument that rights are relative to social context, it should. The arguments are formally identical, and both resurrect historic criticisms. The other major contemporary movement to recall the historic criticisms of rights is the communitarians. They argue that persons are socially constituted or "encumbered" selves and so restate the ontological objection to rights, namely, that rights arise as a matter of social convention rather than nature. Indeed, though not formally identified with the movement but a frequent philosophical source for those who are, Alisdair MacIntyre goes so far as to say that belief in human rights is on a par with belief in witches. Others in the school stress that the liberal view of autonomous individuals freely choosing their own ideals of the good life-so central to liberal doctrines of rights-is simply wrong. Individuals, they rather maintain, are socially constituted and thus "encumbered"-but hardly free.

Communitarians have also made much of the social chaos that has allegedly arisen as a consequence of the West's over-promotion of rights. Although their focus has been primarily on practical consequences rather than the rights-as-ends problem, the more theoretical criticism is sometimes broached. Thus Michael Sandel sharply criticizes what he calls the "procedural liberalism" of the U.S. This is the view that rights take precedence over all other substantive goods-a view that Sandel (echoing Stephen) tries and finds wanting.

Communitarians also draw upon another source of the criticism of rights in Western history: nineteenth-century republicanism. While neither republicanism nor an interpretation of the American as republican (rather than liberal) is essential to the communitarian argument, many draw from these sources to reinforce their social agenda. Specifically, communitarians advance the argument that the United States was not founded on an ideology of rights-based liberalism but on republicanism, and did not become a decidedly rights-based liberal state until the turn of the twentieth century or so. Until then rights were considered neither good, but neither an absolute nor the highest good. It was in fact widely acknowledged that rights could be enjoyed only in the context of a good society. Hence, the good brought by rights existed in relation to the good of society, with republicans believing that the two rose or fell together.

Whatever the historical reality of republicanism, it is used by communitarians to strike a blow against the idea that the modern state can be completely rights-based. Sandel for example asks how a rights-based state can handle religion. If it is completely neutral it must be secular. But from the standpoint of religion secularism is not neutral but anti-religion. Sandel and Bell also ask about gay marriage. If the state is neutral with respect to the life plans of its citizens as a theory of universal rights demands then it cannot prohibit gay marriage. But it cannot prohibit polygamy either, for that too involved the imposition of a moral judgment on citizens and so violates their rights.

It ultimately follows that the state has no business involving itself at all in marriage. To this example Bell adds the problem of state subsidization of the arts. His question is on what grounds the genuinely neutral rights-affirming state can subsidize theater but not professional wrestling. Unless the state imposes a notion of good entertainment on the public, thus failing to respect its rights, it cannot. Although there may be ways for the rights advocate to respond to these and similar criticisms, recourse to a rights-based democracy may not be among them. As one of the most ardent contemporary republicans, Robert Bellah, put the matter, a truly liberal state devolves into a parliamentary cacophony of self-interested voices and crisscrossing coalitions.

What most Americans think of as a "democratic" solution to these problems is thus really a republican or communitarian solution-that is, one in which a substantial number of citizens devote themselves to a public good that transcends their own narrow interests. But to believe in a public good larger than the aggregation of individual rights is also to embrace a public philosophy larger than rights-based liberalism. It is also interesting to note that both Sandel and Bellah single out religion as especially problematic from the standpoint of a rights based liberal political philosophy. For it was in responding to the Wars of Religion following the Reformation that liberalism first arose triumphant.

To find contemporary critics of liberalism challenging liberalism on just this substantive area is to suggest that the division between the camps is a wide one indeed. Most of these communitarian critics of rights stop well short of endorsing the conservative label of their most articulate historic predecessors. Those most susceptible to the label even go to great lengths to reject it. Bell for example suggests a curious and not quite clear contrast between the "tradition" that he claims to favour and the "traditionalist" outlook of Edmund Burke. Regardless of the label, the ideas are familiar-and subject to the same criticisms.

A CRITIQUE OF THE CRITIQUE

Weaknesses in the rights camp do not mean that the opposing camp is strong. Actually, the critics of rights also confront two troublesome problems. One is that while the opponents of rights generally support a modest range of rights they give no reason for doing so. This weakness runs through the conservative tradition as well as its contemporary reincarnations. Edmund Burke may well have been a supporter of both the English and American revolutions as well as an Irish sympathizer, and he may thus have opposed the French Revolution not so much because he opposed all rights but because he feared their wholesale celebration at the expense of other goods.

Indeed, he writes that liberty "is good". But why should Burke have favoured any rights at all? His philosophy gives no reason for doing so. The same criticism applies to Stephen, who claimed to be no defender of caste or slavery, but who gave no reason for that position. It applies as well to feminist "difference theorists." Although they may be correct to reject the application of a universal scheme of rights to women and men, some notion of rights must underlie their feminist agenda. And the criticism applies especially to contemporary communitarians, who glibly accept the achievements of liberalism while calling for a "moratorium" on future rights. By what rationale do they accept some (existing) rights but not other (future) rights?

All critics of rights do not succumb to this inconsistency, but most do. Even those who avoid it, however, may still stumble over the apparent fact that something like a notion of human rights seems to appear as a moral maxim in many cultures. Thus, the Confucian principle of reciprocity and the Christian golden rule are each closes enough approximations to Immanuel Kant's "categorical imperative" to prompt some observers to propose them as universal instances of rights-like morality. To be sure, the existence of such maxims is hardly evidence for the universality of rights, which if they have existed have also been more often violated than maintained in the several traditions that profess them.

Yet, since most traditions uphold some notion of rights as goods, the burden falls on the critic to explain why this should be the case. But of course the burden weighs heavier on those who concede that rights are goods but give no justification for the concession. This problem is also found among proponents of "Asian values." After arguing that the Western-style rights agenda is mistaken, Singapore's Kausikan declares that "the hard core of rights that are truly universal is smaller than many in the West are wont to pretend," and that "a focus on a more restricted but precise core of basic human rights ... is a more productive approach."

The question that he nowhere addresses, however, is by what rationale he concedes even a "hard" or "precise core" of human rights. This leads to the second criticism of most rights opponents: they offer no criteria for evaluating traditions. Since they clearly prefer traditions that are supportive of some rights, they are obviously willing to evaluate traditions by some external criteria of justice. But what are these criteria and from where do they arise, unless it is the very rationalist moral sense that they otherwise deny?

It is no out to suggest, as Walzer does, that some traditions are "deeper" and therefore more just than others. Nor can the problem be avoided by using what Bell calls "transitional arguments." (These are arguments that compare alternative cultural practices in order to choose the morally superior one.) Both strategies ultimately beg the question. Unless there is some criterion of justice independent of cultural practice it is impossible to decide which argument is "deeper" or which "transition" is superior to another. Once again, rights critics are forced into a rationalist corner if they wish to evaluate moral practices- which of course they do.

To these objections there are only two rejoinders. One is to plead ignorance. This is a main theme in the conservative tradition, and at least intellectually honest. Confronted with even an appealing philosophy-as most conservatives believe some theory of rights is-the conservative tends to worry that it might not work as expected because of unforeseen problems. The tendency is to proceed with changes slowly lest they backfire and destroy the goods already enjoyed. When the new idea strikes them from the start as potentially problematic, conservatives are even less inclined to support its implementation. The safest course is to continue with traditional ways since the changes could be worse.

The other rejoinder is, obviously, to posit a notion of the good that can be used to evaluate traditions. This is the strategy of Bentham and Marx - as well as innumerable utopians throughout history. But of course by positing a notion of the good, utopian theorists invite criticisms of their positions. But neither rejoinder applies well to contemporary circumstances. The world of the "Asian values" debate is hardly a static one in which, motivated by prudence, the thoughtful leader can simply stay the conservative course. It is rather a dynamic, ever-changing arena in which new states are born, traditional cultures are overrun, and questions of rights or other criteria for cultural evaluations are unavoidable.

Moreover, neither feminists nor communitarians want to preserve the status quo. Whatever the value of prudence in a more static world, it is neither an option nor normally an aim in our world. But the utopian alternative-a society in which there is agreement on a good that transcends rights-is hardly foreseeable either. Fukuyama may have overstated the case for a globe bereft of alternatives to capitalist liberalism, but few would want to return to the last time the West experienced a serious threat to rights-based liberalism, the fascist era. Against it liberalism prevailed for the same reasons it arose two centuries before: Not because it was the most cogent philosophy, but because it was preferable to the allegedly "utopian" alternative.

The strongest case for human rights, as well as for liberalism generally, has long been this practical one: that it is superior to all alternatives. Yet it is precisely against this case that the proponents of "Asian values" strike their most decisive blow. For they arguably demonstrate what neither fascism nor Marxism could, namely, that a more harmonious and prosperous society is possible on the basis of an alternative moral philosophy. To make a case for human rights in this context requires more than a restatement of the practical arguments. Required is rather a cogent, theoretical argument. If such a case must be more measured than has been necessary historically, it is because the criticisms of it must now be taken into account. Even so, because the criticisms contain weaknesses too, a tempered affirmative argument can be advanced.

A COMMUNITARIAN THEORY OF RIGHTS

There is only one way that a theory of human rights can be reconciled with the main criticisms of them outlined above (that rights can neither be derived from a universal rationalist principle nor can stand as any society's highest good). It is to accept these criticisms as valid but to propose that more or less universal features of human experience nevertheless make a rights-like moral scheme available to people on occasions when they seek a moral alternative to their existing social traditions.

If such an argument can be plausibly sketched it will address the weaknesses of the critics' accounts, namely, that they give no reason for supporting the rights they do support and that they fail to specify criteria for evaluating cultural traditions. Yet by emboldening them it will bring them closer to their opponents' camp. The result will not be a defence of rights as automatic trumps, but it will be the establishment of a framework for including rights as a criterion of justice in any discussion of cultural values. More importantly, the framework will be one that the critic of rights will be compelled to concede.

The opposite procedure-to begin with the affirmative case for human rights and then to temper it with an appreciation of cultural traditions- cannot produce the desired results. Rights advocates may want final moral authority and believe that it is available to them on a rationalist basis, but they have no rebuttal to those who simply deny the rationalist argument. Worse, even if the rationalist argument is accepted, rights activists have no way of explaining how so pristine a moral sense can lead to the more complex and contextualized notions of moral ends that humans everywhere posit. Although it is logically possible to begin by conceding the strong case for rights, the procedure stumbles into both snares of the critics and thus offers no avenue for reconciliation. Parsimony if not persuasion weigh in against this approach.

The first approach will therefore be pursued. It may be called communitarian because it builds upon the historic criticisms of rights generally endorsed by communitarians while answering their desire to support rights, but avoids the confusing connotations of other labels. Neo-conservative would fit equally well were the label not already taken (and many neoconservatives not to have departed from the historic conservative critique of liberalism). Republican might also be used, but it risks raising confusions with the various tributaries of thought already coexisting within that tradition. Feminist is obviously too narrow. The communitarian label is therefore adopted.

The theory must begin by conceding the fundamental communitarian case: People are not primarily autonomous, rights-bearing selves, but the products and carriers of social traditions. The case should also be deepened. The traditions that mould people are unavoidably hierarchical, even necessarily coercive. They are hierarchical because, for a tradition to be meaningful, it must select from the array of possible values those that it will emphasize and so arrange them hierarchically. To value everything equally is to value nothing in particular. Then, since social traditions are not simply abstract ideas but lived social practices, the arrangement of values requires that normal social roles and institutions express them.

In other words, the society must be hierarchical in ways that express and embody the group's values. Because of this hierarchy of both values and social practices, coercion-or what might appear to be coercion from the standpoint of those outside of or simply disaffected with the tradition-is unavoidable. "Coercion" is of course a strong word and no argument is here advanced that it must be especially brutal or onerous. But it does no good to pretend that a meaningful social order can avoid denying some individuals certain liberties in some situations. If people are to be socialized to embrace their culture and to socialize others to that embrace, they must be moulded and mould others to it. Although this might more politely be called "education" rather than "coercion," short of the postulate that education appeals to a metaphysical logos which coercion may violate (the sort of rationalist supposition rejected here) the two are the same thing.

According to this view of persons and cultures people conceive as their highest good as participating meaningfully in and maintaining their hierarchical society. How then does a notion of rights arise-and with it the ability to criticize one's culture? The answer lies in two universal experiences: the norm of reciprocity and the idea of human equality. The norm of reciprocity is thought to be universal. Although it may therefore suggest rationalist foundations, inferring these is unnecessary. The pioneering theorist of the emergence of rationalist-like qualities of thought from social experience is probably Emile Durkheim, whose student and nephew, Marcel Mauss, extended the approach to the analysis of exchange relations. To Mauss as for later generations of theorists, something like a norm of reciprocity is a universal feature of social life even though it need not be derived from a priori mental categories.

By itself, however, the norm of reciprocity cannot account for human rights. Although the norm does dictate that interactions proceed according to a moral logic of equivalence, which is a notion akin to rights, it typically operates in morally structured contexts in which the exchanging participants seek equity only according to predetermined roles. So, for example, reciprocity may govern relationships between ruler and subject, men and women, or father and son-none of which in most contexts presume equal rights. Indeed, certain displays of authority and deference may be considered reciprocal insofar as the participants are fulfilling role obligations more or less predetermined by their society. Conversely, the assertion of a universal right by either party may actually reflect a breakdown of reciprocity-a violation of the norm-insofar as it represents a rejection of more widely shared moral ideas about the appropriate ranking of various persons and their mutual obligations.

However, if the norm of reciprocity is coupled with a belief in the equality of the interacting parties, it will result in a rights-like idea of justice. Since neither of the interacting parties in cases of equality is defined by social circumstances to be superior or inferior to the other, the only moral criterion to which they can appeal is the norm of reciprocity itself. But in a condition of equality, reciprocity is but another way of saying human rights. That is, parties have exactly the same social privileges and social obligations as the other, so each is obligated to treat the other as he or she expects to be treated.

This reasoning is consistent with the usual liberal argument that the idea of rights presupposes a notion of equality. However, most liberal inferences about the basis for notions of human equality are too ambitious for the communitarian. Any posit of a rationalist basis for equality is of course suspect. But even the conjecture that humans arrive at a notion of equality by crediting one another with the "dignity" that attends each person's need to fashion a meaningful life is overly optimistic.

This kind of conjecture smacks of a reified concept of the person that a communitarian must deny even as it presupposes what it purports to explain. In order to credit another with this kind of dignity, it must be assumed that persons everywhere struggle to fashion a meaningful life and recognize that others do as well. But the bulk of humanity-evens the bulk of humanity in liberal societies-probably does not think of life's meaning this way. Surely most think of it as socially given rather than individually chosen. Even in the rare situations in which life's meaning does arise as an individual problem, the awareness of that problem does not by itself explain why people would be prompted to grant dignity to others for confronting it too. That extension of dignity to others presupposes universal experiences of fellow-feeling that incline persons to sympathize with one another.

The better basis for a notion of human equality may therefore be found in certain common experiences of fellow-feeling. Hobbes's thesis that the common fear of death is such a leveller comes immediately to mind, although Mencius's belief in the universal capacity for sympathy also suffices. The important point is that equality be understood to be based upon certain experiences that really are universal-not merely rationalist posits or heuristic inferences. Since all people are cognizant of death and can empathize with suffering, such experiences may therefore be said to be universal. Based upon them (and perhaps others) a rudimentary notion of equality can be plausibly posited.

Although such experiential bases for equality are plausible and under most circumstances may be operative, they may be too weak to generate a rights conviction by themselves. It is not clear, for instance, that a Hobbesian fear of death is a sufficient basis for a belief in equality sturdy enough to support human rights. History provides too many examples of both murder and suicide justified by social values to believe that it is. The reservation is similar for Mencian compassion. Surely suffering may sometimes elicit the requisite fellow-feeling for a notion of equality to develop, but just as surely it does not uniformly do so.

Again, history offers countless examples of indifference to and even infliction of suffering upon others. Enemies and oppressors may "dehumanize" their victims before inflicting harm on them-the literature on atrocities suggests they do-but history shows that this is a process that is accomplished fairly routinely. It also merits mention that neither Hobbes nor Mencius developed theories of human rights based upon the positions of fellow-feeling. Therefore, while it is plausible to conjecture that some and perhaps most people across cultures develop ideas of human equality based upon fellow feeling; in themselves these experiences do not suffice to establish the convictions firmly.

The problem, as Max Scheler notes, is that the persons expected to make these moral judgments are themselves socially constituted. Looking inward, they see their society and its hierarchical values. These values trump the appeal of equality, although it remains an accessible experience. To translate common experiences into a norm of equality sturdy enough to support rights therefore requires a social value conducive to doing so. The question is: Under what conditions might such a value arise?

The easiest answer is when people find it to their advantage to cooperate across cultural boundaries, that is, where they agree to disagree. Such conditions may arise in postmodern societies where individuals struggle for personal meaning, sympathize with others they assume to be similarly struggling, and thus arrive at a rough notion of the liberal right to fashion one's own life plans unhampered by others. But not too much should be made out of a scenario like this one, which either reifies the concept of persons by stripping them of their cultural moorings or describes a situation in which cultural constructions of personhood themselves paradoxically create this image of the existentially autonomous person. Better scenarios are those in which persons do understand themselves to be culturally constituted adherents of particularistic values, but also desire to cooperate across cultural boundaries for specific, limited purposes.

The paradigmatic example of this situation is that of cross-cultural exchange. In this situation cultural differences are given. Persons do not expect to agree with one another's socially constituted values but agree to see themselves in their similarities rather than their differences for the promise of mutual gain. Voltaire may have described this situation best: "Enter the Exchange of London, that place more respectable than many a court, and you will see there agents from all nations assembled for the utility of all mankind. There the Jew, the Mohammedan, and the Christian deal with one another as if they were the same religion, and give the name of infidel only to those who go bankrupt." That this description is echoed by Karl Marx's objection to rights as a mere convention of the bourgeoisie underscores its force. Both defender and critic agree that in situations of cross cultural economic exchange the common humanity required for rights may arise.

Perhaps more importantly, this description roughly corresponds both to the classic instances of reciprocity studied by anthropologists and to the religious pluralism that marked the rise of human rights in Europe. In the first instances an ethic of equivalent reciprocity has been found to characterize the initial contacts of different cultures when cooperation rather than conquest was the aim. In the second instance it was precisely the desire to halt the wars of religion that prompted Europeans to subscribe to a notion of rights. In neither instance were rights held to be "trumps" in the sense of being the "highest good," nor did the posit of equality go so far as to encompass a notion of "dignity" in the contemporary individualistic sense. But in both a notion of rights arises as a compromise substitute for a moral code when agreement about higher goods is impossible.

These instances illustrate the argument, which in short is that the foundation of human rights lies in universally available notions of equality enacted into social practice when situations call for reciprocity across cultures differences. If this argument is accepted, then a communitarian case for rights has been made. It is a case that bases rights on a more solid moral foundation than their critics allow but a more fragile foundation than their advocates allege. On the one hand human rights are said to arise from experiences that are more or less universally available to humanity.

They are therefore sturdier than mere convention. But on the other hand the enactment of rights depends upon a foundation of human agreement or positive law which can by definition be only situational rather than universal. Rights are therefore weaker than arguments based upon natural law allow. In all, this reasoning suggests that rights are within the universal moral repertoire of humanity, but not universal in the rationalist sense normally credited to them by their advocates.

A communitarian defence of rights like this one has, I believe, a certain intuitive appeal. It makes sense of both the claim that rights are "merely" matters of convention and the claim that they are moral trumps. It reconciles these claims by rooting rights in agreements which, in effect, proclaim them to be trumps. The proclamations do not alter the prior ontological or teleological status of rights-hence the critics' suspicions that they are philosophically unsound. But by codifying a moral position that is within the universal repertoire of humanity the agreements carry more weight than could be accorded to convention alone.

If it follows that the idea of rights is within the grasp of the bulk of humanity based upon experience and may be enacted by agreement, it also follows that a supra-cultural criterion for evaluating cultural traditions is also universally available. This criterion is the ideal of equality and rights in conditions of moral pluralism. This is not, it must be stressed, a stance that is automatically morally superior to others within the tradition.

But it is a universally available moral position from which traditions can be evaluated-and the only such universally available position. It is thus the standard that can and should be used to assess cultural traditions, even though these assessments cannot be presumed to by the last words on the matter. In this way as in others, a communitarian theory of rights gives more play to them than the critics of rights allow while simultaneously restricting their use to the advisory role of a default position. Some of the implications of this position can be sketched by way of conclusion.

IMPLICATIONS OF THE COMMUNITARIAN SYNTHESIS

The gist of this synthesis is to ask that rights not be considered as ends- much less as trumps-but only means for establishing a rough sort of justice where other ends collide. It suggests, therefore, that there is a higher good than human rights, namely, a meaningful cultural life. This subordinate status of rights to cultural meanings can be reinforced by examining one of the instances in which rights seem to arise in their fullest: cross-cultural exchanges. These exchanges have revealed a curious phenomenon for those who assume that exchange relations based upon equality result in equal outcomes.

For with some regularity exchange partners offer each other goods of greater value than they receive. Why should the norm of reciprocity under conditions of equality result in imbalanced exchanges, an apparent voluntary loss? The answer generally given is that the extra measure "lost" in the exchange is a contribution to the building of the relationship, which the loss does by obligating the recipient to future exchanges. But this in turn may suggest something more fundamental: that asocial equality is a condition that people find discomforting, and when in such situations they move to cement normative and hierarchical relationships within which shared meanings rather than formal equality can govern their interactions.

If this is true, then the argument that an entire society can be based primarily upon a morality of rights looms as implausibility. For people appear to be uncomfortable with such a morality and try to move beyond it. That this is true of people is illustrated by evidence from the West. The equal rights so often touted in the West are, upon closer examination, rarely as equal in reality as they are in rhetoric whether an informal group of friends in the neighbourhood or even the formal equality of a jury, research has consistently demonstrated the quick emergence of a rigid power and prestige order.

How much more farfetched is the notion of, say, equal rights before the law or in the political process? Few would maintain that every defendant in a criminal trial and every voter actually enjoy equal rights. Westerners, no less than others, inhabit of a culture in which equal rights are sharply skewed by hierarchies of values substantiated by social practices. That we say that we possess equal rights and occasionally base moral claims upon that conviction is no evidence that we typically enjoy such rights or even want to. Indeed, the belief may not be too far removed from the inhabitants of Salem maintaining that witches were in their midst.

Even more troublesome for the rights advocate is the realization that for every situation that produces a rights-like moral compromise there are others that evidence plunder and the imposition of hierarchical values. To be sure, from an external point of view a rights-like moral creed is a morally preferable solution for the interacting of divergent cultures. But from a perspective within one or another of the interacting cultures, ethnocentric and material advantage may be the more appealing ethic.

To dismiss these aims as merely immoral is short-sighted. They are immoral only from the fairly narrow standpoint of universal rights. But since this standpoint is not the one to which most people are oriented most of the time, nor the one that supplies them with compelling moral ends, it is mistaken to dismiss the violation of rights for the sake of one or another socially constructed morality as immoral. The lesson that should rather be derived is the one that recognizes the moral limits and necessary fragility of an ethic human rights in a world where people rightly demand richer meanings embedded in social practices.

Even so, the rights advocate is not bereft of moral voice. Since the appeal to rights is within the universal repertoire of humanity, the assertion of rights is one that must be granted a moral hearing. This is so especially where sub cultural groupings within a cultural tradition themselves resist a certain imposition of values and their corresponding behavioural requirements, or where cultural conflict itself arises.

These situations offer prima facie evidence of the failure of the tradition to provide a coherent moral framework for all its members. On such occasions, there is every justification to evaluate the tradition from the universal standpoint of human rights and, assuming the differences are otherwise unreconcilable, to urge the adoption of these moral standards instead of the contested ones. Although the standard of rights cannot be a final one (and it is morally dubious, to say the least, to seek to implement them where cultural traditions remain harmonious and reasonably free of dissent), a rights-based morality clearly has a role to play in instances marred by cultural conflict and dissent. Indeed, it is the only moral vision that can be called upon.

It follows that rights-based moral reasoning has a large part to play in the pluralist nation-state. For these states by definition demand a moral scheme appropriate to cooperation across cultures and subcultures. Whereas rights advocates should appreciate that even the liberal state can in no way be completely neutral with respect to moral ends, they may nonetheless confidently call for a state that errs more on the side of rights than it does on the side of restrictions. The argument can only be partial and pragmatic, but it can be confident: the pluralist nation-state is by definition an entity that must appeal to the morality of rights since no other moral strategy is universally compelling.

More extreme implications also follow, namely, that there is no valid communitarian distinction between negative and positive, civil and social rights. A pluralist regime like the United States which is established in large part on principles of equality and rights cannot thereby justify the huge discrepancies between rich and poor that it maintains. Rights, derived not from any mystical doctrine of natural law but from the norm of reciprocity based upon common human experience, pluralist exchange, and positive law may just as easily demand equal access to health care and economic security as they do the choice of physician and entrepreneurial opportunity. The difference is not in kind or even in degree. It is solely one of realpolitik.

It is also the case that rights are an entirely legitimate criterion for justice in the international arena. To be sure, rights proponents should avoid promoting the arbitrary cultural values of the West under the guise of rights and, in particular, avoid the promotion of individualism that is so attached to Western ideas about rights. Rights as here defended by communitarian reasoning are in no way properties of individuals but are rather properties of individuals as embodiments of cultural traditions. To avoid a "clash of civilizations", proponents of rights must be especially careful to avoid confusing what is merely one culture's conception of the person with a legitimate claim to rights.

Nevertheless, it is entirely appropriate for Westerners or others to insist that a rights-based agenda, properly articulated, be a major element of and even condition for international cooperation. Indeed, the essence of human rights is now, as it should be, the articulation of a minimal moral code that all cultures can be held to despite their legitimate differences. As Bryan S. Turner put this matter when contrasting human rights with citizenship rights, "human-right concepts can be seen as a progressive paradigm which is relevant to a world system. The point about human rights is that they are extra governmental."

Even so, advocates of rights must be careful-more careful than they have hitherto been-to distinguish their use of rights as a means for adjudicating cultural disputes or evaluating social traditions and the promotion of rights as ends in themselves. The repertoire of rights is intuitively available to humanity. But people also want that which makes their lives meaningful: a coherent hierarchy of values and the social and institutional arrangements that realize and sustain them. These values and arrangements are by their very essence indifferent respecters of rights, and rights provide no substitute for them.

A remark by Edmund Burke about the "curious character" of his Protestant nemesis, Dr. Price, may illustrate this point. He is "so earnest for setting up new churches," noted Burke, "and so indifferent concerning the doctrine which may be taught in them." A minister who one would presume would be committed to promoting a moral vision of life's ends was identified by Burke as one solely committed to promoting the means. Surely a humanity that on occasion justifiably demands the right to select its church also wants that church, once selected, to disseminate the truth as it understands it. For the meaningful life does not arise from the selection of the church but from the doctrines of value theoretical taught therein. And these are not "selected."

The ultimate task of social criticism is thus not to foster rights but to fashion theories of inequality and value that are morally palatable. But rights advocates are by definition not such theorists; nor can they be. Their goal must rather remain the more limited one of suggesting instances in which greater equality and more rights may be desirable across cultural divides. Tempered by recognition of its limitations, this goal is nevertheless a worthy one. Indeed, it is the only universally reliable moral guide.

2

Reconciling Civil Religion

As the new century begins international human rights have become a central focus of international relations, law and politics. Article 1 of the Universal Declaration of Human Rights 1948 declares that 'all human beings are born free and equal in dignity and rights' and that we should all 'act towards one another in a spirit of brotherhood'. But what do these words mean? Who are human rights for? What standards whether individual or collective can be accepted as universally applicable to everyone? What does a 'spirit of brotherhood' imply? In other words, what constitutes the 'humanness' of human rights?

We have come to understand that what we took to be humanly inclusive problematic, concepts, theories, objective methodologies, and transcendental truths are in fact far less than that. Instead, these products of thought bear the mark of their collective and individual creators, and the creators in turn have been distinctively marked as to gender, class, race, and culture. Western cultures favoured beliefs mirror in sometimes clear and sometimes distorting ways, not the world as it is or as we might want it to be, but the social projects of their historically identifiable creators.

One of Western culture's most favoured beliefs is in the existence of inherent and universal human rights. Yet, after more than fifty years of effort by the United Nations and other bodies the world is still far from the full adoption and implementation of universally recognised human rights for all. The Universal Declaration was meant to be a lasting statement of basic human rights. Nevertheless, when it came to implementing these standards into a binding convention two main covenants had to be drafted (the International Covenant on Civil and Political Rights (1966) or 'ICCPR' and the International Covenant on Economic, Social and Cultural Rights (1966) or 'ICESCR'). Many subsequent treaties on human rights indicate that turning universally acceptable standards into enforceable norms is very difficult.

This fragmentation and contention over what human rights might mean is particularly curious with regards to the United Nations Convention on the Elimination of All Forms of Discrimination against Women 1979. Women constitute more than 50 per cent of the world's population. If the Universal Declaration, covenants and other conventions are inadequate in dealing with women's rights then whose human rights are they? As Hilary Charlesworth has noted, there has been a rather embarrassed silence within the halls of international diplomacy and law-making concerning women's rights.

The fiftieth anniversary of the adoption of the Universal Declaration by the United Nations General Assembly occurred on 10 December 1998. Leading up to the anniversary there was considerable discussion about altering this most basic document better to represent differing cultural perspectives on human rights. Asian countries were particularly insistent while most so-called 'Western' nations responded with horror. But regional documents on human rights indicate the existence of significant differences over what human rights are and what they might mean.

The African Charter on Human and Peoples' Rights contains civil and political rights similar to those in the European Convention on Human Rights (1950) and the ICCPR. It also contains economic, social and cultural rights as in the European Social Charter, the ICESCR and other conventions. In addition, however, Articles 19 to 24 contain a list of peoples' rights. These include the right to self-determination, the right to dispose freely of a peoples' wealth and natural resources, the right to development, the right to peace and the right to a satisfactory environment.

This is the only major human rights treaty that explicitly recognises peoples' rights (other than Common Article 1 of the ICCPR and the ICESCR recognising the right of self-determination), but the reiteration of the other rights is similar to most other regional and global conventions. Although political and civil rights are generally treated separately from economic, social and cultural rights, as in the two main covenants, the African Charter is not alone in grouping them together. But because of the emphasis on group rights peculiar to this Convention the individual human rights that are enumerated cannot in fact be seen in the same light as in, for example, the ICCPR or the European Convention.

Individuality, so central to human rights in Western Europe and North America, has a much less central role in the rights of Africans - or at least as they are expressed in the African Charter. In addition this convention sets out a list of duties for each individual covered by the Charter. These include duties towards 'the family and society, the State and other legally recognised communities, and the international community'. The rights and freedoms contained in the African Charter must be exercised 'with due regard to the rights of others, collective security, morality and common interest' (Art. 27). This hybrid formulation illustrates how difficult it is to identify human rights as universally binding in the light of culturally specific or regional needs, whether as an inheritance of a colonial past, or as part of the desire to create a post-colonial present and future.

A major gap in many analyses of human rights is the lack of any deep or complex awareness of the historical context in which they developed. International human rights are intimately connected to a range of issues. The expansion of Europe, including the economic, political, scientific and technological values that have accompanied it, is a crucial factor, although perhaps in ways less obvious than is usually accepted within international human rights discourse. Religious and ethnic struggles are an important issue.

Less generally recognised, however, are the changing nature of the patriarchal family in Europe and elsewhere, the development of printing, the chronology of empire through mainstream history, the connection between citizenship and militarism, and the establishment of human rights within Euro-American literate cultures. Where histories of these structures have been referred to they tend to be dominated by one history - the rise of Europe - whose dominance is taken as axiomatic.

In one sense a focus on the history of European institutions and traditions is an accurate portrayal of the development of such supposedly 'Western' traditions as international law and international human rights. But the dominance of the West is not a matter of economic, technological, scientific, political or legal superiority. The 'lever of riches' in the West was the colonial conquest of most of the rest of the world. Despite considerable academic debate over the relative costs and benefits of colonisation and imperialism in Europe it is no coincidence that 'the rise of Europe' accompanied its expansion outside the boundaries of western Eurasia.

This expansion involved the dispossession and appropriation of most of the rest of the world. Whatever the particular expenses and burdens this may have imposed on specific European states the overall impact for colonial Europe was access to and acquisition of the world's resources. This resulted in the transformation of European states into centres of world capital, political development and control over legal discourse, including discourses of international law and human rights. This monopoly on the language of power was extended to European colonial settlements established by the English, French, Spanish, Portuguese, Russians, Dutch, Danish, Belgians, Italians, Germans and the United States. Even today only Japan really qualifies as an exception to this centralisation of power.

Its economic pre-eminence is both dependent on the European models it adopted with enthusiasm from the mid-nineteenth century onwards, and inherently fragile because of this dependence. International law and human rights are closely connected to this wider colonial history. Part of this connection is reflected in the disturbing lack within human rights discourse of the histories of those people who have been silenced within and because of the Western 'meta-narrative', i.e. women, children, the poor, the colonised, the indigenous, the 'disappeared'. These are the 'people without history' in Eric Wolf's evocative phrase. These are the people who, when they are brought within the reach of Western rationalist narratives, are treated as objects, static, unchanging, their 'development' dependent on biology or nature or tradition and, above all, the guiding hand of white European man.

Although it is necessary to place human rights within the very complex context of European colonial history it is not my intention to demean or destroy the deeply transformative effect human rights or a belief in their efficacy can have. Shirley Scott has posited that international law can be seen as ideology. Human Rights may also be seen as an aspect of the ideology of international law - as ideas that have power and can enable action. But these ideas are also subject to processes of re-examination and reimagination. They are not immutable.

The following are meant as an exploration, a kind of archaeological dig through the past and present of human rights within international law. In particular I would like to examine the 'humanness' of rights and how the characterisation of this humanity from a Euro-American perspective affects who gets to be fully human and who doesn't quite make it. My intention is to take a critical perspective. As Charlesworth has said on another occasion:

> While there have been lively debates about the relationship between the generations of rights and the best methods of implementing human rights law, there has been a general reluctance to question the basis or value of the international human rights system itself. Analyses of the

foundations and scope of international human rights law frequently lapse into heroic or mystical language; it is almost as if this branch of international law were both too valuable and too fragile to sustain critique.

Decolonising human rights, and creating a global community that is conducive to the well-being of all humans and the earth that we share, requires a radical restructuring of our ways of thinking, researching and writing. Linda Tuhiwai Smith describes these processes as 'indigenizing' research, or they might be described as 'feminising' traditional discourses. The point is not to replace one perspective with another but to decentre our focus of attention in the hope that human rights can be expanded and strengthened. It is an uncomfortable but necessary project.

A critical evaluation of the history of international human rights can be very difficult to sustain. A visit to the Holocaust Museum in Washington, DC, provides a vivid example. The depiction of loss represented within the Museum is sometimes overwhelming in its intensity - the names of European villages emptied of their Jewish populations engraved on the glass walls of the walkways from one exhibit to the next; the tower of photographs from the stetl in Lithuania out of which no survivors came; Eisenhower's determination to visit the camps so that he could be a witness ensuring that no one could deny this, no one could forget; the Temple of Memory on the ground floor with its candles, the flame of remembrance, the names of the death camps around the six sides of its warm orange walls, the quiet dome, the cool silence.

The display of Nazi photographs of Aryans and non-Aryans - human and sub-human - is particularly chilling and very familiar. Similar photographs were common within anthropological and ethnographic studies of the late nineteenth and early twentieth centuries and the same representations can be seen in books and documentary films on Australian Aboriginal people, the indigenous peoples of the Pacific, American Indians, Africans and non-European populations more generally.

Individuals from these groups were measured and photographed and their lives dissected in the name of science and the acquisition of knowledge. On the walls of the Museum the faces of the less human are exhibited and compared with the Nazi ideal like mug-shots or a police line-up with no apparent awareness of their resemblance to anthropological representations common in Western academic and popular documents of the time.

The genocide that the twentieth century gave us is most appalling when we realise how familiar it is, how common it has become. The word itself is quite recent, invented by Raphael Lemkin during the worst years of the Second World War. His new word and ideas about what it meant first gained currency as the Holocaust ended and an attempt at understanding was first attempted. He and a small group of like-minded scholars and activists were largely responsible for the drafting and passage of the Genocide Convention through the United Nations General Assembly on 9 December 1948, just one day prior to the General Assembly's adoption of the Universal Declaration of Human Rights.

The definition contained in Article 2 of the Convention, for all its flaws, is now generally accepted as the legal definition of genocide in international law. But the resonance of the images of dehumanisation that occurred during the Holocaust is also a construction, a careful representation of the past designed to recall and move. Such representations are necessary and dangerous - necessary because we forget our past at our peril, dangerous because this history is itself a form of forgetting, a burial.

Gypsies, gays and lesbians and the physically and mentally disabled were also targeted for elimination by the Nazi regime. Yet they receive little attention in the Washington Holocaust Museum. One small set of displays tucked into a corner acknowledges their loss. History is never 'just history'. The twentieth century may have given us the word but the practice and policy of genocide is much older. Nor did it end in 1945. We seem to have ended the old century much as we began it: debating humanitarian principles and the nature of international law while preparing for war; using humane impulses and the rhetoric of concern as well as the fervour of nationalism to justify the use of force.

To this list we have added denial of our own complicity with violence and exploitation while proclaiming our belief in universal rights for all human beings. We continue to struggle with ideas about the rule of international law while breaching such rules because of the apparent impossibility of resolving our differences in any other way. Three events in 1999 seemed to encapsulate the difficulties of reconciling history, human rights, violence and the desire to move away from the tragic consequences of the past.

On 24 March 1999 NATO began its aerial bombing of Yugoslavia in response to the political stand-off over Kosovo. On that same day the House of Lords announced its second attempt to resolve the problem of General Pinochet's extradition from the United Kingdom to Spain on criminal charges of torture, kidnapping and murder during his term as head of state in Chile. As the world's attention was focused on the Balkans and the legal difficulties of a former South American dictator another unfolding chain of events, the process of self-determination in the former Portuguese colony of East Timor, was struggling with the meaning of autonomy and human rights.

Despite months of harassment and violence nearly 80 per cent of East Timorese people voted for independence on 30 August of that same year. Without the harassment and terror the vote may well have been higher. Close to 100 per cent of all voters lined up to cast their ballot on that day. In some polling stations half the registered voters were waiting as the blue UN ballot boxes arrived early on that morning. Reports of UN monitors, journalists, Catholic Church workers and volunteers with non-governmental organisations tallied with the images that appeared on television screens around the world. Women wore their Sunday best and whole families, including small children, came.

The elderly, the young, women and men stood in line with their registration papers and identification in hand waiting to cast their vote of condemnation of Indonesia's rule and their hopes for the future. One old man was quoted afterwards: 'Now I have voted; now I can die.' Over and over again the people said they knew they would suffer for this but they had voted for their children. The militia and Indonesian army personnel hovered just out of sight of the cameras. Remembering that close to a quarter of a million East Timorese, around a third of the population, had been killed or had died of starvation and mistreatment during twenty-four years of Indonesian rule made the affirmation of democratic rights all the more poignant and dramatic.

The day of 'Popular Consultation' was peaceful, but the preceding weeks and months of violence were a mild foretaste of the havoc, murder, terror and intimidation to be inflicted by the pro-Indonesian militias (armed and directed by the Indonesian military) within hours of the announcement of the final tally. It soon became apparent that another Kosovo-type intervention by 'like-minded countries', in the words of the New Zealand Minister of Foreign Affairs, or a 'coalition of the willing' in the words of the Foreign Minister of Australia, would be necessary to curtail the violence. Two weeks later, after an appalling level of killing, rape and forced removals, the UN finally intervened.

Human rights are often assumed to include only a narrow range of civil and political rights applicable in a relatively confined type of situation. But they have become much more than this. Human rights are an eclectic mixture of civil, political, economic, social, cultural and collective rights engaging us all in an ongoing debate over priorities, relevance and implementation and, at a deeper level, on the meaning of civil society and a humane world. As we enter a new century of economic globalisation these are the issues that will need to be addressed.

We can all agree that torture is a serious infringement of human rights, and many of us support Amnesty International in its efforts at eradicating this practice. The decision of the House of Lords in upholding at least part of the case against General Pinochet, refusing to allow him to hide behind the shield of state sovereignty, was surely right. But what about children sold into sexual slavery, handcuffed to beds or kept in cages and brought out for the benefit of tourists and businessmen who want anonymous sex without the fear of HIV/AIDS? Is this torture? Is the abuse of women, children and even men in the home, or harassment in the workplace, a breach of international human rights?

Are the violent dispossession and removal of indigenous peoples and peasants from their land in the name of economic development or national cohesion contrary to international law? If the Albanian Kosovars of Yugoslavia or the East Timorese have a right to be free of violence, 'ethnic cleansing' and abuse, then do not these rights also apply to Aceh and West Papua, Tibet, the Karen peoples of Burma, the Kurds, the Palestinians, the Chechens? Are human rights and decolonisation only applicable to the exotic and the strange? Do the Basque people of Spain and France, the Québecois, the Polynesians of Hawaii, the Spanish-speaking population of Puerto Rico also have rights to self-determination?

Human rights are not only about these more obvious forms of violence. Is hunger an abuse of the human right to an adequate standard of living and if so how can this be implemented? What about the high death rates of children from malnutrition, disease and neglect in many parts of the world? The UN Convention on the Rights of the Child has been ratified by every nation on earth with the exceptions of the United States and Somalia. And yet children suffer and die in the thousands every minute of every day.

The holocaust of HIV/AIDS is destroying whole generations of the young and strong in much of Sub-Saharan Africa, the Caribbean, South and Southeast Asia, Latin America and Eastern Europe. The world has been frighteningly slow to respond effectively. This is not only an issue of the right to health but also of the corporate rights of pharmaceutical companies and the power of economic globalisation, the clash with cultural diversity, sexuality, gender, even mass murder. What about the renewal of so-called 'fundamentalist' religions demanding specific codes of behaviour for women in particular?

Why is the veiling of Islamic women described as a breach of human rights by so many Western commentators, but the reduction of abortion services or the censoring of the 'media' in First World countries in the name of 'family values' and Christianity not? What of the abuses committed by multinational corporations and other private investors in co-operation with governments and international institutions in their search for profit? There is ample evidence that the disparity between the very rich and the very poor is widening, that the middle is eroding and that poverty is getting worse not better.

Is this a question of human rights, or is it merely a matter of the operation of blind market forces moving inexorably towards a world of free trade and unfettered corporate investment? The history of international law and human rights and their association with the projects of European colonialism, decolonisation and globalisation. Colonisation began in Europe itself more than a thousand years ago and continued with its expansion throughout the world by the beginning of the twentieth century.

This has resulted in a resolutely Eurocentric perspective in most disciplines including international law and human rights. The word 'Eurocentrism' has been defined to mean the imaginative and institutional context that informs contemporary scholarship, opinion, and law. As a theory, it postulates the superiority of Europeans over non-Europeans. ...On a global scale, this results in a world with a single center - Europe - and a surrounding periphery. Europe, at the center (Inside), is historical, invents and progresses, and non-Europe, at the periphery (Outside), is ahistorical, stagnant, and unchanging.

'Eurocentrism' is not limited to Western Europe but also includes former white settler colonies in North America and elsewhere, principally the United States but also including the rest of North and South America, Australia, New Zealand and southern Africa. For this reason I prefer to use the phrase 'Euro-American' unless the context warrants otherwise. But it is meant to be synonymous with this geographically expanded definition of 'Eurocentrism'.

The relationship between supposedly 'universal' values embedded in international human rights law and the complications and challenges posed by cultural difference is also discussed. As Antony Anghie has pointed out, the 'universality of international law is a relatively recent development'. It could not be said to have been really established until 'the imperial expansion that took place towards the end of the "long nineteenth century"'. Questions of universality cannot therefore be properly addressed without facing squarely the history of European colonialism.

Surprisingly, relatively little attention has been paid to the relationship between colonialism or imperialism and international law, including human rights, until very recently. Anghie postulates this as a problem of sovereignty. As European states became increasingly rigid embodiments of sovereignty they contrasted themselves with sites of 'non-sovereignty' in the rest of the world. Once the colonial project was largely complete (by 1900) the entire world, with a few exceptions, was subject to Euro-American authority. Most of the world's population therefore could be seen as 'non-sovereign' and unproblematic in terms of legal theory if not in terms of political reality. My own view is that this historical blindness is much more complex and has much more significant social, cultural and even psychological reasons lying behind it. As Anghie also notes, sociological perspectives preceded questions of sovereignty for European colonisers. The resulting failure to accommodate difference without conquest or violence has profoundly shaped our world.

'Sovereignty' is, according to Martti Koskenniemi, an extremely ambiguous term. He divides sovereignty into 'external sovereignty' or 'independence' and 'internal sovereignty' or 'self-determination'. By the end of the nineteenth century states came to represent the principle of independence in international law, meaning the power to exercise the functions of a state to the exclusion of all other states within defined territorial boundaries. It was not, however, until after 1960 that this principle of sovereignty was applied to most of the world's peoples through their exercise of a right of self-determination in achieving external sovereignty, or independence, as nation-states.

This process of decolonisation or nation building was presumptively built on the post-war international legal order's return to a natural law theory of rights pertaining to individuals, not just to states. New nation-states formally adopted principles of human rights directly from international law (principally from the Universal Declaration of Human Rights) into new constitutions and regional human rights arrangements in Europe, the Americas, Africa and even Asia. Since then human rights appear to have become the new civil orthodoxy of morality in international politics and law.

But this process of nation building essentially grafted the older positivist notion of state sovereignty onto a plethora of new states most of which are culturally non-European. Even where Europeanisation was deeply entrenched most states have begun to depart from their colonial pasts as decades or even centuries of European colonialism begin to disintegrate and native or home grown social and cultural traditions resurface or are newly invented in the quest for an anti-colonial or 'post-colonial' national identity.

Human rights, supposedly 'universal' in application, have suffered through lack of implementation and enforcement, neglect or, more controversially, through a lack of cultural 'fit' (or so it is sometimes argued) between mainly civil and political rights and the demands of new national orders. Nation-states continue to grapple with the complexities of modern political structures that are often antithetical to pre-existing cultural or social patterns and political arrangements. In addition the weight of Euro-American economic superiority, most recently 'universalised' through the process of globalisation, has increasingly buried new nation-states under mountains of debt, poverty, disease and dysfunction.

Both new and old patterns of social structure frequently collapse through civil and interstate war, famine, environmental devastation, expropriation of land, and rapid urbanisation. Human rights are fundamentally about challenges to the notion of state sovereignty. The late twentieth-century expansion of economic trade and financial arrangements across international boundaries is also a significant challenge to state sovereignty. The trajectory of law and international relations in the twenty-first century must deal with these two major forces and how they can be reconciled (or not) with the sovereignty of the state.

Although economic globalisation is frequently seen as the more significant of these challenges, political and legal globalisation through international law, labour law, human rights and environmental regulation is rapidly developing as the twin force for change. Disruptive riots in Seattle, Melbourne and Quebec City have highlighted this uneasy relationship. In fact economic decisions are primarily political and legal in nature and major international economic players (including states) are becoming increasingly aware of this, partly through the noisy insistence of the millennial street fighters.

Human rights and environmental regulation within international law are developing as the constitutional framework for global governance by which economic liberalisation might be tamed. States, especially new nation-states, are caught in the middle. The theoretical construct of the state in international law is struggling to adapt to these twin challenges. The impact of these revolutionary processes on indigenous peoples, women, children and other disadvantaged groups has often been devastating. This book focuses on indigenous peoples and women in an attempt to deconstruct and perhaps reconstruct the meaning of 'humanness' as it applies to human rights within international law. I would suggest that decolonisation is an immensely more complex process than international law has hitherto acknowledged. It involves seriously questioning the meaning of universality and its association with European humanism and the Enlightenment as partners and beneficiaries of the colonial mission overseas.

As decolonisation continues to undermine the long history of European colonialism different cultural patterns will continue to emerge making the applicability of international law and human rights more and more complex. To dismiss this trend as a misconceived and fuzzy idea called 'cultural relativism' or, more bleakly, as a descent into chaos is to miss the great challenge that the new cultural renaissance of the twenty-first century presents. The changing nature of state sovereignty, a global marketplace, human rights (including labour standards), the environment and the effect of burgeoning and often aggressively defended cultural difference are the five interrelated pillars of historical change through which we are currently moving.

It is proposed that a much more complex process took place in which indigenous peoples and women played a prominent, though often hidden, role. Nevertheless, the weight of European colonialism buried this more complex history under the notion of the universality of international law and human rights. Ideas about 'humanness' that developed in European debates on the meaning of civil society borrowed from indigenous sources while genocide, slavery and misogyny flourished.

To question the fundamental premises of human rights looks like a dangerous thing to do given the precarious nature of human freedom, security and solidarity around the world. But without questioning our basic assumptions about human rights we leave ourselves vulnerable to inaccurate assumptions about the nature of human identity, cultural diversity and the hangover of colonial thinking posing as universality.

As we stumble into a new century the rights discourse seems to have been momentarily captured by Western commentators who maintain that human rights are coterminous with corporate capitalism and individual initiative. Anything else is dismissed as a form of 'political correctness' antithetical to 'real' human rights. Individualism is seen as axiomatic to human rights, essential to the competitive nature of 'Man', and any reference to collective or co-operative values is dismissed as a laughable or even dangerous degeneration into romanticism, socialism or cultural relativism. In some senses this conservative view of human rights has become the new ideology of the post-Cold-War world.

We still seem to be caught in the illogic of our own passionate attachment to divergent ideas about nationalism, universality, humanitarian concern and the rights of both individuals and peoples. During the past hundred years or longer the call for equal rights by women, former slaves, indigenous peoples, the poor, the disabled, gays and lesbians, and even children has become a powerful force for political debate and legal change. Too often, however, human rights discourse is constrained by boundaries which make the rights of the vast majority of human beings seem marginal, 'alternative' or irrelevant. International human rights can be a necessary tool in bringing all human beings into the centre of discussion over the division of resources and power in this world, or they can be used as a rhetorical device for sidelining most humans into a kind of international darkness.

As war began in March 1999 with nightly bombing in Kosovo and Serbia (brought to us in intimate and uninformative detail by the technological miracle of the televised military briefing) the massive war in Central Africa was almost completely ignored. On that memorable northern spring day of 24 March 1999 another announcement of another atrocity on the borders of Uganda appeared in small print on the back pages of the American national press. Member-states of NATO and their allies (such as Australia) prepared to take in thousands of Kosovar Albanian refugees.

At the same time hundreds of thousands of Africans displaced by war, famine and terror in Sierra Leone, Sudan, Somalia, Ethiopia, Eritrea, Rwanda, Burundi, Angola, both

Congos and many surrounding states were left to their misery in almost complete obscurity. People struggling for self-determination and human rights in Asia, the Pacific, Africa and the Americas are still routinely dismissed and ignored. In former President Clinton's words, we cannot leave any people behind based on the belief that this is 'just how they are'. At the end of the twentieth century East Timor, after centuries of colonial rule by Portugal and decades of violent oppression by Indonesia, seemed on the point of tremendous hope and potential horror - again - while the world focused its attention on another tragedy in southern Europe. Then, early in the new century, one old man did finally catch his flight from London to Santiago.

Human rights have become a kind of civil religion to many, especially in the West. Conor Cruise O'Brien borrows the phrase from Rousseau as meaning 'the religious dimension of the polity' or the 'cult of liberty' best represented by the American experience of civil rights and freedoms. O'Brien suggests that the phrase can be generalised to mean a belief in human rights going beyond law or political freedoms. International human rights have developed into a powerful ideological device both for and against the peaceful resolution of disputes and the equitable division of political and economic power. They are also a foundational principle of legal order in the world competing directly with older patterns of realpolitik, economic development and state sovereignty.

Human rights cannot be dismissed simply as the colonialist imposition of Western values or the cynical manipulation of an outdated 'meta-narrative' of Enlightenment. Nor should they be relegated to the level of propaganda in the modern temple of law and political grandstanding posing as principle. Despite British Prime Minister Tony Blair's assertion that the action against Yugoslavia over Kosovo could be described as 'compassionate bombing', rights cannot be established or maintained through force. Only the long hard work of sustained self-examination, negotiation, reciprocal respect, responsibility, imaginative law reform and the input of significant political and economic resources can achieve some measure of peace, stability, equity and freedom in this deeply damaged world.

THE UNIVERSAL DECLARATION OF HUMAN RIGHTS

Where do human rights come from? A full history of the debates, deals, failures and triumphs of human rights within the bureaucratic maze of the United Nations would be a fascinating one but it is beyond the boundaries of this book. The foundation for the human rights principles contained in the Universal Declaration of Human Rights is the American Bill of Rights and the French Declaration of the Rights of Man and the Citizen, but this is far from being the full story. Although the search for origins is probably futile some understanding of the different threads that have gone into the making of human rights might help to ground the current debates over their relevance and implementation.

The idea of an international 'Bill of Rights' goes back to the 1920s or earlier. The introduction of human rights into international law was an important feature of the post-war years, although this may be more a product of hindsight than a genuine reflection of the priorities of the time. Franklin D. Roosevelt's 'Four Freedoms' speech in his State of the Union address in 1941 is often credited with laying the foundation for the incorporation of human rights in the post-war international order.

Human rights first became a significant part of international law under the Charter of the United Nations 1945 and the Universal Declaration of Human Rights 1948. The Declaration is a resolution passed by the United Nations General Assembly, not a binding treaty. But, as Louis Henkin has noted, even in 1948 some saw it as elaborating on references to human rights contained in the Charter itself. Since then it has almost certainly crystallised into customary international law. Some provisions may even have achieved the status of jus cogens or 'peremptory norms' of international law taking priority over all other customary law and even treaty obligations.

The vote for the Declaration was forty-eight countries for, none against, two absentees (Honduras and Yemen) and eight abstentions. Honduras later stated that if its representative had been in the General Assembly at the time the vote was taken Honduras would certainly have voted in favour of the Declaration. The list of those who abstained is revealing. Byelorussian SSR, Czechoslovakia, Poland, Ukrainian SSR, the Soviet Union, Yugoslavia, Saudi Arabia and the Union of South Africa all found it impossible to vote either for or against the Declaration.

Byelorussian SSR and the Ukrainian SSR are now the independent states of Belarus and Ukraine. At the time they were both part of the Soviet Union but still had separate votes in the General Assembly. It is interesting to note that these countries, although they disagreed profoundly with some provisions of the Declaration, did not want to vote against it. This was considered significant at the time as an indication that even those who disagreed with some provisions were not prepared to reject it in principle.

Not only Eastern bloc countries had their doubts. Canada also nearly abstained in the final vote even though Professor John Humphrey of McGill University had participated in writing the first draft of the Declaration and strongly supported its passage. In a preliminary vote in the Third Committee of the General Assembly on Social, Cultural and Humanitarian Questions Canada *did* abstain, shocking nearly everyone. Canada finally voted in favour of the Declaration in the plenary session of the General Assembly on 10 December 1948, thus avoiding the permanent embarrassment of having abstained in the company of the communist Eastern bloc and apartheid South Africa. But the Canadian government, offering a rather weak *ex post facto* explanation, remained sceptical.

States that took a positive role in the drafting of the Declaration included Australia, Chile, (pre-communist) China, Cuba, France, India, Iran, Lebanon, Panama, the Philippines, the United Kingdom, the United States and Uruguay. Afghanistan, Burma, Ceylon (now Sri Lanka), Ethiopia, Iraq, Haiti, Liberia, Pakistan, Syria, most of Latin America and all the Allied powers were members of the UN General Assembly at the time and voted in favour of the Declaration. South Africa did not vote for the Declaration in view of its developing policies on apartheid that would eventually lead to its expulsion from the United Nations, the Commonwealth and most other international groups. Its stated reasons were that the provisions were too broad and would give rise to legal liability in international law. This may well lie behind Canada's near-abstention. As Humphrey points out, the South Africans were right about the document creating legal obligations.

The wide representation of nations voting for the Declaration portrays perhaps a surprising unanimity among a range of different political and cultural traditions. Ensuring that the Declaration was sensitive to 'differing religious traditions, political philosophies, legal systems and economic, social, and cultural patterns' that were represented among the fifty-eight members of the UN at that time was a primary goal of the drafters. These included eminent international figures such as Eleanor Roosevelt and leading international scholars and diplomats such as René Cassin of France, P. C. Chang of China, Hernan Santa Cruz of Chile, Charles Malik of Lebanon, Omar Loufti of Egypt, Hansa Mehta of India, Carlos P. Romulo of the Philippines and Alex P. Pavlov of the Soviet Union.

The hope was to reach as wide a consensus as possible and this seems to have been achieved with the exception of the Eastern bloc. It should not go unnoticed, however, that most of the principal drafters were male. It was mainly a few determined women in delegations from the developing world and smaller nations, such as Hansa Mehta of India or Jessie Street of Australia, who pursued issues of sex discrimination within the UN at this time.

The Declaration went through extensive discussions and revisions before reaching a vote in the General Assembly plenary session on 10 December (under the warmly supportive chairmanship of Australia's H. V. Evatt). From the first drafting or 'nuclear' committee of the newly formed UN Human Rights Commission, to the full Commission (both under the guidance of Eleanor Roosevelt), and finally to the Third Committee of the General Assembly the debate included all member-states of the UN. The debate in the Third Committee lasted nearly three months. Every article was thoroughly discussed.

The claim by some cultural relativists that this document represents a Western imperialist imposition of standards on non-Western cultures is weakened by the widespread support for the Declaration in the General Assembly in 1948. It is true that most of Africa and much of Asia and the Pacific were still under colonial rule at this time so could not be represented in the drafting or passage of the Declaration. Nevertheless there was, significantly, broad support among a range of different cultural and political traditions including Islamic, Asian, Latin American and African. The discussions were by no means dominated by the Western powers although they obviously played an important role.

In an incident recounted by both Eleanor Roosevelt and John Humphrey, Chang took an early opportunity to establish that the Universal Declaration could not be a simple reflection of Western philosophy - and to that end, he advised UN staff to embark on a study of Confucian thought. Chang was remembered and appreciated for two kinds of contributions. On one hand, he regularly caught the attention of other delegates by referring to Chinese practice or quoting a pertinent Chinese proverb. Official records reflect some of these contributions, and in some instances they appear to have had the effect of helping delegates appreciate an alternative perspective and move beyond an impasse. Third Committee records note his advice to sweep the snow in front of one's own doors and overlook the frost on others' roof tiles.

Representatives from Latin America, the Soviet Union and the Middle East ensured that the Declaration contained economic, social and cultural rights going beyond an

Enlightenment view of human rights as civil and political rights only. Humphrey himself had put such rights into his original draft. Both Eleanor Roosevelt and the British delegation supported them. The most controversial issues revolved around whether to include some reference to the Deity in the Declaration, and over the substance of Article 18 on religious freedom. In the end no reference to either 'God or nature' was made in the Declaration. The Article 18 reference to the right to change one's religion was hotly contested by representatives from Saudi Arabia, Lebanon, Afghanistan, Iraq, Pakistan and Syria.

In the Third Committee [Arabia's representative] Jamil Baroody had said that the provision in Article 18, which recognizes the right of everyone to change his religion or belief, was contrary to the rule of the Koran, an interpretation which was challenged in plenary by Sir Mohammed Zafrullah Khan, a Pakistani Moslem. At the plenary session, however, only Saudi Arabia among majority Muslim nations abstained.

The Declaration and the development of binding human rights law were seen by some as a possible means of maintaining global peace and security as well as creating a more just and equitable world order. The backdrop against which the UN Charter and Declaration were drafted was, however, one of deepening schisms among the Allied powers themselves. By 1948, when the Declaration was passed, the Cold War had already begun. The expansion of nuclear weapons symbolised by the acquisition of the 'Bomb' by the Soviets increased this sense of threat.

The starry eyed delegates and self-congratulating diplomats present at the Palais Chaillot, in the shadow of the Eiffel Tower, at the birth of the first New World Order in December 1948 failed to notice that the Berlin airlift had just begun, made necessary by Stalin's petulant decision to seal the city against road and rail transport. ...The Soviet ambassador to the UN gave a tight, abstemious smile as he explained the Soviet abstention to the newsmen: the Declaration, he said, was 'just a collection of pious phrases'.

It is too easy to romanticise the efforts of the drafters of the Charter and the Declaration. There is no doubt that the horrors of world war were very much on their minds in attempting to establish a peaceful and humanitarian global regime. The prominence of human rights within the UN was not, however, the original purpose of the organisation. The 'Great Powers' were intent on creating another version of the League of Nations, but one with a little more muscle. It was only after 'last-minute pressure exerted on the US delegation by a group of American non-governmental organizations (notably, the American Jewish Congress and the National Association for the Advancement of Colored People)' that human rights were elevated into a primary purpose of the UN.

The role of NGOs generally was crucial to the drafting of the Declaration. But, as Mark Mazower has reminded us, anti-Semitism did not disappear in Europe or elsewhere after the Holocaust was revealed to the world by Allied soldiers in 1945. Indeed it appears to have intensified as Jewish survivors tried to re-establish their lives either in their old homes (which had frequently been taken over by others), or as immigrants overseas; or as they tried to reclaim their property, a process which is still continuing.

Racism of another kind has remained a problem in Europe and elsewhere despite gains made from the early 1960s onwards. Sexual discrimination against women is still inadequately dealt with despite the demands of women's rights activists and feminists that gender discrimination is as serious as racism in most societies. This form of human rights abuse did not receive any significant attention until the 1970s. This was so even though the elevation of a sub-commission on women's rights (set up under the UN Commission of Human Rights in 1946) into a full-blown Commission on the Status of Women was, at the time, a considerable achievement. Other major human rights abuses such as genocide, torture, even slavery continued throughout the second half of the twentieth century and remain unresolved problems in international and national affairs.

THE HOLOCAUST

In writing a book about international human rights, and especially one that purports to offer some sort of historical explanation for their manifestation and expression, it is impossible to avoid a discussion of the Holocaust. Yet, like Inga Clendinnen in her superb portrayal Reading the Holocaust, I still come away baffled and silent.

In the first two years in which a colleague and I offered International Human Rights as an undergraduate unit of study at the University of Sydney in Australia we invited a Jewish survivor of the death camps to come and speak to our students. The first year he came he described his own experience as a young man. He had fled Austria when it became clear that the Nazis were about to take over, sought refuge in Switzerland (which was denied) and ended up in France where he managed to evade detection for a number of years. Eventually he was sent off by railway to various different camps including Auschwitz.

He described the killing work, the brutality of the guards, the cold, the lack of food and how desirable it was to get the last bit of soup because it was more nutritious. He said he only slowly realised that he and the others were not meant to survive - that their prisons were in fact death camps. He described his striped uniform and shaved head and how ordinary people in the streets would literally not see the work gangs of concentration camp inmates when they passed. At the end of his talk he gave us just one horrifying detail meant to shock - his description of a pile of bodies heaped up in a corner of a yard that had not been disposed of before the Allied troops came and liberated the survivors.

I do not know whether our guest ever really came to terms with what had happened to him or, like Primo Levi's suicide seems to indicate, had merely learned how to speak of it in quiet language that hid ongoing anguish. He told us that he had not started to speak about his experiences until fairly late in life. This seems to have been a common part of the biography of many survivors. Talking to groups, especially groups of university and high school students, was, he said, one way for him to fulfill his obligations to those who had not survived, which included most of his family. He emphasised that the experience in the camps was deliberately designed to dehumanise the victims. His view was that it had in fact dehumanised those who were committing the crimes. He expressed pity for the guards who had become brutes, no longer human.

The documentation on the Holocaust is overwhelmingly thorough and detailed. The record is very clear that Jews were targeted for elimination. But so also were gypsies or Roma people. Many others were of course also caught up in this system: civilians from all nations conquered by Germany, especially Poland; communists; gays and lesbians; the mentally and physically disabled; political agitators; pacifists; anyone deemed deviant by the German state. Even Allied servicemen were sent to the camps contrary to existing laws on the treatment of prisoners of war. By 1942 when the 'Final Solution' was begun in earnest 2 million Russian prisoners of war had already been shot or had died of exposure and starvation.

Although we tend to think of Hitler and Nazi Germany as a horrifying aberration in European history, I believe this is a mistake. The recurrence of fascination with this topic in academic, literary and popular culture (including the continuing debate over whether the Holocaust 'really' happened) indicates that we are still trying to come to terms with what the Holocaust means. By the early twentieth century Western Europeans had convinced themselves that they did indeed represent the pinnacle of human achievement; that Europe really was the centre of the earth; that the peak of civilisation really did exist in Europe alone.

The 'white man's burden' was the extension of this civilisation to the rest of the world. People genuinely believed this. Not just blatant racists, or xenophobes, or imperialist oppressors, but ordinary men and women had been convinced of the truth of this racially based propaganda. These included my own forebears and many others from all classes and nationalities of Europe and where European settlement has multiplied, as in the United States, Canada, Australia, New Zealand and southern Africa. Indeed many Europeans and people of European descent still believe this. It has become so ingrained that most of us are not even aware of our own Eurocentrism.

The Holocaust was a horrifying event that cut a deep wound down the middle of twentieth-century Europe. That wound is not, however, as some have maintained, a great chasm dividing us irrevocably from our brutal past. It is a very thin line. We have crossed it many times. If one is in search of memorials to the killing fields of the past and the present one should not limit one's travels to Auschwitz. Indigenous peoples in the Americas, Australia and elsewhere around the globe have their own memories of horror to deal with as do the citizens of Armenia, Cambodia, East Timor, China, and Russia, much of Africa.

A treeless valley in South Dakota, a sluggish stream in central New South Wales, a river bank in Rwanda, a small forest village in Vietnam - each are quiet memorials to an unspeakable past. Indeed it is hard to find a place on this earth which has not witnessed mass murder. Human rights were designed as an attempt to halt the killing. They have grown well beyond this aim. At the same time the international human rights movement appears to have failed to fulfill even this most basic goal, as witnessed by the dead of Rwanda in 1994. Arguments that somehow these other examples of mass murder and terror are not 'holocausts' seem to those who still suffer from them to be a heartless quibble over terminology, or an attempt at another kind of 'holocaust denial'.

The Holocaust was, among many other things, a terrible awakening. But it has also paradoxically induced an even more terrible blindness and denial. It demands that we understand that the violence of ethnic tribalism is not confined to Africa, or Asia, or the Middle East, or the cities of Eastern Europe -

it is here, at home - We are the Savage. For many of us of West European ancestry this is still impossible to accept. International human rights provide one mechanism whereby we might atone for this terrible denial.

The second time our guest came to talk to our students he did not talk about his personal experiences but rather about the historical background to the Holocaust. He discussed the transformation of empires in Europe, the position of Germany, the movement of history across the continent in an attempt to explain what had happened. This account was less moving on one level but perhaps more revealing on another. How does one come to terms with such experience? How does one 'explain' the Holocaust?

For Europeans the Second World War and the mass killing of civilians was a revelation. It was easy for them, and for us, to forget the extent of murder that had gone on in overseas colonial territories both before and after the war. Europeans had created an image of themselves that could not accommodate such barbarity. To discover that the 'heart of darkness' was not in Central Africa, but in Central Europe, was a stunning realisation.

After the first talk ended each and every student came up and spoke to our guest at the front of the classroom. They also each had to touch him. Every student shook his hand or touched his arm or in some way made physical contact. My colleague and I both noticed it, indeed we did the same ourselves, but I still cannot explain it. Nor can I explain the tone of forgiveness in which this survivor spoke of his persecutors. I have heard this same note of forgiveness in the voices of indigenous people discussing their own sense of loss.

It is not that anger and despair are not part of the emotional response any human being would feel if confronted by such experience, but rather as if, in order to continue as a human being, the anger and despair must somehow be transformed into something else. I felt then, and feel now, that human rights are not just a set of legal doctrines or idealistic principles but are in fact part of a journey. This journey began in earnest long before the drafters of the Declaration were first shepherded into agreement by Eleanor Roosevelt or John Humphrey scribbled his first draft of a document on a piece of notepaper.

DECOLONISATION AND HUMAN RIGHTS TREATIES

The world order that was envisioned after the Second World War was also built, over the profound objections of France, Belgium and other colonial powers, upon an agenda of decolonisation. Self-determination and conflicting definitions of human rights were made part of the post-war rebuilding agenda mainly through American and Soviet initiatives carried against the immediate wishes of older European colonial powers.

This had also been an important part of the settlement after the First World War with a notable lack of success. Although the concept of 'self-determination' was not invented by President Woodrow Wilson (it owes more to Lenin) he nevertheless made it an important part of his plan for a post-war settlement that would guarantee lasting peace under the Treaty of Versailles and the League of Nations. But Wilson could not even convince his own Congress of the wisdom of this plan.

Decolonisation became the principal expression of self-determination after the Second World War. Neither of these terms is present in the Declaration, although as Waltz points out, newly decolonised states seized on the drafting of the Declaration as an opportunity to extend human rights protection beyond the control of the colonial powers. With the brief exception of the United Kingdom under Clement Attlee's post-war Labour government, Europe was not anxious to divest itself of its colonial possessions. Self-determination and decolonisation came, however, to be defined as the right of human beings, contained within collective entities called 'peoples', to achieve the status of citizens within newly created nation-states or some other connection to an existing nation-state (UN Charter, Preamble, Arts 1, 2 and 55 and Chapters XI, XII and XIII).

This principle was crystallised in Common Article I of the two main UN covenants on human rights in 1966. But the law of self-determination developed slowly only as it became clear through protracted anti-colonial wars in French Indochina, Algeria and elsewhere in colonial Africa and Asia that the old European empires could not be maintained. After 1960 the drive towards decolonisation and the creation of new nation-states accelerated rapidly. This was reflected in the attention paid to this process by the UN particularly with the backing of the Soviet Union and the Eastern bloc.

By the late 1940s the United States had retreated towards a more conservative position and tended to see claims of self-determination in terms of the Cold War and the spread of communism. The division of the world into blocs unquestionably had a distorting effect, not only on the decolonisation process itself, but also on the development of human rights and their division into separate categories of rights.

Extensive treaty obligations have been created by the UN and other international bodies both globally and regionally since this early expression of human and peoples' rights. The rights protected include classic civil and political rights explicitly derived from Bills of Rights formulated in France and the United States in the late eighteenth century. These include freedom of expression, freedom of religion, the right to a fair trial, the right to participate in political affairs and other rights. International human rights also include economic, social and cultural rights developed as a result of Marxist, socialist and anti-individualist movements of the nineteenth and twentieth centuries.

These rights include the right to work, the right to equal pay, the right to an adequate standard of living, social security, health, education and participation in cultural life, all of which are in the Declaration. Finally, and more contentiously, collective or 'peoples' rights have been added to the individual rights with which we are most familiar. These include the right to self-determination, a closely associated right to democracy, the right to development, the right to control of natural resources, the right to a clean environment and the right to peace. Besides the two UN covenants specific conventions were drafted on genocide; refugees; human rights violations against civilians during times of war or armed insurrection; racial discrimination; women's rights; indigenous populations; the rights of the child; and migrant workers.

There are also conventions dealing with specific infractions of human rights such as torture. The Rome Convention 1998 provides for a permanent International Criminal Court to try individuals for war crimes, crimes against humanity, genocide and crimes of aggression. Conventions are in force dealing with human rights violations on a regional basis in Europe, the Americas and Africa. The Asia-Pacific remains the only part of the world that does not have its own regional human rights system.

The European system was originally designed to cover Western Europe only but since the collapse of the Eastern bloc and the Soviet Union from 1988 to 1991 many former Eastern European countries have joined or are attempting to join European human rights structures. The American Convention is applicable to countries in the Western Hemisphere. Neither Canada nor the United States has ratified it. Nevertheless, they are bound by the American Declaration of the Rights and Duties of Man 1948. The Inter-American Commission on Human Rights can address complaints made under the American Declaration against a non-state party to the Convention under certain conditions.

The two main covenants have a contentious history. The Declaration is supposed to represent global consensus on human rights, but when there was an attempt to create a binding convention incorporating the standards set in the Declaration it was not possible to draft a single document. The process of creating binding and to some extent enforceable human rights provisions within the UN took another eighteen years. Two covenants instead were necessary mainly owing to disputes between Western and Eastern blocs over the priority to be given to civil and political versus economic, social and cultural rights. But temporary political differences do not provide a full explanation for the proliferation of human rights documents, or deep divisions over the content and standing of particular human rights or indeed any human right.

THE BRETTON WOODS SYSTEM AND HUMAN RIGHTS

International economic law was also being transformed at the same time as human rights and self-determination became major principles in international law. But the two discourses rarely if ever conversed with each other. It is as if the international law of human rights and the international economic law of globalisation and development have been progressing within parallel universes. They eerily replicate similar principles (the universality of basic Euro-American economic and political principles; rights to control of natural resources and development; massive incursions into the concept of state sovereignty; the general spread of international law both within and between states) but never seem to touch.

The one area of human rights that does directly address economic issues, economic and social rights, seems to have had no influence on the development of international economic law. The massive post-war internationalisation (or globalisation) of currency values, monetary policy making, banking and trade developed out of the Bretton Woods Conference initiated by the United States and the United Kingdom in 1944. The World Bank and the International Monetary Fund were both created as a result of this Conference.

A parallel trade body failed, but the General Agreement on Tariffs and Trade provided a mechanism for the regulation of international trade until 1994 when the World Trade Organisation was established. The original goal of this system was to encourage the removal of trade barriers, rigid monetary and fiscal policies and gross inequities in wealth that, it was believed, would drag the world into another 1930s-style Great Depression after the Second World War.

'Keynesian economics', inspired by the work of British economist John Maynard Keynes, was the new orthodoxy.

This included high levels of government intervention in fiscal policy through the manipulation of revenue raising and distribution and the creation of a secure social safety net. A more equal distribution of wealth would in turn, it was thought, encourage consumer spending. The thinking proved to be largely correct for European, North American and Australasian economies as the boom years of the mid-twentieth century attest. These were largely driven by massive increases in consumer spending as well as rapid industrialisation fuelled by this spending, and by the expansion of the 'military industrial complex' (in the words of President Eisenhower), the aerospace industry and new technologies during the Cold War.

This 'boom' came to a dismal halt in the early 1970s as 'stagflation' (combining inflation with recession, previously unheard of), the 'OPEC' oil crisis, and the increased removal of favourable trade arrangements between Europe and its former colonies brought seemingly impervious First World economies back to reality.

The Bretton Woods System went through substantial changes in the early to mid-1970s. During this period fixed exchange rates, co-ordinated economic stimulation and use of the US dollar as the world's reserve currency were abandoned and development policies shifted to structural adjustment programmes in the new nation-states of the developing world. The World Bank had been set up to provide long-term financial assistance to countries in post-war reconstruction.

After 1970 it refocused its attention on Third World development. Those states that gained independence after 1945 played no part in the setting up of these organisations and, as a result of weighted voting in which the interests of the major economic powers are safeguarded, still have little say in their management. Weighted voting means simply that the more a country contributes financially to the organisation the more votes it has, with the United States having by the far the greatest say. The WTO has abandoned such a system and all members now have an equal voice. The UN system provided an alternative structure that was more heavily influenced by developing nations but which has had little real power in economic policy formation.

But there are signs that the separation of economic thinking and human rights may be diminishing. The IMF was sharply criticised for the severity of the fiscal and monetary measures that it attempted to impose on Indonesia after the economic downturn of 1997-1998. These measures included a severe reduction in public spending, the removal of food subsidies and drastic measures to clean up corruption and 'crony capitalism' that had become endemic in Indonesia under Suharto. During the 1999 East Timor crisis the IMF also insisted with unprecedented vigour that the human rights of East Timorese people must be respected. Indonesia's inability to implement many of these policies contributed to Suharto's fall from power in 1998.

It also forced a certain modification of the stringency of fiscal measures the IMF was imposing on Indonesia. Although rooting out corruption and dealing with a serious banking scandal remain priorities of the IMF, and of the post-Suharto Indonesian government, the IMF has also been forced to reappraise seriously the social consequences of its policies. As a result the restructuring programme instituted for Indonesia has arguably proven less economically punitive than other so-called 'recoveries' in the past. In 1991 the World Bank accepted the broad concept of development defined in the UN Declaration on the Right to Development (1986).

The World Bank has committed itself to development policies that [encompass] not only higher incomes but also better education, higher standards of health and nutrition, less poverty, a cleaner environment, more equality of opportunity, greater individual freedom, and a richer cultural life.

The World Bank is prohibited in its Articles of Agreement from straying into political or 'non-economic' territory. For example, in Article IV, paragraph 10 the Bank may not 'interfere in the political affairs of any member. ...Only economic considerations shall be relevant to their decisions' (1944 International Bank for Reconstruction and Development, Articles of Agreement, Art. IV, 10; Shihata 1992:30). In addition the Bank must ensure that the proceeds of any loan are used only for the purposes for which the loan was granted, with due attention to considerations of economy and efficiency and without regard to political or other non-economic influences or considerations.

In the past such provisions have been used to limit the Bank's mandate to narrow considerations of economic efficiency and acceptability. The inclusion of broader issues is a new and promising step in the direction of the Bank's activities. Reduction of poverty became at the end of the twentieth century of much greater importance to Bank policies (World Bank 2001). In addition in 1996 the Bank and the IMF launched a programme to reduce the level of debt owed by the poorest countries.

This, in combination with a greater awareness of the impact of Bank policies on the poorest, particularly women and children, has meant a reduction in spending on 'mega-projects' such as dams and greater attention to grassroots work. NGO consultation, through more open Bank processes of public scrutiny and review, also instituted in the early 1990s, has seen a positive change in the operation of the Bank towards the incorporation of civil society in its policy formation.

The consequences of IMF and World Bank policies on the economic well-being of a country can still be severe. Currency devaluations often translate into inflation as foreign imports rise in price. The aim is to make national exports more attractive, but where a country has little to sell overseas or where it relies on one or two commodities controlled by First World cartels the result may simply be a drastic lowering of the standard of living. Reduction in public spending may decrease a country's debt burden but the principal losses will usually be in the areas of education, health care, social assistance, poverty relief and the provision of basic supplies of food, shelter, clean water and reasonably priced fuel. Women usually have the primary responsibility for providing these essentials to their families. Where the state retracts from assistance in these areas the increased burden falls on women.

Development as it is channelled through the financial, monetary and trading wings of the 'Bretton Woods System' has tended therefore to entrench and extend a Western free market economic model in both the First World and the Third World. This capitalist model depends on growth and expansion, the proliferation and export of First World technology, the gearing of developing economies to servicing First World industrial needs and the exploitation and frequently despoliation of Third World economic, social and cultural structures as well as the environment.

Women, children and indigenous peoples, because of their invisibility within the international economic system, have tended to suffer a disparate proportion of the burden. Even more seriously the traditional unpaid labour of women as household workers, subsistence farmers and marketers, and as the providers of basic services, provides the safety net and supporting infrastructure for the international economic order. Without the exploited labour of women the system could not function.

THE DEVELOPMENT OF INTERNATIONAL LAW

Divisions over the importance of civil and political versus socio-economic rights have continued since the end of the Cold War, carried on now mainly between North and South or between the developed and the developing worlds. This is partly due to reluctance by many countries to provide adequately for the enforcement of civil and political rights, seeing these rights as a threat to the legitimacy of existing regimes that may have little or no popular support. The law of international human rights will generally only intervene where a state fails to live up to internationally binding obligations prohibiting interference with the private rights of individual citizens.

Rights involving a more complicated relationship between individual and state, such as economic, social and cultural rights, present serious ideological problems for that 'most public of public realms', the international legal order. Collective rights are also inherently threatening to this primary relationship between the state and the individual, or between public institutions and private citizens. Self-determination, the most well recognised of collective or peoples' rights, is built on the premise that distinctive groups will inevitably move towards statehood or a formal relationship with a state that can be relatively easily accommodated within international law, as the proliferation of new nation-states since 1945 attests. Other collective rights, such as the right to development, the right to a clean environment, the right to peace and security, are viewed with enormous suspicion within the circle of the former colonial powers.

It was these powers, situated primarily in Western and Central Europe, who can be said to have invented modern international law with the Treaty of Westphalia in 1648. These European powers and their colonial settler offshoots (mainly the United States) have dominated its development up to the present. The treaty signed at Westphalia established the primacy of states based on territorial control. The primacy of the state has been the basis for all international law since. The nation-state, with ethnic or cultural unity as a goal, came much later. The settlement represented by the Treaty ended the Thirty Years War that had engulfed most of Central Europe for the first half of the seventeenth century.

Peripheral but no less radical shifts of power away from a continent splintered by competing aristocratic influences and religious schisms and towards absolutist monarchies (in France) or bourgeois governmental regimes (in England) were occurring at the same time. These included the English Civil Wars and Revolutions of the 1600s and the French religious wars of a slightly earlier period. Significant aspects of the dispute began to spread overseas involving control of the principal trade routes (as in repeated wars between England and the Netherlands at this time) and the early establishment of European beachheads in Asia, Africa and the Americas.

The Treaty also ended the assertion of political power by the Roman Catholic Church and began a process of sublimating European religious disputes into overseas evangelisation and colonisation. Violent confrontations over religion had largely disappeared in Europe by 1800, partly because of the transformation of these disputes into 'missions' among the 'savages'. The religious wars of the Reformation and Counter-Reformation in Europe could be safely set aside once they were transferred overseas.

The supremacy of the state and the dominance of natural law created the idea of natural rights for states protected by international law, and natural rights for individuals protected by domestic law. This was the prevailing balance within the 'law of nations' until the nineteenth century. After the Congress of Vienna 1814-1815 the division of territorial states came to be dominated, not by naturalist theories of states' rights, but by positivist claims to the development of specific international legal norms based on each state's individual self-interest. Over-arching principles of natural law or divine ordinance were largely dismissed as 'nonsense on stilts' (in Jeremy Bentham's famous phrase).

If the Westphalian period was the era of Hobbes, Locke, Grotius and de Vattel, the Vienna settlement was the era of Bentham, Metternich, Marx and Bismarck. Human rights as an aspect of natural law theories went through a significant decline only to be revived after the end of the last, great, modern European war in 1945. This conflagration seemed to show that positivist theories of legal development were inadequate in preventing major conflict and massive violations of humanitarian concern. The law of international human rights is therefore partly the product of a strong revival of natural law theories. But this time natural law has been used to transpose the natural rights of individuals from domestic protection to the international regime. Therefore the 'law of nations' now incorporates human rights. This represents a dramatic shift in international law.

The relationship between the development of international law, the expansion of European colonialism and the direction of European economic development has not been sufficiently highlighted among commentators and analysts. It is clear that one of the foundations of the Peace of Westphalia and other treaties of the period was the retention of lucrative colonial possessions already obtained by France, Spain, Portugal and the United Kingdom. There is no doubt from treaties of the time that this purpose was intentional and that European claims to overseas territories were accepted as fundamental to the law of nations. For example, the 1670 Anglo-Spanish Treaty of Madrid, confirmed by the Treaty of Utrecht of 1713, stated:

[T]hat the most Serene King of Great Britain, his heirs and successors, shall have, hold, keep, and enjoy for ever, with plenary right of sovereignty, dominion, possession, and propriety, all those lands, regions, islands, colonies, and places whatsoever, being or situated in the West Indies, or in any part of America, which the said King of Great Britain and his subjects do at present hold and possess. Grotius, de Vattel and other seventeenth- and eighteenth-century commentators tended to ignore indigenous claims while espousing principles of war and international law that furthered the colonial project. The significant exception was the very early Spanish commentator Francisco de Vitoria in his De Indis Noviter Inventis in 1532.

PROPERTY AND THE PUBLIC/PRIVATE DICHOTOMY IN HUMAN RIGHTS

Human rights were incorporated into international law after the Second World War based primarily on their European roots in theories of natural law. But such theories carry with them significant limitations, at least for women and non-Europeans. Some ideas about natural law stress a proprietary basis for their existence. The genesis of rights within the American tradition is derived from the work of John Locke whose discussion of rights was centred on 'Man's' inherent rights to property in himself and what he produced by his own labour. Inherent rights to 'life, liberty and the pursuit of happiness' were strongly influenced by the desire of white men in the American colonies clearly to own and control property, including slaves, without state interference. The US Constitution was particularly designed to limit governmental interference in the private sphere with property rights underlying the whole.

A closely related ideological foundation for human rights is the division between public and private. Usually this division is characterised as the separation of the state from interference in the 'private' realm of commerce and individual initiative. The effect is, at least theoretically, to protect property from state regulation. The separation of the public and private realms is also the basis on which the state is obliged to refrain from interfering in 'natural rights' such as freedom of expression, religion or privacy itself. The 'private' sphere also includes the home, or the domestic sphere, the putative domain of women and children. The key social structure within the private sphere, the middle-class family, itself went through a profound transformation from the sixteenth to the nineteenth centuries and again into our own time within European societies.

During the political, religious and economic revolutions of seventeenth-century Europe the position of women became ruthlessly subject to an ideology of extreme patriarchy. By the end of the eighteenth century in Europe the more brutal aspects of this patriarchal rule were disappearing, at least in theory. The familial model became the closed, nuclear, bourgeois family, the site of 'virtue', affection, comfort and graciousness. Middle-class and aristocratic European women and children were confined to the home to a much greater extent than in previous centuries and their economic role or value outside the home diminished. Women were not seen as participants in the public world of 'rights' and political and economic achievement.

What few privileges they had previously had in relation to property or public participation disappeared. The subordination of women to patriarchal structures did not end with the development of liberal, or even later socialist, theories, but was entrenched in the new political order and conceived of as 'natural'. In 1776 (the year of the American Declaration of Independence) Adam Smith could write in his book Wealth of Nations:

> There are no public institutions for the education of women, and there is accordingly nothing useless, absurd or fantastical in the common course of their education. They are taught what their parents and guardians judge it necessary or useful for them to learn; and they are taught nothing less. Every part of their education tends evidently to some useful purpose; either to improve the natural attractions of their person, or to form their mind to reserve, to modesty, to chastity and to economy; to render them both likely to become the mistress of a family, and to behave properly when they have become such.

Connections between the development of international law, European colonialism, theoretical bases for 'natural rights' and notions of proprietary control go a long way to explaining why there was and remains such a major disjunction between the international economic law of trade and development and the international law of human rights. The 'Bretton Woods' agreements and the UN human rights system represent major attempts at globalisation, but their shared theoretical basis requires a radical division between public and private.

Human rights (including socio-economic rights) developed within the public sphere of the UN while international economic law seeks to reform and deregulate the operation of market forces in the private sphere of trade and development. Social, economic and cultural rights clearly indicate that this division is artificial and increasingly irrelevant. The impact that the freeing of money flows, banking practices and the unregulated operation of large corporations has in the public realm, such as in the apparent erosion of state sovereignty, further dissolves this dichotomy. As international economic and political structures move closer in the regulation of economic practices and their impact on human rights, labour rights and the environment this division will disappear. International law is now a major force for change across these lines.

THE EUROPEAN ENLIGHTENMENT

It is impossible to understate the importance of the Enlightenment on the development of modern human rights. In some ways it may be said that human rights represent the highest expression of Enlightenment philosophy. This philosophical tradition can be dated more or less from the end of the seventeenth century to the end of the eighteenth century. René Descartes' establishment of principles based on intuitive understandings prior to any empirical observation, and the division between intellectual and physical endeavour are important aspects of this transformation.

The entrenchment of the belief in universal principles based on rationality, and the primacy of the individual thinker and actor personified as the rational European man, were also major developments during this time. Human and ecological diversity could be subsumed within this wider field of universal Truth and the contingency or ambivalence of reality could be ignored or characterised as an incomplete (as yet) manifestation of this Truth which would gradually be revealed so long as rational principles of scientific logic were applied.

The particular understandings of indigenous peoples and others were seen as childish, mythical or inaccurate if they did not accord with the Truth as it was revealed to mainly European male discoverers and researchers. The subject 'Self' of this perspective was the rational, self-aware, unified and sovereign individual best exemplified by European Man himself. All other human beings, along with existence more generally, were relegated to the category of objects to be observed, studied and analysed.

The nature of this kind of subjectivity necessarily meant that, as human rights were developing as the natural birthright of 'Man', they could be confined to those individual men who created, benefited from and best represented this form of 'selfhood'. Women, indigenous peoples and many others were not seen as fully human. Their status further declined as they became objects of rational observation and their identities disappeared as autonomous subjects. The objectification and dismissal of most human beings as neither rational nor (as a logical consequence) autonomous became entrenched as a significant component of 'enlightened' thinking, so much so that it is extremely difficult to move beyond this paradigm even now at the supposed end of the colonial period.

The nature of Enlightenment subjectivity was seen, however, as a priori and universal, i.e. it was not theoretically dependent on cultural, racial or sexual variables. Thus, while it was always determinedly local and specific in content it could eventually be characterised as universally applicable to all human beings. The cultural specificity of this form of subjectivity became buried and masked by its claims to universality. Although human rights were originally devised in France and the United States as very specifically class, race and gender bound, their connection to universal Truth meant, at least theoretically, that they could be expanded to include all human beings.

On the one hand this has tremendous liberating potential for human beings oppressed within social, cultural or political systems that devalue and denigrate the worth of the individual. On the other hand, the form of subjectivity underlying human rights is itself culturally and temporally bound to a very short period of Western European history.

The expansion of this particular model of subjectivity, in the shape of human rights or constitutional forms of democratic government or other types of political and economic 'progress', can also be justified on the grounds that the revolution of European Enlightenment is being given to the non-European world. International law can therefore see colonialism as inevitable and natural. More typically descriptions and analyses of international law have simply ignored its ties to colonialism even when discussing significant treaties or judicial decisions that are precisely about colonial relationships. International human rights cannot be seen as somehow separate from the colonial history of Europe more generally, or of international law more specifically, but is a quintessentially important part of this history.

IMMANUEL KANT

A key figure of the Enlightenment in the development of ideas about human rights and civil society (including the idea of the state based on rational principles) is Immanuel Kant. Kant did not fully develop his principles of political or constitutional structures, human rights or international law. He did not believe in the efficacy of revolutionary action. But the ideas of the late eighteenth century obviously greatly influenced his political thinking. Some of these thoughts can be found in The Metaphysical Elements of the Theory of Right first published in Königsberg in 1797.

Kant talked about 'right' as opposed to 'rights' but the relationship between the two concepts is apparent from his description of 'right':

The Universal Principle of Right - 'Every action which by itself or by its maxim enables the freedom of each individual's will to co-exist with the freedom of everyone else in accordance with a universal law is right.' Thus if my action or my situation in general can co-exist with the freedom of everyone in accordance with a universal law, anyone who hinders me in either does me an injustice; for this hindrance or resistance cannot co-exist with freedom in accordance with universal laws.

Right is therefore the sum total of those conditions within which the will of one person can be reconciled with the will of another in accordance with a universal law of freedom.

'Right', however, in order to be protected, must be contained within a system of positive law or 'public right' in which universal laws of freedom can be protected. Kant's notion of public right is intimately connected to his discussion of private right, or property. According to Kant, private rights to property can only exist where public right exists to limit external freedom. In a 'state of nature' possession can never give rise to property but is only ever provisional. Public right and private rights are therefore intimately connected through civil society, the state and, ultimately, international law where any one of the three spheres of public right fail adequately to contain unfettered external freedom the whole system will collapse.

The authority of the state relies on the legislated will of the people. This in turn is based on rights to citizenship including 'fitness to vote' which is crucial to the operation of the system. But 'fitness' depends on what type of citizenship a person has:

> The legislative power can belong only to the united will of the people. For since all right is supposed to emanate from this power, the laws it gives must be absolutely incapable of doing anyone an injustice. ...The members of such a society (*societas civilis*) or state who unite for the purpose of legislating are known as citizens (*cives*), and the three rightful attributes which are inseparable from the nature of a citizen as such are as follows: firstly, lawful freedom to obey no law other than that to which he has given his consent; secondly, civil equality in recognising no-one among the people as superior to himself...and, thirdly, the attribute of civil independence which allows him to owe his existence and sustenance not to the arbitrary will of anyone else among the people, but purely to his own rights and powers as a member of the commonwealth.
>
> Fitness to vote is the necessary qualification which every citizen must possess. To be fit to vote, a person must have an independent position among the people. He must therefore be not just a part of the common-wealth, but a member of it, i.e. he must by his own free will actively participate in a community of other people. But this latter quality makes it necessary to distinguish between the active and the passive citizen, although the latter concept seems to contradict the definition of the concept of citizen altogether.

The following examples may serve to overcome this difficulty. Apprentices to merchants or tradesmen, servants who are not employed by the state, minors (*naturaliter vel civiliter*), women in general and all those who are obliged to depend for their living (i.e. for food and protection) on the office of others (excluding the state) - all of these people have no civil personality, and their existence is, so to speak, purely inherent.

The woodcutter and the blacksmith in India who goes from house to house with his hammer, anvil and bellows to do work with iron, as opposed to the European carpenter or smith who can put the products of his work up for public sale; the domestic tutor as opposed to the academic, the tithe-holder as opposed to the farmer; and so on - they are all mere auxiliaries to the commonwealth, for they have to receive order or protection from other individuals, so that they do not possess civil independence.

The class, race, age and gender lines are absolutely explicit here. Civil and political rights, as the guarantors of private rights to property, are dependent on the possession of active citizenship rights or 'civil independence'. 'Independence' means 'not dependent', i.e. as having sufficient property so as not to be dependent on others for a livelihood.

Kant is careful to point out that the possession of civil independence and consequent civil and political rights does not mean that all others are denied freedom and equality as human beings. The attainment of civil independence is something that 'all men' may be allowed to work their way towards. Women do not seem to be included in this general respect to be accorded to all human beings on the basis of universal laws of freedom. Also, the assumption is that all those males who are servants, children or dependent in some way must naturally wish to live in the kind of society Kant is postulating and must all want to attain the political rights of full citizenship.

It is not clear how such passive citizens may actually demand any respect from anyone. The characterisation of those who possess active citizenship is clearly dependent on expectations about property rights and the possession of a certain class position which can only be attained by wealth or related status. Passive citizens are those who do not have sufficient property rights to justify their active membership in civil society. This clearly reflects late-eighteenth-century expectations about property rights, citizenship and the connection between property and civil rights.

Kant's characterisation of a 'state of nature' as prone to violence and injustice, although milder in its tone than others of the period, clearly harks back to an earlier understanding of the commonwealth and the state as discussed, for example, in Hobbes's Leviathan (1651). This thinking was clearly drawing on the colonial experiences of Europeans in the Americas. It was there that humans living in a 'state of nature' were thought to be really observable. By characterising indigenous peoples as 'savages' and non-Europeans, servants, women, children and others generally as, at best, passive citizens dependent on the will of others to ensure their equality and freedom within civil society or the state the colonial mission was justified and entrenched.

This included the increasing sequestration of middle-class women and children in the home and the gradual stripping away of any property, public rights or privileges that women, servants and others may have previously held. What it ensured was an extension of the benefits of a patriarchal state to a brotherhood of middle-class male citizens while explicitly excluding others from those benefits and justifying the continuing subservience, dispossession and silencing of the majority of human beings.

The inheritance that human rights owe to the formation of civil and political society in eighteenth-century Europe indicates a profoundly uneasy ideological base for their existence. It also indicates the main reason why, at least in the West, civil and political rights take such precedence over other kinds of rights. The roots of this division lie in the colonial history of Western Europe and the justification of the colonising project through the development of ideas about subjectivity, universality, public right and private property.

Kant himself is a significant figure in the development of human rights not only because of his ideas about political participation, constitutional law and the law of nations but also because of his more general ideas about the nature of human beings. For Kant, the dignity and worth of human beings stems from the internal autonomy of subjects who are 'ends in themselves' rather than means to some external end. This internal unified subjectivity is the quality of all rational beings. It means that each individual is unique and priceless as a matter of moral certitude.

> Thus virtue [*Sittlichkeit*] and humanity to the extent that it is capable of it, is that which alone has dignity. Skill and diligence in work have a market price. Wit, lively imagination and humor have an affection price. But faithfulness in promises and kindness out of principle (not instinct) has an inner value. Absent these, neither nature nor art can set anything in their place.

It is, however, important to be aware of the inner contradictions contained in Kantian thought. Although Kant's principles of morality and political reason are posited as universal there are significant 'loopholes'. Drusilla Cornell insists that we can adapt Kant's notion of 'freedom' (the capacity to coerce others so as to ensure their freedom harmonises with our own) to ideas of freedom for women. But, are women faithful and kind 'out of principle' or do we behave from 'instinct'?

Even if we can expand this logic to include women, are we not sacrificing necessary and common features of humanity in the process? Why does acting kindly out of instinct (whatever this might be) disqualify any human being from being treated as unique and priceless? Why do these qualities rest on 'rationality'? By segregating human experience along lines separated by what is mental or spiritual from what is corporeal or material we replicate and reinforce distinctions between ourselves (as human) from the non-rational 'natural' world. We are also replicating yet again the division between public (rational) and private (material). Those humans, who are deemed less rational, closer to nature, will necessarily fall more and more into the category of creatures that are not ends in themselves but means to ends, as chattels, tools, vessels, objects.

JEFFERSONIAN CONTRADICTIONS

Thomas Jefferson is a compelling, even poignant, example of the deep contradictions at the heart of the Enlightenment revolution in political thinking that he most vividly represents. On the one hand Jefferson was one of the earliest and most ardent supporters of the principle of liberty and of stringent limitations on governments in interfering with individual freedoms. The Declaration of Independence, although not the first such statement of the importance of freedom, is nevertheless one of the clearest and most eloquent examples of this principle of liberty.

Freedom, according to Jefferson, takes precedence over all other human rights including rights of equality and solidarity (*égalité et fraternité*) which were also being developed at the end of the eighteenth century. It is clear from the Declaration itself and from the subsequently drafted Constitution and Bill of Rights that liberty is closely associated with the inherent right to own property which men acquire through their physical, but especially intellectual, labour. Lockean principles influenced Jefferson's thinking. Liberty is defined as the right to be left alone, to do what one wants, to engage in 'the pursuit of happiness' at one's own discretion, to speak freely in political matters and to participate as a freely determined equal in the public sphere.

These principles are at the heart of the American ideal of constitutional government and human rights. This legacy of liberty strongly coloured the drafting of the Universal Declaration of Human Rights in 1948 and all subsequent instruments outlining civil and political rights. These rights are arguably the pre-eminent expression of individual human rights in the world, taking precedence over socio-economic and collective rights. Indeed, in extreme versions, they are said to subsume socio-economic rights and the rights of the collective ('We, the people…') under the promise of individual freedom, personal accumulation and ownership of private property, and democratic political participation.

The stress on individuality and the right to create conditions of socio-economic prosperity and happiness for one's self without interference are clearly inconsistent with the aims of egalitarian redistribution and sharing of material benefits and solidarity which are at the heart of social, economic, cultural and peoples' rights. But in a discussion of Thomas Jefferson and the 'civil religion of liberty' Conor Cruise O'Brien points out the deep and seemingly intractable contradictions apparent in Jefferson's own life.

The principal problem as O'Brien sees it is the deep contradiction between Jefferson's views regarding liberty as the fundamental article of faith in the new Republic, and his own inability to recognise the right to liberty of others who were not white male property-owners like himself. Jefferson's views on anti-slavery are well known. They are, however, according to O'Brien, greatly misunderstood. On the Jefferson Memorial in Washington are inscribed the words:

> God who gave us life gave us liberty. Can the liberties of a nation be secure when we have removed a conviction that these liberties are the gift of God? Indeed I tremble for my country when I reflect that God is just, that his justice cannot sleep forever. Commerce between master and slave is despotism. Nothing is more certainly written in the book of fate that these people are to be free.

O'Brien points out that the last sentence of this statement is in fact taken from a different source than the first four sentences, i.e. Jefferson's Autobiography, where the passage continues:

> Nor is it less certain that the two races, equally free, cannot live in the same government. Nature, habit, opinion has drawn indelible lines of distinction between them.

For Jefferson the solution to slavery was the removal of all Africans back to Africa or to some other place outside of America. Liberia was set up in the early nineteenth century as an American colony where freed slaves were sent to establish a homeland for all African-Americans. The creation of the English colony of Sierra Leone (whose capital is still called Freetown) performed a similar function for part of its history. Jefferson saw the institution of slavery as inherently corrupt, but the solution was not the recognition of the humanity, equality and freedom of African slaves as fellow Americans, but their removal.

What most struck Jefferson and his contemporaries was the extreme difference between white and black, with the African seen as barely human. To some slave-owners (not including Jefferson) slavery was seen as a benevolent institution bringing Africans into the enlightened European values of Christianity, appropriate forms of labour, sexual morality and civilisation. For Jefferson slavery was a disease eating into the heart of Republican values, not because it destroyed the freedom of Africans, but because it betrayed the ideal of freedom for white slave-owners such as him.

Jefferson's views on slavery and the rights of those held in slavery, and of freed slaves, appear to have been strongly coloured by his own inability to see Africans as human beings. As O'Brien points out, Jefferson was responsible for legislative proposals in Virginia restricting the freedom of liberated slaves and of severely punishing sexual relations between black men and white women. This was despite his notorious relationship with one of his own slaves. Although Jefferson was an ardent foe of the slave trade he himself bought and sold slaves at will and was at least as unrelenting in pursuing runaways as his contemporaries were.

For Jefferson the right of liberty so radically proposed for 'all men' was not applicable to everyone. Slaves or freed slaves (inevitably African), women, the 'dependent' poor, children, or anyone else who did not fit Jefferson's own persona of the white, property-owning male had a much more tenuously recognised right to liberty or freedom than Jefferson's ringing phrases are usually credited with. The interesting exception to these views was his tolerance towards and even admiration of Native Americans.

Women were clearly disappearing into the private realm at this period in history and even white middle-class women were losing rights over property, public participation and economic viability just as the 'rights of Man' were being consolidated and limited democracy was gaining acceptance. Slaves, children, foreigners were all largely excluded from the libertarian ethic.

Even freed slaves or men of colour who were not defined by their status as chattels or dependants were not entitled to rights usually associated with liberty, such as ownership of property, the right to vote, the right to participate in public processes, freedoms of expression and assembly, etc. Institutions of freedom remained limited even in post-Revolutionary America, and the more radical ideals of liberté propounded during the early years of the French Revolution were quickly contained within the bourgeois limits of white, middle-class, male privilege.

3

From Intention to Action

Lawmaking or prescription within the area of international human rights has proliferated rapidly since World War II, but the problem of applying or enforcing human rights norms has remained a major difficulty. Most scholars concern themselves with the rules and not with the actual process under which international rules, including human rights rules, operate. A number of human rights standards are also viewed as international labor rights standards. They include freedom of association, the right to organize and bargain collectively, abolition of forced or compulsory labor, establishment of a minimum age for child labor, nondiscrimination in employment, and minimum acceptable conditions of work regarding wages, hours of work, and workplace health and safety.

Because labor is an input in the production process of goods that enter the international trading system, various scholars, unions, and national governments have argued that violations of international labor standards should be enforced through trade sanctions.

Unfortunately, most of these proposals are extremely vague and ill defined. This chapter proposes the establishment of an enforcement system jointly administered by the International Labor Organization (ILO) and the World Trade Organization (WTO), the successor organization to the General Agreement on Tariffs and Trade (GATT), which enforces GATT rules and standards. This joint enforcement system would rely upon the expertise and cooperation of both organizations to prevent violations of international labor rights.

The ILO has emerged as the principal 164 international body with expertise in the area of labor issues. It's well-developed, integrated, and intricate standard-setting and enforcement machinery has produced positive results in persuading states to adhere to their obligations with respect to international labor standards, including those involving human rights concerns. However, the tools that the ILO currently has available to attain member compliance are limited to moral persuasion, publicity, shame, diplomacy, dialogue, and technical assistance. While able to enforce some standards and obtain positive results from some states, gross and persistent violations of international labor standards, including those classified as human rights standards, continue in a number of countries.

The GATT/WTO has become the premier international institution for the regulation of international trade. Within the GATT, a large body of international trading rules and standards has developed. An effective and frequently utilized dispute resolution system has also evolved. The GATT/WTO has been largely successful in its objective of liberalizing international trade through reducing trade restrictions. Thus, the international trading system, largely as a result of the activities of the GATT/WTO, has flourished by increasing the volume of international trade through the enforcement of a set of mutually beneficial rules and standards of conduct. In contrast to the ILO, the GATT/WTO uses procedures that permit trade sanctions for violations of its rules.

Whenever the idea of establishing and enforcing labor standards has been introduced in the GATT, it has always been rejected. In fact, the establishment of a working party to even broach the issue has been repeatedly refused. Besides contending that such an approach is a form of disguised protectionism, a number of members claim that the establishment and enforcement of labor standards properly resides in the ILO. Alternatively, whenever the idea of linking the enforcement of international labor standards with international trade is mentioned in the ILO, it has been rejected as being beyond the expertise and mandate of the organization. In addition, neither the GATT/WTO nor the ILO has the expertise in both the international labor and international trade areas. If one organization attempted to regulate conduct pertaining to both areas, it would encroach upon the other's area of expertise.

"Supervision of compliance should be entrusted to those organizations with the greatest technical competence in the field." Since the ILO is the most competent organization in the field of international labor and since the GATT/WTO is the most competent organization in the field of international trade, combining these two organizations would create the most effective enforcement regime in terms of establishing adherence to international human rights and labor standards with respect to goods that enter the international trading system. This synergistic linkage, relying on each international organization's expertise, could be used as a model to demonstrate how cooperation between multilateral organizations can be effectively utilized to effectuate international human rights and labor rights policies, and optimize world public order.

JOINT ILO-GATT WTO ENFORCEMENT REGIME

A synergistic combination of ILO and GATT/WTO expertise, creating one enforcement mechanism, would provide the most effective means of preventing violations of fundamental labor rights in the production of goods that enter the international trading system. The ILO is the premier body to examine the implementation of labor standards. It has over seventy years of experience, through its reporting and contentious supervisory procedures, in determining whether basic international labor standards are being observed and the degree of that compliance. It has an established technical cooperation component to complement its supervisory activities. Thus, the ILO should contribute these resources, its supervisory and technical cooperation expertise, to this joint enforcement regime.

The GATT/WTO is the principal body that regulates international trade. Its expertise is in determining the existence and extent of unfair trade practices, such as dumping or subsidies that breach existing GATT/WTO obligations or nullify or impair the receipt of reciprocal trade benefits. It also supervises the cessation of those practices through the imposition of countermeasures and economic penalties. Therefore, the GATT/WTO should bring its expertise on trade practices and its well-developed dispute settlement system and enforcement procedures to this joint enforcement regime.

This enforcement regime would operate with a bifurcated procedure. The first phase of the procedure would be the determination phase. The object of this phase would be to determine whether gross and persistent violations of labor rights occur in the production of goods that enter the international trading system, and the extent of those practices if they are found to exist. The second phase of the procedure would be the remedial phase. It would determine what measures - technical cooperation programs, certification procedures, and possible penalties -need to be established to eliminate those practices, and under what timetable compliance can realistically and fairly be achieved.

Although the procedure itself would be bifurcated, the organizations should not bifurcate their activities under this enforcement regime. In the first and second phases, both organizations' expertise would be required. During the first phase, the ILO has the competence to determine whether gross and persistent violations of basic labor rights occurred and the extent of those violations. The GATT/WTO, in this first phase, has the knowledge to interpret the existence and impact of those practices in terms of trade flows, just as it does in cases involving dumping or subsidies. During the second phase, coordination by the ILO and the GATT/WTO would be essential to eliminate such practices from the international trading system.

The organizations need to work in tandem to execute this enforcement regime since neither organization by itself has the expertise to administer either phase of the enforcement regime. This cooperation would benefit both organizations by creating possible synergies and would result in a greater appreciation of the symbiotic relationship between trade and labor practices. The standards used to determine if a violation had occurred would be whether gross and persistent practices that violate fundamental labor rights occurred in the production of goods that entered the international trading system. This standard is distinct from those situations where random and isolated violations of these practices occurred that did not involve complicity by the state in either a direct or negligent manner.

Countermeasures and economic sanctions would be viewed as a last resort, only to be used against recalcitrant states that did not respond to less drastic means. First, a technical cooperation program, administered by the ILO, would be put in place. A certification program might also need to be instituted to ensure that products made under conditions involving labor rights violations would not enter the international trading system. A timetable would need to be placed on the utilization of these programs before countermeasures and economic sanctions would be activated so that violating states could not delay implementation under the pretense of cooperation.

Economic sanctions would be applied only in the most extreme cases and their application would need to intensify over time. These sanctions might range from banning the importation of the specific products produced under conditions that violate labor rights to a wider ban on other products. This entire process of remedial measures would be coordinated by the ILO and the GATT/WTO so that a fair and realistic timetable would be put in place. Access to the enforcement regime would include states as well as employers' and workers' associations. Allowing only states to initiate complaints would be insufficient to prevent labor rights violations. This is because states are reluctant to criticize each other on matters that may be perceived as being merely human rights concerns.

This problem is somewhat ameliorated since these practices bear upon the international trade in goods that directly affect each nation's material interests. Yet states may still remain hesitant to confront each other on the use of these practices for fear that such action would be seen as a hostile and potentially volatile. Therefore, carefully filtered and controlled access by certain employers' and workers' associations, such as is used in current ILO practice, would be used. Not only would greater use and, therefore, more consistent compliance result; but as the use of this procedure became more frequent, it would appear less politicized, so that the initiation of complaints would not appear to be hostile, biased, and based upon totally unfounded acts.

A PROPOSAL TO PRODUCE EFFECTIVE COMPLIANCE

Any state that is a member of the ILO or of the GATT/WTO, or a bona fide employers' or workers' association from a state party of either organization would be able to file a complaint, thereby initiating the enforcement regime process. The first stage of the process would be to screen the complaint for admissibility. An admissible complaint would trigger the determination phase and the establishment of a joint ILO GATT/WTO Dispute Panel. To be admissible, a complaint must meet the following criteria:

1. The complaint must be in writing and addressed to the International Labour Office or the GATT/WTO Secretariat;
2. It cannot be anonymous;
3. It must be filed by either a state that is a member of the ILO or of the GATT/WTO or a bona fide employers' or workers' association from a state that is a member of either organization;
4. It must concern activities in a state that is a member of the ILO or of the GATT/WTO;

5. It must allege that a pattern of gross and persistent practices of labor rights violations exist in the implicated state that results in the production of goods that enter the international trading system;
6. It must specify the manner in which the state has failed to secure effective observance within its jurisdiction of the prohibition against violations of fundamental labor rights, indicating whether the violation is caused by direct state action or by a failure of the state adequately to police infractions of the standard in accordance with appropriate domestic legislation;
7. It must allege in which industry or sector these violations are occurring and which products are implicated; and
8. It must provide some documentary evidence that these violations are actually occurring. Mere allegations without proof would be insufficient to trigger the determination phase of this process.

Admissibility would be determined by a permanent "Admissibility Committee." This committee would be composed of nine members appointed in equal numbers by the ILO and the GATT/WTO. Members of the committee would have expertise in either international labor matters or international trade matters. They would be appointed for staggered two-year terms and would serve in their individual capacities. After being appointed, the members would be required to declare that they would perform their duties honorably, faithfully, impartially, and conscientiously. The committee would specifically be appointed as follows: four members would be appointed by the chair of the ILO Governing Body (GB); four members would be chosen by the chair of the GATT Council (Council); and one member would be a joint appointment of the ILO and the GATT/WTO Directors-General.

The duties of the Admissibility Committee would be to decide if a complaint is admissible based on the eight aforementioned criteria. The Admissibility Committee, in their discretion, could communicate the complaint to the member state concerned so as to afford the government an opportunity to reply. Once a determination had been made, a notice to that effect would be sent to all parties concerned: the party that initiated the complaint, the party or parties implicated by the complaint, the GB, and the Council. The determination of the Admissibility Committee would be final. If declared inadmissible, all further deliberations regarding that complaint would cease.

Once a complaint had been declared admissible, the determination phase would be triggered and a joint ILO-GATT/WTO Dispute Panel would be established. The Dispute Panel would be quasi-judicial body composed of seven prominent and professional persons who would serve in their personal capacity. Members of the committee would be chosen on the basis of their expertise in either international labor matters, or international trade matters. They would have a judicial temperament, a reputation for fairness and objectivity, sufficient formal training or practical experience in the operation of international legal rules, and good character and excellent ability. After being appointed, the members would be required to take an oath in which they would swear to perform their duties honorably, faithfully, impartially, and conscientiously.

The ILO and the GATT/WTO would each appoint three members to this Dispute Panel, with the remaining member being a joint appointment of the ILO and the GATT/WTO Directors-General. The ILO panelists would be selected from the current members of the ILO Committee of Experts or from a specially created pool of potential panelists formulated by the ILO. The GATT/WTO panelists would come from the current list of governmental and non-governmental panelists.

In the case of an interstate complaint, the states would be given the opportunity to agree on the ILO and the GATT/WTO panelists, using the respective pools of panelists that each organization would have made available. If the parties could not agree on the panelists within twenty days, either party could request the ILO or the GATT/WTO Director General to appoint the remaining panel members within ten days from the date of the request. The Directors-General, in selecting the remaining panelists, would be required to consult with both parties, but would make the final determination. In the case of a complaint initiated by an employers' or workers' association, the ILO Director-General would appoint the ILO panelists and the GATT/WTO Director-General would appoint the GATT/WTO panelists. The remaining panelist would still be a joint ILO-GATT/WTO appointment. This method of appointment would be used to ensure complete impartiality, independence, and objectivity.

The duties of the Dispute Panel would be to consider fully the complaint and make an objective assessment of the matter. It would prepare a report that would include its findings on all relevant questions concerning the issues implicated by the complaint. The report would indicate what the panel perceived to be a reasonable period of time for compliance, recommendations and programs to aid in the attainment of compliance (i.e., technical assistance programs and certification procedures), and possible countermeasures. The timeframe for compliance, the aid programs, and retaliatory measures could be made part of the adopted report.

The panel would fulfill these duties by engaging in a quasi-judicial inquiry into the matter, allowing sufficient flexibility for all parties to prepare their submissions while ensuring that the matter would be resolved in an expeditious manner. The panel, after consultation with the parties, would fix a timetable for presentation and deliberations within one week from its establishment. Normally, each side would submit written submissions to the panel with the complainant or complainants submitting first. The respondent party or parties would receive a copy of the complainant's submission and would have an additional twenty days to prepare its submission.

After receiving the submissions, the panel would hold oral hearings during which each side would present their arguments and answer questions with the other party present.

After this first round of written submissions and oral arguments, another round of simultaneous written submissions followed by oral hearings would take place. The panel also would have the right during this investigatory stage to listen to and examine witnesses, who would appear at the request of the parties or at the request of the commission. The panel could seek information and technical advice from outside experts; utilize the reports of the Committee of Experts and other international bodies; and conduct on-the-spot investigations, field visits, and field hearings. Other states, not directly involved in the complaint, would be asked to place any relevant information that they possessed at the disposal of the Dispute Panel. Those member states either bordering on or having significant trade relations with the country or countries involved in the complaint would be called upon to furnish any relevant information.

In the case of complaints initiated by employers' or workers' associations, the submissions and oral hearings would be performed by a joint-complainant committee of GATT/WTO and ILO officials, with expertise in dispute resolution procedures, appointed by the Directors General of the ILO and the GATT/WTO. These appointed officials could not have been involved in any matter that would prevent them from effectively representing the ILO and the GATT/WTO in these proceedings.

The task of this joint-complainant committee would be to uphold the interests of both the ILO and the GATT/WTO in preventing violations of international labor rights in the production of goods that enter the international trading system. They would prepare the case in consultation with the original complainant party. Yet they would be responsible for representing their organizations' interests. The Dispute Panel could accept written submissions from the original complainants and could even allow them to appear before the panel as witnesses. Yet the original complainants would have no standing before the panel. In the case of interstate complaints, the complainant would be the state or states that filed the complaint.

Panel deliberations would culminate in the drafting of a panel report. The report would be drafted in three sections. The first section would describe the disputants' arguments and would include findings of fact. This section would be submitted to the disputants for their comments before the final report would be completed. The second section of the report would include a determination by the Dispute Panel as to whether gross and persistent violations of fundamental labor rights had occurred and, if so, the industry, sector, and products implicated by the violation. The third section of the report would indicate what the panel perceived to be a reasonable period of time for compliance, recommendations and programs to aid in the attainment of compliance (i.e., technical assistance programs and certification procedures), and possible countermeasures. The completed reports would usually be submitted to the disputants before submission to the GB and the Council.

The determination phase from establishment of a panel to completion of the final report would normally not exceed nine months and would never take longer than twelve months. The Dispute Panel report would be circulated to all members of the GB and the Council. Any state that is a member of the ILO or the GATT/WTO could also receive a copy of the report. The "consensus" rule would be followed with respect to Dispute Panel reports. Under this rule, the first two sections of the Dispute Panel report, dealing with findings of fact and a determination as to whether a violation had occurred, would be automatically adopted unless a consensus of either the Council or the GB decided to withhold adoption or delay consideration.

The Council, at the meeting following the report's presentation, could decide to withhold adoption or delay consideration. Likewise, at the next meeting of the GB, automatic adoption of the report could be delayed or denied. The report would be adopted unless a consensus by members of either the GB or the Council decided to reject the report. If this rejection by either the GB or the Council occurred, the dispute process would be completed and no violation would have been found to exist. Thus, no subsequent actions would need to be taken by any state concerning this matter.

Any contracting party with an objection to the report would be required to detail their objection in writing and circulate the writing to all GB or Council members at least ten days before the meeting of either body at which the panel report would be considered. The disputants would have a right to participate in the GB or the Council deliberations concerning the report and their views would be recorded. The entire dispute settlement process from the filing of a complaint to the decision on the Dispute Panel report should not exceed eighteen months. If the report were to be adopted, the date of adoption would be the ending date of the meeting of either the Council or the GB, whichever occurred later, in which the report had not been rejected nor had consideration delayed.

If the report was adopted, the state implicated by the report would have up to three months to appeal the decision of the joint ILO-GATT/WTO enforcement regime to the International Court of Justice (ICJ). The ICJ could affirm, reverse, or vary any of the findings and conclusions contained in the adopted Dispute Panel report. The determination of the ICJ on this matter would be final. During this three-month period, the implicated state would also have the opportunity to formulate and develop a technical cooperation program with the ILO. This technical cooperation program would be specifically geared to eradicating any violations of fundamental labor rights.

This program would be required to be approved by the ILO Director General and the appropriate state official within six months from the period in which the Dispute Panel report had been adopted. The technical cooperation program could involve a number of activities. These could include rewriting existing domestic legislation; imposing stiffer penalties against domestic violators; strengthening the labor inspectorate and state enforcement mechanisms; instituting public education and other campaigns targeted at employers, workers, religious institutions, schools, judges, law enforcement officials, and others; developing efficient production processes to produce the goods without violating labor rights; generating poverty eradication programs; and instituting compulsory education programs.

The technical cooperation program would incorporate a timeline for compliance. The timeline would include a number of interim phases in which the program's implementation could be evaluated. While the technical cooperation program would allow for some flexibility in terms of achieving compliance with the adopted Dispute Panel report's rulings, a period of no longer than two years from the date of adoption of the panel report would be permitted before either full compliance would be achieved or an export ban on all products made in violation of basic labor rights would be instituted.

Besides the development of a technical cooperation program, the GB and Council with the assistance of officials from the International Labor Office and the GATT/WTO Secretariat would meet and jointly decide upon the actions the violating state would need to take to comply with the adopted report's ruling. These bodies would also oversee compliance monitoring of the violating state. A joint ILO-GATT/WTO remediation committee would be established. It would consist of ten members: five from the GB and five from the Council. The members would be appointed by their respective chairs in consultation with their respective Directors-General. The committee would be established within ten days from the date at which the Dispute Panel report had been adopted.

This joint ILO-GATT/WTO remediation committee would decide upon a timetable for compliance, the actions that the government would be required to take to achieve compliance, and a timetable for countermeasures and economic sanctions. The committee would use section three of the Dispute Panel report as the initial starting point for developing this remediation plan and timetable. The committee could either accept or alter the Dispute Panel's recommendations. They would be required to complete the remediation plan and timetable within a period of two months from the date of their creation.

Once devised, the plan would be submitted to the GB and the Council. This remediation plan would be adopted automatically unless a consensus of either the Council or the GB refused to adopt the plan as formulated by the joint ILO-GATT/ WTO remediation committee. If the remediation plan was rejected as written, it would be revised until an acceptable plan would not be rejected by consensus of either body. In the event that the new plan of the joint ILO-GATT remediation committee was rejected a second time, the plan would be formulated by a special unit consisting of the two Directors-General and the chairs of the GB and the Council. They would seek input from all interested states, but would make the final determination as to the content of this remediation plan. They would complete the development of this plan within two months.

Compliance would normally occur within one year from the adoption of the Dispute Panel's report. It would, in no event, take longer than two years. If violations continued beyond the period of time designated in the remediation plan for full compliance, countermeasures and/or sanctions would be instituted. First, a countermeasure would be activated. This measure would ban any products made in the state where the violation had been found to exist if those products continued to be produced under conditions violative of fundamental labor rights.

Only products implicated in the adopted Dispute Panel report that have been certified as having been produced without such violations would be permitted to enter the international trading system. In other words, only those products that satisfied a strict certification procedure could be exported. If, after an additional period as specified in the remediation plan, the violating state had still not stopped producing goods that enter the international trading system under conditions that violate labor rights, wider trade sanctions or bans would be instituted. These sanctions would intensify until the violations had ceased.

In addition to these measures, a certification procedure would also be developed. This procedure would be constructed so to certify that the products implicated in the adopted Dispute Panel report were not actually made under conditions that violate labor rights. If the mechanics of this certification procedure could not be arranged to the satisfaction of the joint ILO-GATT/WTO remediation committee and included in the remediation plan, a ban of all implicated products would occur as soon as the period for compliance in the remediation plan had expired.

To be operative, this certification plan would require mandatory inspections by a joint inspection team, composed of International Labor Office and GATT/WTO Secretariat employees. The inspection team could enter and inspect all facilities where the implicated products are being produced, including the facilities of subcontractors and other intermediate producers. These mandatory inspections would take place periodically and could occur without prior warning. Only those products certified as having been produced without labor rights violations to the satisfaction of the procedures agreed to in the remediation plan as worked out by the violating state and the joint ILO-GATT/WTO remediation committee would be permitted to be exported.

The progress of the violating state would be periodically reviewed by the ILO and the GATT/WTO. The joint ILO-GATT/ WTO remediation committee would have primary responsibility for monitoring progress with respect to the remediation plan. They would meet once every three months to discuss the progress of the violating state with regard to the adopted Dispute Panel report's rulings and the remediation plan. They would expect to receive a mandatory report from the violating state on the progress it had achieved with regard to compliance.

If the violating state had entered into a technical cooperation program with the ILO, a report by the ILO would detail the progress achieved with regard to the technical cooperation program and the eradication of the offending practices. If a certification procedure had been implemented, then a report on the status of that procedure, including reports by the inspection team, would also be delivered to the remediation committee. The joint ILO-GATT/WTO remediation committee could also seek information and hear witnesses from any other pertinent sources in order to evaluate the compliance of the violating state. States that are members of the ILO or the GATT/WTO and bona fide employers' and workers' organizations could furnish information to the committee.

On-the-spot visits could also take place either by the joint ILO-GATT/ WTO remediation committee or by a joint surveillance team composed of International Labor Office and GATT/WTO Secretariat employees with the permission of the violating state. If such visits occurred, reports of the findings of those visits would be presented to the committee. Based on all the information received, the joint ILO-GATT/WTO remediation committee would draft a report to the GB and the Council.

The GB and the Council would consider compliance four months after the remediation plan had been approved or implemented. The GB and the Council would review the report of the joint ILO-GATT/WTO remediation committee every four months and oversee the remediation committee's activities. This review would continue until full compliance had been achieved. The chair of the joint ILO-GATT/ WTO remediation committee would be present at each of these review sessions to present the committee's report and to answer questions. If monitoring efforts were deemed ineffective, the chair of the remediation committee would meet with the chairs of the GB and the Council and the Directors-General of the ILO and the GATT/WTO to formulate a revised monitoring strategy.

Again based upon all the information received, the joint ILO-GATT/WTO remediation committee could decide that the implicated state had fully complied with the rulings reflected in the adopted Dispute Panel report. Alternatively, the implicated state, at any time, could declare that it had achieved full compliance and could request that a joint ILO-GATT/WTO inspection team visit to verify compliance. If an inspection occurred, the report of the joint ILO-GATT/WTO inspection team would be submitted to the joint remediation committee. Full compliance would occur when the implicated state ceased from violating labor rights to produce goods that enter the international trading system.

Once the joint ILO-GATT/WTO remediation committee determined that full compliance had been achieved, it would file a report to the GB and the Council, certifying its finding. The GB and the Council would each discuss the matter and adopt the recommendation of the joint ILO-GATT/WTO remediation committee that full compliance had been achieved unless a consensus of either body determined otherwise. If either body refused to ratify the recommendation of the joint ILO-GATT/WTO remediation committee, then the monitoring procedure and the remediation plan would remain in place.

If the GB and the Council adopted the remediation committee's recommendation - namely, that full compliance has been achieved by the implicated state - then all economic sanctions and any bans on export goods would cease immediately. The certification procedure, however, would remain in place. The implicated state would continue to be monitored by the joint ILO-GATT/WTO remediation committee for a period of one additional year. The GB and the Council would continue to receive reports from the remediation committee and review their activities every four months for the additional one-year period.

During this one year period, periodic and unannounced on-the-spot visits of the country and inspections of all facilities that were suspected of violating labor rights in the production of goods that enter the international trading system would take place. If, during the additional year, no gross and persistent violations of labor rights were uncovered that produced goods that entered the international trading system, all countermeasures, bans on exportation, and certification procedures would be terminated.

The international trading system and the world economy would benefit by the enforcement of international labor rights standards. The international trading system would signal its seriousness and impartiality in regards to enforcing rules that promote fair competition and fair trade. The benefits of an open trading system would accrue to all, not only those who are exploiters. More human resources would be available to increase the efficiency of and expand the world economy. Indeed, a multilateral enforcement regime of international labor standards would increase the amount of world trade controlled by multilateral institutions and would decrease calls for protectionism.

Perhaps most important, developing countries would be able, more effectively, to promote social and economic advancement within their countries without having to compete against other nations that do not respect these standards. Thus, a country would not have to fear being penalized in the international marketplace for respecting the labor rights, human rights, and dignity of its people. Although many developing nations are currently opposed to the enforcement of violations of international labor standards, a number of developed countries are moving toward enforcement of these standards on a unilateral basis. The United States has already included worker rights provisions in its trade laws and has taken unilateral action against a number of countries. Rather than dissipate, these demands will only increase in the future. Thus, a multilateral enforcement regime that replaces what has been called "aggressive unilateralism" would be in the best interests of developing nations.

It would allow them to participate in the formulation and implementation of objective multilateral procedures, rather than be at the mercy of the procedures and actions devised by the developed nations. By viewing violations of international labor rights not only as human rights violations but also as unfair trade practices, states could more readily recognize the implications of these practices on their material interests. Strong incentives would thus be created for states to protect their interests by sanctioning transgressor states and preventing future violations. In effect, the self-interest of each state would be harnessed to promote and enforce human rights for all.

THE CASTRO ALFARO CASE CONVENIENCE AND JUSTICE

The dissenters argue that it is inconvenient and unfair for farm workers allegedly suffering permanent physical and mental injuries, including irreversible sterility, to seek redress by suing a multinational corporation in a court three blocks away from its world headquarters.... The "doctrine" they advocate has nothing to do with fairness and convenience and everything to do with immunizing multinational corporations from accountability for their alleged torts causing injury abroad.

Proclamations of a "new world order"; the signing of the North American Free Trade Agreement (NAFTA) and the General Agreement on Tariffs and Trade (GATT) Uruguay Round pact; controversy over the Maastricht Treaty; recent international summit conferences on ecology and development in Río de Janeiro, on population and development in Cairo, on sustainable development in Stockholm, and most recently on women in Beijing, are all indicators of a fundamental shift toward a more systematic integration of the global economy. Before this shift, global trade patterns developed with minimal planning or regulation at the international level. Instead, national governments set tariffs and otherwise managed their trade interests. There was virtually no supranational "lawmaking" or other form of regulation of multinational enterprise.

The "legalization" of this integration of capital at the international level through various trade agreements is now provoking demands for regulation of global economic activity from advocates for those interests most affected by the new dynamic, and so far most voiceless - workers, trade unions, the environment, indigenous peoples, and women (who provide the majority of the workforce in many of the multinational, especially "maquila"- type assembly industries). The Social Chapter of the Maastricht treaty, environmental and labor "side agreements" to the NAFTA, and consideration of labor rights and environmental protection on the agenda of the new World Trade Organization are prominent indicators of the demands for increased responsibility on the part of the transnationals for the effects of their policies and products.

Requiring corporations to assume responsibility and pay the costs of their labor, health and safety, and environmental policies is a relatively new challenge for advocates working within the framework of existing United States law. Achieving such a goal when the corporation is U.S. based and the affected persons, communities, and resources are in Costa Rica or India or Korea heightens the challenge. Lawyers who advocate in this area have to break new legal ground, learn new skills, and combine litigation with other forms of advocacy like effective use of the media, coordination with grassroots organizations, education, lobbying, and other tactics needed to change public perception and policy. They also need an understanding of cultures very different from that of North American (and European) lawyers, and perhaps more than anything, humility of conduct to match boldness of concept.

This chapter discusses the Castro Alfaro case not so much for its controversial holding (defendants may not invoke forum non conveniens in Texas state courts to escape liability for personal injuries inflicted abroad to foreign nationals), but as a prototype for worker rights cases brought against U.S.-based transnationals on behalf of men and women whose language, culture, and history differ radically from the one that created the system of law we use in attempting to vindicate their rights.

As one of a growing number of cases involving efforts by foreign plaintiffs to seek legal redress from the judiciary of the transnationals' home country, Castro Alfaro also contains vital lessons for transcultural litigation. It underscores the importance of recognizing that the legal system of the "North," where redress is sought by workers from the "South," is part of the wider system, encompassing both law and economics, that created those workers' jobs, then harmed them, all the while shaping our attitudes, work habits, and assumptions about human nature.

Lawyers and those who assist them in developing ways to make corporations responsible for these injuries face tremendous challenges as well as great rewards. The challenges are not all from the opponent; some are the fruits of our ignorance of other cultures and the arrogance that is part of the "developed world" culture. The rewards are not all monetary; they include not only the few precious legal victories, but also the opportunity to learn other values and world views that may, in the end, offer more hope for the future than the ones that produced the tragedy at Bhopal or the pain, mental anguish, confusion, and loss, as well as physical damage, done to the protagonists in the case discussed here, the men, women, and children who have lived and worked on the banana plantations in Costa Rica.

THE CASTRO ALFARO CASE

Castro Alfaro concerns a group of farm workers from Standard Fruit Company's Río Frío banana plantation located in Costa Rica's tropical Atlantic region. These first plaintiffs were men and their spouses or partners, who, born into a life of poverty, regarded the multinational plantations as an opportunity to improve their living standards, earn a minimum wage, have access to potable water, visit a medical clinic, and even learn to read and write at night school. Río Frío is an immense plantation composed of approximately fifteen large farms where row upon row of banana plants are grown within an infrastructure of railways and cabled passageways (for banana transport only) that go on as far as the eye can see, converging at the horizon.

Standard Fruit Company began breaking ground for the Río Frío plantation in the late 1960s. The initial labor force was comprised mostly of young men ages fourteen to twenty-five. By 1971, after a two-month strike, banana workers' unions were recognized and the first collective bargaining agreement was signed. The banana workers' unions became the strongest unions in Costa Rica, encompassing 70-80 percent of the workforce by the late seventies. They achieved modest company-owned housing, transport to the fields, and greatly improved working conditions.

In the late 1970s, however, Standard Fruit began engaging in antiunion activities, including persecution and arbitrary firing and blacklisting of union activists. After the triumph of the Sandinista revolution in neighboring Nicaragua, the multinationals became much more aggressive, mounting a major campaign to eliminate the "communist" unions and introduce a new employer-worker relationship - "solidarismo." In a successful effort to destroy the banana unions in Costa Rica, and as the final response to a long and violent strike in 1983, United Fruit Company closed down its extensive plantations and left the country crossing over the southern border in to Panamá. By the mid-1980s, the unions had lost most of their membership and union leaders were permanently banned from entering the farms. By the early 1990s, there were virtually no active banana worker unions functioning openly inside the farms. Workers have little bargaining power and very few recognized rights.

During the 1960s and 1970s, thousands of Costa Rican banana workers were required to handle dibromochloropropane (DBCP), a highly toxic, but effective pesticide (nematicide) that kills nematodes that attack the roots of the plants. DBCP was manufactured in the United States by Dow Chemical, as Fumazone, by Shell Oil, as Nemagon, and by Occidental Chemical as Anvac and furnished to the banana companies for export. The application of DBCP to the banana plants contributed millions of dollars in increased profits for the defendant companies, increasing banana production by a phenomenal 35 percent. DBCP helped to eliminate crop losses caused by nematodes and ensure blemish-free bananas grown for export to the United States.

DBCP also virtually ensures sterility in men who are exposed for as little as one hundred hours in sufficient doses. It also causes injury to testicles and birth defects in children fathered by DBCP-exposed men. Women also blame their sterility upon DBCP exposure. DBCP may cause cancer and is suspected of causing neurological damage. Sterility has provoked emotional and psychological effects, impotence, and a great social cost including the dissolution of families and social alienation of the victims.

The toxicity of the chemical was known to the manufacturers at least from the late 1950s on, when Shell and Dow researchers and independent scientists found that inhalation killed rats and, at much lower levels, produced liver damage and atrophied testicles. The manufacturers successfully avoided a strong warning label that would have required the use of protective apparatus when handling the chemical. The information remained buried in technical journals and not provided as part of either Shell's or Dow's product data summary, much less to the workers who manufactured or applied it.

During the mid-1970s, plant workers at Occidental Chemical Company's agricultural products division in Lathrop, California became aware that they were sterile. In 1977, the Environmental Protection Agency (EPA) announced its intention to ban all food-related use of DBCP in the United States, shortly after the Occidental factory workers began to pursue their legal action, which eventually won an average of over $1 million per plaintiff for the DBCP-related sterility.

Standard Fruit and other banana growers redoubled their efforts to secure their DBCP supply. Dow and Shell, although reluctant after the Occidental scandal, continued to ship their products overseas for almost two years after the U.S. ban as Standard threatened breach of contract action. Workers were never told about the dangers of handling the chemicals, even after the problems at Occidental were known.

Thousands of the Costa Rican banana workers handled the DBCP with absolutely no protection, not even gloves.

Workers responsible for preparing the diluted mixture to be applied to the plant handled full strength DBCP by pouring the liquid from large barrels into smaller plastic jugs and adding water. The substance always spilled onto their bodies and clothing. Although spills stung the skin and fumes caused dizziness and nausea, the warehouse workers who performed these tasks were paid more and their chores were less physically demanding than was the field work. Besides, if they complained they were either demoted or fired. In the field, workers utilized a large syringe-like plunger to inject the DBCP mixture into the root of the banana plants. They, too, were constantly being splattered and directly exposed to the toxic substance.

No news of the Occidental workers' injuries was transmitted to the banana workers in Costa Rica. The first complaints about sterility of the workers at the Río Frío and other plantations were publicized in 1978 but Standard Fruit continued using DBCP for another year and a half until receiving pressure from the Costa Rican authorities, and Dow and Shell stopped selling it to them in 1979. By that time thousands of Costa Rican men had been exposed for a decade or more.

Costa Rican urologists and toxicologists presented the case to colleagues in the United States, who referred them to a Texas law firm specializing in large-scale personal injury lawsuits. Representatives of the firm visited Costa Rica and after meeting with workers and local health and legal professionals agreed to take the case on a contingency basis. Domingo Castro Alfaro was one of the afectados (the term in Spanish commonly used to refer to the DBCP victims in Costa Rica, literally meaning "affected ones"). In 1984, the law firm filed a products liability suit against Dow and Shell in Texas on behalf of Castro Alfaro and forty-six other banana workers and their wives or partners from Standard's Río Frío plantation. Similar suits were also filed in state courts in Florida, and California.

The complaints were based on tort claims of product liability and negligence, and subsequent claims included

Standard as a defendant as well as Dow and Shell. Defendants universally responded by removing the cases to federal courts, where they asserted a forum non conveniens procedural defence - that while there might be technical jurisdiction of the case in a U.S. court, the inconvenience of litigating here outweighed the technicality. "Let Costa Ricans sue in Costa Rica," they argued. The problem with this position was that, at the time, the maximum recovery available to plaintiffs under Costa Rican law was less than $1,500. As one of the judges who finally rejected that argument in the Texas Supreme Court wrote:

The plaintiffs, who earn approximately one dollar per hour working at the banana plantation, clearly cannot compete financially with Shell and Dow in carrying on the litigation. More importantly, the cost of just one trip to Houston to review the documents produced by Shell would exceed the estimated maximum recovery in Costa Rica. In other words, "If successful, Shell and Dow...would have secured a largely impenetrable shield against meaningful lawsuits for their alleged torts causing injury abroad."

The Texas Supreme Court's decision to reject the assertion of forum non conveniens was not just a procedural nicety. It really determined the outcome of the case, since the evidence of negligence and injury was irrefutable. Faced with unassailable scientific evidence of the toxicity of DBCP, and their prior knowledge of this, accompanied by proof of their failure to warn or protect the workers, their only defence was to try to demonstrate that individual workers could not prove that they had been exposed to the toxin. Given such a weak defence, settlement discussions began within a year and a half of the Texas Supreme Court's decision, and an agreement was reached among U.S. attorneys for the plaintiffs and defendants in June 1992. This agreement was then offered to local counsel and plaintiffs.

The concept of negotiating about one's rights, like the concept of plea bargaining, is utterly foreign to the Costa Rican legal system, and to the culture of the plaintiffs. Suffice to say that negotiating a settlement in a lawsuit - always exceedingly difficult, even for those of us inured to the process - is especially troublesome to those not used to it, particularly in a culture where corruption, bribes, and sell-outs are not uncommon. This is a stage of the litigation process at which sensitive communication, listening to the clients, and careful explanation of the real alternatives are critical.

ABOUT FORUM NON CONVENIENS

Dow and Shell invoked the traditional discretion of courts not to hear controversies in cases "in which the Court may consider it more proper for the ends of justice that the parties should seek their remedy in another forum." Here defendants' interest in "the ends of justice" must be measured against their unwillingness to produce their personnel in Costa Rica, thereby defeating even the reduced recovery that may, theoretically, have been possible there. Like so many procedural devices cited by the powerful to resist the claims of the less powerful, application of the forum non conveniens doctrine is outcome determinative, because in this case there is no other adequate forum.

The Costa Rican workers sued in Texas not because it was convenient, but because they had no other hope of justice. Their case represents not just the advisability of using United States courts to make U.S. based transnationals responsible for damages inflicted in the developing world. It also confirms the imperative to develop additional forums and alternative theories while the lessons of Castro Alfaro are analyzed and incorporated into practice.

The nine justices of the Texas Supreme Court permitted the suit to proceed to the merits, based upon a reading of the Texas statute. The legal issues were neither novel, complex, nor difficult, but the decision appears as a majority decision with two special concurrences and four separate dissents, with some of the most passionate (and at times insulting) dialogue found among jurists in their written opinions. And all this controversy was over a procedural motion about whether to provide a forum.

The U.S. law firm, local Costa Rican counsel, toxicologists and medical experts based in Dallas, Texas, and their Costa Rican counterparts, legal workers, law students, and liaison personnel who worked on Castro Alfaro and related cases put tremendous energy, effort, and resources into finding a forum in which the workers' injuries could be aired and, perhaps, partially redressed. Their victory puts transnational companies on notice of their responsibility and liability for the time-honored tradition of "us[ing] the Third World...as the industrial world's garbage can."

But the decision in Castro Akaro, together with the efforts of plaintiffs and counsel in other ground-breaking cases like Labor Union of Pico Korea v. Pico Products, Inc. and Labor Rights Fund et al. v. Bush, discussed elsewhere, merely help us open the door to the courthouse. It will take several more years of experience and learning to begin to fashion these experiences into a way of making litigation an effective tool on behalf of victims of the transnationals' power and mobility.

This article does not purport to shed light on forum non conveniens, removal, pre-emption and other doctrines, or other defences that those who litigate in United States courts on behalf of victims of U.S.-based transnationals will meet. Rather, it attempts to distill some practical lessons from the experience of working as part of the Castro Alfaro legal team, lessons to avoid practical, legal, and human problems that may prove as dangerous to successful litigation as the forum non conveniens doctrine.

These transcultural lessons include the importance of developing the right combination of humility, empathy, and sensitivity necessary to serve as advocates within the United States legal system for those who have no other forum, but little understanding of how it works and how it will treat them. Finally, a measure of introspection and openness to learning about other cultures may be the only ways to avoid exporting some of the same culture, habits, and attitude that permitted Dow and Shell to profit from DBCP use in Costa Rica and other developing nations.

PLAINTIFFS AND DEFENDANTS IN A GLOBAL ECONOMY

"I am not only mourning my personal loss of the son I could never have.... This injury is a loss to society of a whole generation of people." "I am good for nothing; a man who can not give his wife what he used to give sexually does not deserve to live anymore." "I would like to disappear, to escape, to walk forever, to be alone." "Nobody can understand how it feels to be only half a man, inferior to others, abnormal, castrated." "To be a real man you have to have children, I am afraid of the future and that of my wife.... Who will take care of us when we get older?" "Sometimes I think we should separate so that she could have a child, I wish I could kill those guilty at the companies, if only I knew who the people were."

The theory of civil damage actions is that the remedy can compensate plaintiffs for loss and damage suffered as a result of defendants' negligent or wrongful action. When the loss is sterility, fear of cancer, inability to enjoy a sexual relationship, alcoholism, or thoughts of suicide, what compensation is able to make a man, a couple, or a community whole? When defendants can write off several million dollars in damages as a tax on the profits reaped by spreading toxic chemicals that will remain in the Costa Rican earth and water for the next fifty to one hundred years, what compensation is adequate? How do you measure justice in a different culture?

Does it have a monetary price tag? Can the suffering of the Costa Rican workers and the damage to their communities be quantified? These are not merely abstract questions, but ones that a lawyer advocating settlement may be asked by plaintiffs, local counsel, or others concerned about the case. They are questions at the heart of this kind of litigation, which counsel must be prepared to answer in ways that are both realistic legally and humanly real. Again Castro Alfaro is merely an example. By looking at concrete issues and facts, we hope to make the challenge of multicultural litigation clear, and suggest some steps to avoid common errors.

Consider the principle issue in the Costa Rican case. The measurable, irrefutable damage to plaintiffs was sterility. This is more than a physical loss. Domingo Castro Alfaro and his co- plaintiffs are all Latin American men rooted in a rural culture in which virility and fertility are closely related to vitality, which is to say life - social, emotional, and economic life. In this world, the equation of virility with fertility and life is not abstract. Families of five to ten and more children are not uncommon; childless couples and those with one or two children are aberrant, objects of pity.

Men in the United States do not easily talk honestly about sterility and fears of sterility, about impotence, shrinking testicles, and sexual problems, even to their doctors. In the world of the Costa Rican banana workers, husbands and wives rarely exchange words about their sexual relationship, and men are not ready with words about the shame they feel when referred to as "the halfman" or "the gelding" for their failure to procreate. In a society in which the parish priest is the closest thing to a psychologist or psychiatrist these families will ever see, depression and emotional problems are rarely verbalized. Alcoholism, divorce, profound depression, and stigmatization are common reactions to such problems in a society that would find their airing undignified.

The Costa Rican suit was originally conceived as a version of the Occidental litigation, but absent claims of psychological damage: Workers sued for physical loss and their wives for loss of consortium. It was not until a U.S. lawyer who lived and worked in Costa Rica joined the team and began to prepare plaintiffs for depositions that the significance of the psychological damages became obvious and psychologists were called in to evaluate a sample. Intimidated by cultural differences and less common use of psychologists in the society, lawyers may hesitate to explore this dimension with clients when it is often the most significant.

Despite the difficulty of proving such damages, there is no hope of "making the victims' whole" without understanding and looking for remedies to these injuries. This experience in Castro Alfaro underscores the importance of incorporating as a key member of the legal team from the outset a skilled interviewer who is both fluent in the plaintiffs language and culture and understands the concepts of damages and recovery, discovery and proof in the U.S. adversary system. Without such a person, civil actions that survive motions to dismiss will be subverted by weak and contradictory plaintiff's proof. It is impossible to overstate the critical nature of such a person, regardless of how skilled, respected, or close to the plaintiffs and their cause local counsel may be.

One of the problems in chasing the multinational tortfeasor to his domestic judiciary is that the injured must litigate by his rules, which in Castro Alfaro, as in most other transnational litigation, remained a mystery to those whose futures would be determined by them. One of the many jobs of the legal team in these already complex cases is to serve as, or provide for, a cultural intermediary and translator between the United States legal system and the culture, values, and legal system known to the plaintiffs, and from them to the U.S. legal system. Failure to do so can create legal, political, and personal disasters. Consider the following:

- Defendants sought to depose Domingo Castro Alfaro and another plaintiff in Houston. The plaintiffs were brought from the Río Frío plantation to Houston from San José on the first plane either had ever been in. They were welcomed and taken to the hotel, prepared for their interview, and left to rest. These two men had hardly even been in any city, let alone the English-speaking megalopolis of Houston. Lodged on the 35th floor of a high-rise hotel, neither had ever seen an elevator. Their region had recently survived a major earthquake that left it isolated from the rest of the country. Neither plaintiff had ever seen a building with 35 floors, but both knew it was a very dangerous place to be during an earthquake. Intimidated by the electric and electronic "gadgets" provided for their "comfort," the two could not sleep alone in their separate rooms; instead they huddled together in one for reassurance.

- A lawyer familiar with both U.S. and Costa Rican law was hired to prepare plaintiffs for deposition and trial. As part of her preparation, she reviewed each plaintiff's answers to the interrogatories. In the course of the interviews, she realized that they were fraught with factual errors. Dates were inaccurate or imprecise. One plaintiff would give different answers to questions about marital status at different times. This lawyer realized that in the culture of these workers, it was important to give the answer they believed the interviewer wanted to hear, and impolite to say, "I don't know," and that without knowledge of local history, critical events could not be dated. The plaintiffs lived according to the rhythms of the natural world around them and did not need calendars or have date books.
- Several cases were dismissed because adequate arrangements were not made to maintain contact with plaintiffs who may live far from the nearest telephone and work at different sites from one part of the country to another. Dates for plaintiffs to provide information or sign documents came and went with no contact. When U.S.-based counsel advised local counsel that the cases had been dismissed for failure to meet a deadline, local counsel was incredulous.

TRANSLATING JUSTICE

It is easier to write a formula for failure than a formula for success in these cases. The formula for failure is simple. Think first world or "North"; assume your values, experiences, culture, and legal system are (a) universal and (b) best. The consequences will be: frustration felt by all parties; lack of mutual understanding of critical issues; distrust among clients, local counsel, and U.S. counsel; and often procedural and factual errors that may prove fatal to the lawsuit and any hope of obtaining future compensation or curbing transnational corporate criminal and immoral actions.

There is no formula for success because success in these cases depends on learning diversity - learning about and valuing your client's perspective, culture, experiences, traditions, and values. If there is one ingredient without which this litigation cannot succeed, it is humility. So instead of a recipe, we offer suggestions and basic principles about transcultural litigation gleaned from Castro Alfaro and other cases involving litigation in United States courts on behalf of immigrants and others who use different words and different concepts to talk about justice.

Go to your client's country. Go as soon as you possibly can and stay as long as you possibly can. Don't go at the last possible minute to take depositions or interview witnesses. Go in time to think about what you see and learn from it. Visit your clients' homes; get to know their families. If at all possible, learn the language. If you don't know it, find someone who knows both your client's language and your own well enough to answer your questions about problems in communication, which may be cultural as well as linguistic. Preferably utilize the same person so that he or she may get to know plaintiffs and the issues.

One of the most important issues in these cases is that Costa Rica (Colombia, the Dominican Republic, etc.) is not just like some warm part of the United States where Spanish is sometimes spoken. It is a vastly different culture with different roots, different traditions, different values, and a different legal system. You need to learn something about that before you can successfully communicate, even with local counsel, let alone your clients. Successful communication is not about good feelings, although it may help create some. It is about avoiding defaults, issue-preclusion, and the possibility of Rule 11 sanctions as well.

Before you go, read about the history and culture of the country, as well as its economy and political history. The purpose is not to make yourself a better person, but to help you to understand how to communicate with your clients, both substantively and mechanically. It will also make you a more effective advocate in the United States, in relation to the opposing party, the judge, the jury, the public, and the news media.

If you do not take the trouble to do this step, you will, in addition to reducing your effectiveness as an advocate, be reproducing many of the attitudes and practices that led your clients to identify all lawyers from the United States as agents of the corporations responsible for their suffering. Condition yourself to expect mistrust, understand the causes that may justify it, and work to counteract it by being open to learning and honest about your ignorance. Your clients don't need to be impressed about your wealth, your power, your command of the law. They are already impressed, but they are also intimidated by you.

Ask about formalities in the kinds of social situations you will be in. The humblest peasants in Latin America are more formal than most New York City socialites. Greetings and handshakes are exchanged on entering and leaving a room. The proper forms of address are used with strangers. Ask about the common forms of politeness and respect when greeting and leaving, the proper names and forms of address for persons you will be meeting. Be aware that the United States has a very informal culture compared to those of most of the rest of the world, and your informality may be confused with lack of respect. And "respect" is a key word in Latin cultures. To "disrespect" or "lack respect" for someone is to offend deeply.

If lead counsel is in one U.S. state and local counsel is in another, the latter may do little but receive pleadings, file them according to the local rules, and forward responses. Local counsel in San José, Costa Rica will have to do much more. Local counsel will have to serve as chief intermediary and interpreter of both legal systems to the clients. Be sure that he or she is not only experienced with the legal system in your client's country but has some understanding of comparative law and the United States legal system as well, if at all possible. If not, you must provide a running seminar, not only in the theory and procedures that operate in your jurisdiction but also in the Anglo-American, common law system generally.

Usually you can find someone who understands the United States system, at least in theory. Things that are second nature to you - such as the process of cross-examination or the definitive nature of filing deadlines, issue-preclusion, and relevance rulings - are incomprehensible (not to mention counterintuitive) to most people not steeped in this system. Whenever in doubt, explain the purpose of a request or a procedure, and elaborate on any problems you anticipate as well as consequences of not complying with any orders entered or rules of procedure. If feasible, bring local counsel to the United States to observe court in session; their concepts are derived from old "Perry Mason" and "L.A. Law" television reruns.

Whenever possible, local counsel should also be bilingual and understand both cultures as well as both legal systems. He or she will need to help interpret the clients to you and vice versa. Prior to making any definitive decision about local counsel, do some research and some interviewing. Know prospective local counsel's reputation in the local bar, among law professors and constituency groups of your clients (e.g., labor unions); understand his or her place in local politics and society. Find out who past clients have been; your clients will undoubtedly know. Choose local counsel who will be able to interpret the local law for you, so that you will better understand the expectations and preconceptions of your clients, experts, witnesses, and so on.

Visit the offices of prospective local counsel and know what facilities are reliable: photocopier, computer, telephone, fax, modem, or mail? What methods of communication work best from abroad and which can be relied on within the country? How will client contact be maintained? Whose responsibility will it be? Is local counsel's office in a place that is accessible to clients? Will local counsel travel to where the clients are? Are there any dangers to clients as a result of local political situations that local counsel is aware of? Does traveling to his or her office or meeting with him or her jeopardize them in any way, or increase their security? Finally, investigate the possibility of conflict of interest thoroughly. In many societies in the developing world, the concept is marginal, at best, and family loyalties and the traditional social structure virtually require that family, social, and political relationships be reinforced with whatever benefits are obtained from employment.

Once you have chosen local counsel, be as explicit as possible about the scope of the duties and the importance of each. Consider a memorandum of agreement that includes essential points you have discussed and provide copies for local counsel. Ideally, local counsel staff should include a bilingual attorney who understand both cultures and can help translate the demands of discovery and pretrial preparation into complete and accurate responses with regard to every factual situation. Staff must also include someone sufficiently familiar with local resources to identify expert witnesses and others who will be needed to develop the litigation in the plaintiff's homeland.

When considering "local counsel" consider the importance of an attorney who can serve as a bilingual, bicultural "facilitator" who can be responsible for much direct contact with clients (including locating them when necessary). This may be a sympathetic United States citizen living in the plaintiff's country, or one of plaintiff's nationalities with extensive experience in the United States. The "facilitator" function is distinct from that of local counsel, although it may be combined. It is chiefly one of intense client contact, from interviewing and preparation to liaison with expert witnesses and local organizations and entities concerned about or involved in the case.

The agreement with local counsel should include a chart of the responsibilities of all on the local and U.S.-based legal team, with clear descriptions of how information is expected to flow. It undoubtedly will not flow that way, but both sides will start with a map of expectations.

Optimally, part of the job of local counsel and/or staff should be the development of good working relations with sympathetic organizations, popular, political, governmental, religious, academic, and other institutions as well as the public information media. Litigation of this kind involves a great deal more than pleading and client contact. Strong support from significant sectors in the plaintiff's home country can often make the difference between winning and losing an argument, or a case, by generating probative documentary evidence. When local law supports a position or explains the nature of an injury, a term, or concept that becomes significant in the litigation, consider educating the court about it and, when appropriate, incorporating aspects of local law and history to help the court understand the litigation.

Interviewers, whether they are facilitators, local counsel, or paralegals, must understand the purpose of the interview and how the information obtained will be used. The importance of clarity, precision, and honesty over all other values must be made explicit, and communicated to the client. But no interviewer, no matter how well instructed, will succeed without establishing a rapport with the client. Interviewers must be chosen with both criteria in mind.

Many concepts that seem basic to a North American attorney may be different to a client from another culture. It is not merely a question of language and nationality. Urban/rural, educated/unschooled, middle class/poor describe cultural dichotomies that also have a significant impact on vocabulary, style of expression, and ease of communication. The length of exposure to DBCP was a critical issue in the Castro Alfaro litigation, as was proof that DBCP was the exact pesticide to which workers were exposed. Questions about length of employment, duration of work at a particular farm, or assignment to specific tasks, such as injecting the chemical into the ground, all initially produced inaccurate, confusing, and misleading responses to interrogatories. It was not until a person familiar with the language and the day-to-day lives of the plaintiffs began to prepare them for depositions that the legal team began to understand the impact of different experiences and ways of measuring time on the litigation.

Most indigenous and rural people experience and describe time very differently from those of us accustomed to digital watches with alarms. This exchange is hypothetical, but illustrates a situation in which the client understands that his answers are "not good enough" and tries to "guess" the "right answer" to please the interviewer. More objective responses can be obtained by asking the client to describe when he or she began a certain activity in relation to other events in his or her life, and to relate those events to major events in the larger world. For these clients and many who live in the developing world, time is not standardized and is intensely personal. Some relationship may be established between the two chronologies by resort to objective events - history, elections, strikes, floods, earthquakes and hurricanes, the birth of a child, the death of a community leader, and so on.

Social concepts are also relative. Attorneys in Castro Alfaro were surprised to learn that a single client would answer the question "were you married?" (e.g., while handling DBCP) differently at different times. The term and institution of "marriage" means different things to a North American lawyer and a Costa Rican peasant. Are you interested in civil marriage, religious marriage, and common law marriage? Do you want to know if the couple was living together and raising children, whether they considered themselves and the community considered them a stable, established family unit, or whether they had formalized their relationship? Once such a couple/family is established, the woman is "my wife" and the man "my husband" regardless of their civil status - even if one or both is legally married to another. The expression "the father of my child/children" is commonly used to describe the biological father, regardless of whether either or both of the couples sought civil sanction for the relationship.

Clients are not going to find it easy to talk about many aspects of their injuries. Sterility was a major issue in the

Castro Alfaro litigation. Initially the litigation focused on the physical aspects of the men that could be measured by science - zero sperm count, deformed sperm, poor motility, and so on, and also on the wives' loss of their husband's ability to procreate. As interviewers began to re-interview and know the plaintiffs better, other aspects became at least as important: fear of cancer, fear of deformed children in cases of less than complete sterility, fear of sexual rejection and impotence caused by it, shame and regret over not being able to contribute to the continuity of the family and the community.

These were both difficult subjects to talk about and extremely difficult matters to quantify. It was not until plaintiffs found people they could trust to "open up to" that the legal team could even seriously consider seeking damages for psychological injuries, which, in many cases, were the most severe. And it is not until such trust is established that the possibility of any real work toward "making [the client] whole" through counseling and therapy could even be considered. In addition, most of the marriages failed, and it became impractical to maintain contact with ex-partners.

Trust can only be established when respect for the client, on his or her terms, can be conveyed. Whether it is established by person-to-person contact, or through intermediaries - bicultural legal workers and local counsel - litigation such as the Castro Alfaro case must be undertaken with a great deal of sensitivity toward the clients. They believe they are (and often are in fact) risking present and future employment, community ostracism, and often physical danger, not in the hope of recovering millions, but in order to vindicate their rights and see that "justice" is done.

The United States legal system tends to reduce "justice" in tort cases to a monetary award for damages. Victims of the torts and crimes of U.S.-based transnationals in other countries deserve to be "made whole" economically, as well as morally. But they rarely understand the economic compensation as the be-all and end-all of their struggles. This makes the issue of settlement a difficult one, indeed.

Nowhere in the litigation process is trust and accurate communication more important, and respect for the clients more essential. Damage awards can easily be negotiated without exchanging a word with clients, just as cases can be lost without their realizing it for failure to respond to interrogatories on time. The problem of "selling the settlement" can be relegated to local counsel or someone not involved in the tough job of litigating and negotiating. But attorneys involved in transcultural litigation must ask themselves whether this model of "Justice" is very different from the model that resulted in the injuries in the first place. "First world knows best" is a hard attitude to shake, especially for those of us who have honed our skills in an adversary system, believing that using those on behalf of our clients was our best contribution to justice.

The trust essential to ethical long-distance negotiations cannot be created at the last moment, in order to settle the case. It must be built from the first client meeting, and must include counsel's willingness to understand that the feeling that "justice has been done" can be as important to clients as receiving a large damage award. Ethical and financial problems arise when, as in Castro Alfaro, U.S. counsel has spent very large sums of money to litigate on a contingency basis. Who decides when and if to settle? To avoid this dilemma, settlement as a possibility and U.S. legal processes in general must be discussed in depth with local counsel and plaintiffs to the extent possible.

Castro Alfaro brings to light a spectrum of issues concerning workers and human rights in today's global economy. The tenuousness of obtaining any forum for workers in developing countries in order to vindicate their rights against multinational corporations' presents a great challenge for advocates, as do the logistical obstacles discussed above. Multinationals have become "globe-encircling enterprises" affecting people and the environment throughout the world. Advocates for such workers, for indigenous peoples, the environment, and others injured by transnationals must develop new theories of liability and jurisdiction, new forums of accountability, and new ways of using existing laws, both international and national, from both the forum country and the country where the injuries were suffered.

As powerful as governments in many developing countries, the conduct of multinational corporations should be judged at least by the minimum international standards established by the Universal Declaration of Human Rights. At least, they should bear the full human and environmental costs to maximize profits by producing the oversized, blemish-free perfect banana.

4

Advocates for Development

The enjoyment of the totality of human rights calls for the organisation and mobilisation of the poor in developing countries for self-reliant development. Development should be understood as a process designed progressively to create conditions in which every person can enjoy, exercise and utilise under the Rule of Law all his human rights, whether economic, social, cultural, civil or political.

OVERVIEW, 1970-1990

After extraordinary atrocities in the 1970s, the human rights movement came of age. Cambodia's killing fields, South African apartheid, disappearances in Argentina, and widespread torture pricked the global conscience. Human rights NGOs, sympathetic national officials, and international organizations responded together with apparent effect. First the U.S. Congress and then President Jimmy Carter insisted that aid recipients respect human rights. The United Nations began seriously investigating disappearances, arbitrary killings, and torture. A new American Court of Human Rights followed the European model by rendering judgments against defendant states. African governments ratified a human rights convention that established a regional commission. Economic sanctions punished South Africa. Hundreds of new national and international NGOs organized. Amnesty International attracted an unprecedented global membership.

Democratic change arrived first in Western Europe. Portugal, Spain, and Greece removed their dictators in the 1970s. A decade later, Latin American juntas, Eastern European Marxists, and Asian despots fell. By 1990 dictators confronted broad human rights laws that limited domestic jurisdiction; international organizations, aroused citizens, and other governments demanded change. The Cold War, apartheid, colonialism, fascism, and communism were all historic relics. Yet unresolved problems remained. Economic justice was still a distant, improbable goal and old barbarisms continued-war crimes, torture, communal massacres. China, Haiti, Indonesia, Iran, Iraq, and Israel withstood international pressure.

Human rights advocates developed promotion, standard-setting, and protection activities that parallel the public education, lobbying, and litigation of domestic interest groups.

SOCIAL MOVEMENTS AND INTEREST GROUP ENTREPRENEURS

Social movement theorists contend that injustice triggers mass protest. Outraged victims will spontaneously organize and demand radical change. A major study on mobilizing American interest groups found to the contrary that social movements rarely begin as insurgencies by exploited victims against their oppressors. "Distress and anger over perceived injustice are a persistent fact of life among disadvantaged elements of any society and are only one of a number of factors that must exist before a social movement begins." U.S. interest groups typically spread through "the intervention of sympathetic patrons who provide fresh resources and crucial assistance for entrepreneurial leaders at a critical time."

Theories about international politics give conflicting perspectives of the human rights movement. Are idealists correct that mass demands for universal rights contribute to a global consciousness that could doom state sovereignty? Realists forecast an enduring clash of civilizations unaffected by a failure campaign to propagate Enlightenment values in non-Western societies. Are the major battles of the twenty-first century more likely to feature world citizen's assaults on arbitrary state power or Islamic, Hindu, and Buddhist challenges to Western Christendom? From 1970 to 1990, the ICJ systematically cultivated non-Western offshoots, grass roots with uneven growth that put rival theories to the test.

Unlike a social movement, the ICJ mobilized new groups in the same way it had been founded-from the top down. ICJ leaders were elite entrepreneurs who used government, church, and foundation patrons to start third world organization. The ICJ's longest serving Secretary-General was another dominant entrepreneur who came to embody the organization. Nialf MacDermont was a committed internationalist who ardently championed both civil liberties and economic justice.

As a youth in the 1990's MacDermont belonged to the "New Britain Group," which espoused utopian plans for European federation and syndicalist politics. MacDermont completed legal study at Balliol College, Oxford, before enlisting for military duty during World War II. He won the Order of the British Empire for success as a Lieutenant-Colonel in charge of counterintelligence for the Normandy landings. After the war, MacDermont practiced law for eighteen years, joined the ICJ national section, sat as a part-time judge, and became a Labour Member of Parliament. In 1964 his political career blossomed with appointment as Secretary to the Treasury and prospects of promotion to solicitor general.

Instead, MacDermont became the second casualty of a British intelligence agency (MI5) campaign against Labour prime minister Harold Wilson and associates on the political left, MI5 officers possibly bore a grudge against MacDermot for revealing in Parliament that Soviet spy Kim Philby had had an important intelligence position during the war. MacDermot's 1966 divorce and subsequent marriage in Geneva to a half-Soviet, half-Italian U.N. translator provided an opportunity for revenge. Notified of MI5 concerns about MacDermot's wife.

Wilson removed him from the cabinet defence committee and shifted him from Treasury to become Minister of State for Planning and Land. His British political career crippled, MacDermot announced his resignation from the government for personal reasons. With poetic justice, a victim of British intelligence revived the ICJ after its nearly fatal CIA expose and financial crisis. A friendly journalist wrote an admirable personal description of the ICJ Secretary-General.

In many ways MacDermot was an anachronism, a throwback to an earlier era. Long after leaving Britain, he continued to look and act likes a British cabinet minister with his mane of white hair, craggy features, and rich aristocratic delivery. He loved his British-made Rover car, the BBC World Service, and the London Times. His pinstriped suit stood out among the long hair and jeans worn by many other human rights lobbyists. He discouraged intimacy and could be cuttingly rude to people who thought they were his friends. But this only added to the impression of incorruptibility. As a former minister he owed no one any favors. No one talked down to MacDermot, and no one ignored him. Diplomats deferred to him and dreaded his rebukes.

Financial exigency plagued MacDermot for his first five years as Secretary-General. He moved the Secretariat from its spacious offices to a low-rent, five-room residence, where he shared an office in a converted bedroom. An Indian judge once paid a courtesy call at the cramped, suburban office and proposed that on a subsequent visit he would like to see the Secretariat building. First the Spanish and then the French editions of the Review were suspended. MacDermot found commercial publishers for major ICJ conference reports. The shrunken budget would not permit a "triennial" business meeting for six years. Full-time staff declined to seven, and law student interns assumed major responsibilities. The World Council of Churches paid the salary of one legal officer.

Few lawyers became patrons, contributors, or even dues-paying associate members. The ICJ's human rights gentry did not approach wealthy individuals for major contributions.

Modest annual grants from a dozen European governments barely covered operating expenses. Renewal was never assured, and bankruptcy repeatedly threatened. Funds raised and contributed through the AAICJ declined to less than one-third of total revenues. Pressed to recognize the ICJ's urgent needs, Whitney Debevoise relinquished the Executive Committee chair to a more active New York attorney, William J. Butler.

A practicing lawyer, Butler had been counsel and executor for ACLU founder Roger Baldwin. As counsel for the International League for Human Rights, he had testified before the ECOSOC committee reviewing NGOs' consultative status. Butler had joined a fact finding mission to Greece, argued an ACLU school prayer case before the U.S. Supreme Court, and was well connected to the U.S. State Department. MacDermot visited Butler's chalet in Zermatt and discussed the possibility of his becoming Executive Committee chairman.

When Bonsal's regular Commission membership expired, Debevoise invited Butler to a 1975 Executive Committee meeting. He was formally recommended for election to the Commission and continued to attend Committee meetings. When Debevoise announced his resignation from the committee, he asked the members to co-opt Butler. The informal tradition of New York leadership continued under Butler from 1976 until his term on the Commission expired in 1990. Debevoise was elected vice president after his fourteen years as chairman.

PUBLIC AND PRIVATE PATRONS

By the late 1970s changes in Western development assistance and human rights policy generated additional public funding for the ICJ. Foreign aid officials in Western democracies had greater confidence in private NGOs than in multilateral development agencies or recipient governments. Soviet influence at the United Nations and corruption by local officials persuaded Organization for Economic Cooperation and Development (OECD) donors to enlist church groups and charities to disburse relief and development funds directly to grass roots organizations. Legal aid became part of development aid when donor states insisted that recipients respect human rights.

The U.S. Congress pressed the Agency for International Development (AID) to maximize participation by local organizations in development projects and to use private charities to reach those most in need. Butler secured a $100,000 AID grant for an ICJ study on states of emergency. Congressional liberals also made U.S. military and economic assistance conditional on respect for human rights.

The Carter administration began making annual grants to the ICJ which Republican successors continued until 1983. The Reagan administration then sought to involve the ICJ in the National Endowment for Democracy. In Congressional testimony Secretary of State George Schultz mentioned the ICJ as a potential grant recipient. Third world staff denounced the U.S. effort to co-opt ICJ advocates into promoting opposition to pro-Soviet communist governments. MacDermot vigorously protested the unsolicited, unwelcome endorsement, and the ICJ received no politically tainted U.S. grants after 1983.

Grants from European governments were accepted without fear of interference. During the 1980s about twenty-five states made unrestricted grants that ranged between 30 and 37 percent of total annual income. The Ford Foundation's annual $100,000 grant was the next major income source. Those subsidies for the ICJ general budget paid for staff salaries, rent, publications, and administrative expenses. Restricted grants went into a separate special-projects budget for missions, reports, conferences, training seminars, and studies. Special project costs ranged from 24 to more than 50 percent of total expenses. European governments provided the major grants through development ministries and co-financing of quasi-private foundations.

Sweden's socialist government allocated 1 percent of its gross national product for development aid. For popular causes such as human rights and democracy, Parliament mandated spending more than the foreign ministry requested. Sweden's International Development Authority (SIDA) initially funded the ICJ's special project Legal Services in Rural Areas. The agency then paid half of the publications expenses and began providing a reliable base for the general budget. By 1990 SIDA provided over one-third of the ICJ's rapidly growing income.

Indirect government funding through quasi-private charities also increased rapidly. Several governments co-financed foundations administered by Catholic, Protestant, and nondenominational boards-most importantly, NOVIB in the Netherlands and Evangelischen Kirche in Deutschland (EKD) in Germany. Their restricted grants supported relief, development, and human rights projects abroad. ICJ regional legal officers budgeted each project separately, securing multiple sponsors for programs in third world countries where free churches and the professional bar were at risk.

Each special project grant included a share for administrative overhead in the general budget. With the exception of Ford, private foundations contributed far less than those co-financed by European governments. Butler obtained a small Rockefeller Brothers Fund start-up grant for an ICJ Centre for the Independence of Judges and Lawyers (CIJL). As funding gradually improved in the 1970s, MacDermot employed Secretariat legal officers from Latin America, Asia, and Africa, resumed publication of the Review in French and Spanish, and produced a quarterly ICJ Newsletter.

Local cosponsors helped organize regional seminars in English-speaking and Francophone Africa, the Caribbean, South America, the Middle East, and Asia. At each meeting the ICJ expanded its third world contacts, recruited members and staff, and organized regional jurists' organizations, new national sections, and indigenous lawyers' groups. Special-project funding for conferences paid travel expenses for Commission members to hold triennial business meetings at The Hague in 1981, Nairobi in 1985, and Caracas in 1989.

DEVELOPMENT AND THE RULE OF LAW

ICJ advocacy of development as a human right sought to bridge a major North-South divide. Both MacDermot and Butler viewed economic rights as fundamental. Some third world officials insist that human rights begin after breakfast. Famine, disease, and extreme poverty cause more death and suffering than torture or genocide. Southern leaders challenged Northern states to remove trade barriers and provide economic aid during the 1960s, the U.N. Development Decade. Frustrated by slow growth, third world governments next promoted a right to development. The Senegalese jurist who introduced the development proposal at the United Nations, Kéba Mbaye, was elected ICJ President.

The non-aligned movement also demanded a New International Economic Order (NIEO) that would require major reallocation of Northern wealth. Apologists for one-party states insisted that citizens must sacrifice political and civil liberties in order to realize swift economic growth. Western experts attributed slow growth to corrupt management of market economies and sought reallocation of power within third world oligarchies. Many private relief agencies disbursing government funds favored political restructuring that would threaten governing elites both North and South. As dependency theorists and development experts debated economic rights, the ICJ reexamined its rule of law principles.

Most Western lawyers' organizations and Amnesty International exclusively championed political rights. Since 1959 the ICJ had advocated a dynamic rule of law that included economic justice. In a major 1981 conference at The Hague, the ICJ connected development to the rule of law. The Dutch government, which hosted and partially funded the meeting, had also financed the 1976 RIO study on Reshaping the International Order. MacDermot commissioned a conference working paper from Australian Philip Alston, a U.N. consultant on the right to development. His views strongly shaped the ICJ conclusions, as well as a U.N. Secretariat report submitted by the Dutch director of the Human Rights Division, Theo van Boven.

The ICJ repudiated claims that civil liberties must be sacrificed to permit economic growth. The jurists concluded that political and economic rights are inseparable and deserve equal emphasis. Development requires maximum participation by individuals able to associate freely and to speak out on policies affecting their future. Individuals should be the subject, not the object, of development, a human right inextricably linked with political liberty. Beyond third world self-reliance, "industrialised countries should cooperate with the developing nations to achieve a New International Economic Order with a more just and equitable distribution of the world's resources and wealth." Progressive jurists must dismantle structural obstacles to development, such as militarization and export policies that enrich multinational corporations. Pergamon Press published the conference report, and the conclusions appeared in the U.N. monthly Development Forum.

The ICJ's support for a right to development appealed to German and Dutch church foundations and third world elites. Churches used Northern government grants to fund ICJ seminars in the South that promoted the interdependence rather than the incompatibility of political and economic rights. Without formally disavowing its prior critique of socialist legality, the ICJ sympathetically considered how African one-party states could protect human rights. ICJ seminars in Asia and Latin America challenged wealthy landholders and economic exploitation. MacDermot invited Muslim elites to examine how Islam respected human rights. Glasnost led to dialogue with Soviet jurists.

SUB-SAHARAN AFRICA

MacDermot's first major regional conference departed significantly from the multiparty Western parliamentary model celebrated in the ICJ's early Congresses. A 1976 East and Central African ICJ conference promoted "Human Rights in a One Party State." After their independence, Tanzanian and Zambian one-party democracies had experimented with contested elections within the party and professed to respect the independent bench and bar. The ICJ conference report included working papers and speeches by party officials endorsing preventive detention during emergencies, political education, and party direction of the executive, legislature, and judiciary. MacDermot's introduction noted the importance of "changing circumstances" and "the new political philosophy and system."

The report's conclusions satisfied neither Zambia's President Kaunda nor the Commission members who attended the 1977 triennial business meeting in Vienna. Commissioners' objections were appended to the final report. Democratic purists complained that the one-party rule endorsed at Dar es Salaam violated ICJ ideals. For pragmatists, single party constitutions with procedural guarantees for individual rights appeared preferable to the ubiquitous African military dictatorships.

A compromise statement warned of the inherent dangers in both one party system and ineffective attempts to duplicate the Westminster model. The ICJ adopted eleven principles calling for electoral choice, freedom of association, an ombudsman, independent judges, and free expression. A London publisher issued the report and its nonjudgmental recommendations for procedural fairness favorably impressed third world nationalists who resented Western attacks on newly independent governments. In follow-up visits to six countries, ICJ representatives encouraged ministers of justice, attorneys general, judges, and lawyers to implement the recommendations.

For twelve countries in Francophone West Africa, the Senegalese affiliate ASERJ (Association sénégalaise d'études et de recherches juridiques) cosponsored a 1978 regional conference that attracted fortyeight jurists. ICJ President Kéba Mbaye used the session to promote a third generation of solidarity rights, which included the right to development, peace, a satisfactory environment, and a just economic order. Mbaye's personal assistant, Adama Dieng, a Muslim, began his ascent to ICJ Secretary-General at the meeting. After training in law at Dakar University, Dieng worked as an administrative officer and registrar in the Senegalese courts.

He also assisted Mbaye in drafting a proposed African Charter on Human and Peoples' Rights. Dieng completed several research projects on racism as a UNESCO consultant and was a legal columnist for a daily newspaper. After earning a diploma at the Research Center of The Hague Academy of International Law, he taught a course on journalism at the Institute of Human Rights in Strasbourg. MacDermot asked the Senegalese expert on the U.N. Sub-Commission to recommend an African legal officer, and Dieng joined the ICJ Secretariat in 1982.

Dieng managed a new ICJ program to introduce in Africa the type of legal services in rural areas pioneered in Asia and Latin America. The ICJ assisted grass-roots development organizations trusted in rural areas to train paralegals. Litigation would be a last resort. Paralegals from villages, development organizations, or universities would work for legal reform and only involve urban lawyers as needed. Between 1983 and 1990 the ICJ sponsored seven training and follow-up sessions for paralegals in both French- and English-speaking Africa.

From Africa's legal elite, the ICJ elected eleven members in a twenty-year period, including Supreme Court presidents Kéba Mbaye of Senegal and T. O. Elias of Nigeria. Mbaye led the ICJ as its President from 1977 to 1985, campaigning for the right to development and the African Charter. Highly regarded at the United Nations, Mbaye was elected chairman of the Human Rights Commission. He and Elias organized an African Association of International Law for research on decolonization, development, human rights, and humanitarian law. Both won election to the International Court of Justice. ICJ members Rajsoomer Lallah and Amos Wako were elected to the U. N. Human Rights Committee.

Wako came to ICJ notice through his efforts to organize a regional lawyers' organization as the first secretary-general of the Inter-African Union of Lawyers. He served on the Committee of Experts and as Kenya's delegated to the OAU ministerial meeting to draft the African Charter. Following election to the ICJ, he became special rapporteur on summary and arbitrary executions for the U.N. Human Rights Commission, a member of the U.N. Human Rights Committee, and the U.N. Secretary-General's personal envoy to Indonesia after a massacre in East Timor. He was the first African member on the ICJ's Executive Committee.

Human rights advocates have publicly asked whether Wako became a "fallen angel." Opposition lawyers in Kenya learned that he resisted ICJ intervention on behalf of a detained editor who advocated multiparty elections. President Daniel Arap Moi continued repressive measures to preserve one-party rule, but Wako became his attorney general in 1991. In order to avoid potential conflicts, Wako suspended his ICJ membership under a Statute amendment applied during his tenure as a government minister. Promising reforms, Wako released political detainees, lifted a ban on the Nairobi Law Monthly, and secured ratification of the African Charter on Human and Peoples' Rights.

He also supported a constitutional amendment requiring counsel for human rights defendants. Only after Western aid donors cut off assistance did Moi allow multiparty elections, which he won in December 1992. Critics complain that Wako has manipulated law to protect all undemocratic regime and his own power. If so, his career perversely reveals that leadership in the international human rights movement now confers a status coveted by ambitious politicians.

Wako was never active in ICJ's Kenya national section. That group held sporadic meeting and retained its first staff in 1992, when younger lawyers began to challenge one-party rule. At a 1991 seminar organized by the section, an old-guard Kenya African National Union (KANU) minority approvingly cited the ICJ report on Human Rights in a One-Party State.

Kenya's notoriously undemocratic single party routinely violated human rights, and the majority pressed for a multiparty system. U.S. AID funded a major election project in 1992 that employed eighteen thousand poll watchers. The other six registered African affiliates did not send representatives to the ICJ's business meetings, notify the Geneva Secretariat of activities, or provide requested information.

MIDDLE EAST AND NORTH AFRICA

Religious doctrine bedevils human rights advocates in the Middle East. Saudi Arabia did not support the Universal Declaration of Human Rights, and the Organization of Islamic Countries has proposed a regional code more consistent with Koranic law. The IADL organized widely in the region with anti-colonial zeal. The ICJ recruited few members from Arab countries, and none ever played prominent roles in the organization. Israeli Supreme Court judge Haim Cohn was an early member.

The Egyptian member was law professor Boutros Boutros-Ghali, a Coptic Christian whose wife is Jewish. At that time the ICJ had no restriction on cabinet ministers serving as members during their period of government service, and several did so. After Boutros-Ghali became Egypt's minister of state for foreign affairs in 1981, the statute was amended. Thereafter, the Executive Committee on its own initiative or at a member's request could hold Commission membership in abeyance until the official position was relinquished. However much the ICJ might be enhanced by gaining a U.N. Secretary-General as a member, there is no prospect that Boutros-Ghali would resume his affiliation.

To bridge the cultural divide, MacDermot organized a regional conference on "Human Rights in Islam." Kuwait University and the Arab Lawyers Union cosponsored a 1980 conference attended by sixty scholars and lawyers from twenty-six predominantly Islamic countries. Instead of challenging current government practice, MacDermot encouraged general debate on how Islamic law promoted justice. Commission member A. K. Brohi, Pakistan's former minister of law and religious affairs, delivered the keynote address. Free of Western commentary or judgment, the Muslim participants discussed human rights principles in the Koran and Shari'a. One participant, Kuwait's Dean of the Faculty of Law and Shari'a, became one of the first female members but was never active.

MacDermot's U.N. interventions condemning Israeli violations of Palestinian rights won more converts. Unlike other Western NGOs, the ICJ had no dominant Jewish leaders and frequently denounced Israel. A Palestinian group in the Occupied West Bank, "Law in the Service of Man," applied to become an ICJ affiliate. A Ramallah barrister approached MacDermot for assistance in publishing a carefully documented study showing how Palestinians in the occupied territories were subject to secret orders enforced by military courts.

The British-trained activists demonstrated convincingly that lawyers appearing in court had no prior knowledge of the applicable rules. MacDermot was outraged at the practice and impressed that the highly professional non-Muslim lawyers were not fronting for the PLO. "Law in the Service of Man" registered as a corporation to avoid government regulations for charitable societies. The ICJ accepted an application for affiliate status separate from the inactive Israeli national section nominally headed by Haim Cohn.

A Kuwaiti donor funded ICJ publication of the affiliate study entitled The West Bank and the Rule of Law. National sections translated the report into five languages, giving the new affiliate legitimacy and exposure in Europe. The U.N. Human Rights Division purchased five hundred copies for a Special Committee report to the General Assembly; foreign missions in Geneva made bulk purchases. "Law in the Service of Man" took the name Al Haq and received financial support from OXFAM, ICCO, the Ford Foundation, and church groups.

Its offices provided the only public law library in the West Bank, its lawyers took victim affidavits, and its publications systematically exposed Israeli human rights violations. The organization refused all contributions from Arabs and Israelis and limited any single source to 20 percent of the budget. The group became the largest ICJ affiliate, with three times the staff of the Geneva Secretariat. In 1988 the Gaza Centre for Peace and Law affiliated. The Israeli national section discontinued its limited operations, and Jewish activists there founded new human rights groups. A Tunisian group was the ICJ's only other affiliate in a region where governments severely restricted both NGOs and Western influence.

ASIA

In a diverse region of Hindus, Muslims, and Buddhists, many ICJ activists were Parsis, Christians, and women disadvantaged by dominant religions. Legal officer Daniel Ravindran of India began serving India's poor while still a law student. As a member of the All India Catholic University Federation, he taught school dropouts in the slums. After joining the Bar Council he provided legal aid to rural farmers from 1977 until 1981. To gain international experience, he contacted the University of Minnesota human rights intern program.

Based on Ravindran's outstanding resumé, MacDermot hired him for a Southeast Asia regional seminar and Geneva internship, which led to a permanent appointment. Fali Nariman, a Parsi, was elected to the ICJ and its Executive Committee after resigning as India's solicitor general when Indira Gandhi proclaimed a state of emergency.

Most Asian jurists recruited as ICJ members had high status. T. S. Fernando, ICJ President from 1966 to 1977, was president of' the Ceylon Court of Appeal and a former attorney general and solicitor general. Sir Guy Powles of New Zealand and Sir Moti Tikaram of Fiji each served as an ombudsman. Cooperation with Fiji's unconstitutional regime upset Tikaram's reelection to the ICJ after an initial five-year term. At first Tikaram protested a military coup, but he then replaced on the bench independent judges removed for defending the constitution. The ICJ rejected Tikaram's explanation that his appointment could ameliorate an unjust situation. Tikaram attended his final Commission meeting in 1989 when the ICJ protested the dismissal of Malaysian judges who had remained faithful to the rule of law.

Several new women members from Asia breached the all-male bastion. Former law professor and Dean Mrs. Tai-Young Lee of South Korea was elected vice president. As founder and director of the Korean legal Aid Center for Family Relations, she actively campaigned on behalf of "comfort" women enslaved by Japanese troops during World War II. A Muslim woman from Indonesia, Nana Moeljadi, became an administrative mainstay in the Geneva Secretariat.

Australian judge Michael Kirby inherited from his compatriot St. John the gadfly member role, advocated democratizing ICJ governance, and was elected to the Executive Committee. From the bench he promoted domestic application of international human rights norms. The large Australian national section initiated missions to regional trouble spots, occasionally without consulting MacDermot. After one embarrassing incident, MacDermot made clear the Australian section did not speak for the ICJ and pressed the group to apologize for a misstatement.

About ten other national sections and affiliates in Asia were considerably weaker. The predominantly Catholic Philippines offered more fertile ground than Islamic Indonesia, which sought to block Dutch aid for local NGOs. In three countries studied by NOVIB, local activists complained of inadequate feedback and follow-up from the Geneva Secretariat. Sri Lankans appreciated ICJ support when a presidential commission threatened citizen groups. Weak ICJ sections and affiliates in India, Malaysia, and Nepal distributed ICJ publications and arranged occasional conferences.

British and American jurists dominated the ICJ's 1959 New Delhi Congress. The 1980s development seminars were of Asians, by Asians, and for Asians. A 1981 ICJ seminar on "Rural Development and Human Rights in South East Asia" brought forty participants from five Association of Southeast Asian Nations (ASEAN) countries to Malaysia. The ILO, FAO,

UNESCO, and the Economic and Social Commission for Asia and the Pacific all sent representatives. The Dutch foreign ministry and foundations with ties to Indonesia and Catholic churches provided funding. The cosponsoring Consumers' Association of Penang rallied opposition to deforestation, powdered milk, tourist exploitation, and high-technology growth strategies based on production for export. Participants advocated the NIEO, a nuclear free zone, and international protection of the environment.

The ICJ encouraged ASEAN civil rights lawyers to create a Regional Council on Human Rights in Asia (RCHRA). ICJ members Roberto Concepción of the Philippines and Thiam-Hien Yap of Indonesia were among the twelve founders from five countries. The first RCHRA General Assembly issued a strongly worded "Declaration of the Basic Duties of ASEAN Peoples and Governments," which was submitted to the ASEAN Secretariat. After attending the second annual RCHRA General Assembly, Ravindran published the declaration in the ICJ Newsletter. With Ford Foundation support, RCHRA members and staff in the Philippines lobbied for ratification of the international covenants, promoted law reform, worked to free political prisoners, and obtained U.N. consultative status.

A 1982 seminar in Lucknow, India, launched a second ICJ regional enterprise, the South Asian Association for the Right to Development (SAARD). The cosponsoring Human Rights Institute hosted forty participants from five countries and published seminar papers advocating third world development perspectives. Participation by Fali Nariman, a highly respected New Delhi lawyer and former solicitor general of India, revealed the paradox of ICJ elites promoting rights for the oppressed. Seminar advocates for the Asian masses rebuked lawyers who sold their services to dominant groups.

The keynote speaker warned against energy-dependent agricultural systems and heavy petrochemical-based inputs for productivity. Two years later the Bhopal chemical plant disaster took twenty-five hundred lives, and the Indian government sued Union Carbide for damages. Nariman, a member of the ICJ Executive Committee, successfully defended the U.S. Corporation; to the dismay of critics, a negotiated settlement provided only $450,000 for compensation.

At a SAARD follow-up conference in Nepal, Ravindran struggled to make the organization an agent of change for India's untouchables and bonded laborers throughout the region. SAARD adopted a plan of action, but the organization failed to take root. The ICJ expanded its own promotion of legal services in rural areas, with Ravindran organizing twelve training seminars for paralegals in six Asian countries. He edited a handbook that local groups translated for use in the Philippines and India. NGO populists mobilized rural activists to challenge agribusiness, corrupt public officials, and postcolonial legal systems that preserved vast wealth disparities.

[Pathologies] are endemic in the legal systems of most developing countries. Our legal systems are both alien and alienating to our masses.... Access to legal process is usually restricted and available often only through the intermediary of lawyers operating in what is undoubtedly a "disabling" profession.... Our laws and legal institutions seem to have been developed to be geared to the needs and interests of the rich, the powerful, and the transnationals. The cumulative effect of these pathologies has made our legal systems an instrument for the production and reproduction of exclusion, dependency, impoverishment and evasion of accountability.... [W]e must strive for an "alternative" conception of law-law for a society whose vision reaffirms self-reliance, participation, endogeny, redistribution of resources and power, and development, above all else, of the human being. The ICJ promoted a new breed of lawyers to work with social action groups against centralized development projects that oppressed the poor.

LATIN AMERICA

At times ICJ affiliates in predominantly Catholic Latin American countries outnumbered those in Western Europe, although many were organizational shells without substance.

MacDermot recruited Alejandro Artucio as Latin American legal officer. Artucio, a Uruguayan defence lawyer, had been imprisoned and tortured by the junta after representing Tupomaro guerrillas. For eleven months of incommunicado detention he experienced the military's most refined skills-near suffocation in tubs of water, beatings, and days with his head in a hood. Released with head shaved, he was placed on a plane to Paris by a squad of soldiers armed with machine guns. In 1974 MacDermot offered him work, and the World Council of Churches provided his initial salary.

The ICJ's first development seminar in Barbados, though intellectually stimulating, failed to launch the desired Caribbean regional organization. With the Latin American Council for Law and Development, the ICJ arranged a 1979 seminar in Bogotá, Colombia on Human Rights in the Rural Areas of the Andes Region. Sixty-one professors, advocates, academics, unionists, and peasant and Indian leaders from six countries attended. In a rare display of assertiveness, indigenous representatives spoke forcefully of their needs.

The participants concluded that repression of civil and political rights is the cause of economic failure. They called for greater popular participation in agricultural and development policies and advocated agrarian reform, labor legislation, Indian rights, and a regional jurists' association.

MacDermot then invited one leading jurist from each country to be a founding member of the Andean Commission of Jurists (ACJ); he arranged for a Colombian who had worked in the ICJ Secretariat to become ACJ secretary-general. The ICJ obtained $180,000 from foundations and $10,000 from Norway to launch the ACJ. Colombia withheld approval of the ACJ Charter for months, and the secretary- general resigned before the organization was legally registered. MacDermot then contacted the Commission members to appoint a Peruvian national, Diego Garcia-Sayan, as executive secretary. Startup funds deposited in Colombia that could not be remitted abroad were lost as the ACJ became the first international NGO recognized by Peru.

The Lima office quickly became fully independent, with its own foundation and support from Catholic and other European groups. The ACJ published a 323-page seminar report, "International Rules on Human Rights and Internal Law," and lobbied the Peruvian government on behalf of the disappeared in Argentina. The ACJ published a quarterly Botelèin and a monthly Andean Newsletter, and obtained consultative status at the U.N. In 1987 the ACJ cosponsored a Lima seminar on legal services in rural areas of the Andean countries. Peasant and indigenous leaders, lawyers, and social science professionals from five Andean countries attended. After regularly attending ICJ business meetings, Diego Garcia-Sayan was elected to the ICJ and its Executive Committee in 1992. He also joined the U.N. Commission on Human Rights Working Group on Disappearances.

Andrés Aguilar Mawdsley, Venezuela's U.N. ambassador, succeeded Mbaye as ICJ President from 1985 to 1991 and, like his predecessor, was elected to the International Court of Justice. As president of the Inter-American Commission on Human Rights, Aguilar was credited with effectively pressing Argentina's junta to stop the disappearances. With U.N. funding for a conference on an independent judiciary, he hosted the ICJ's 1989 triennial meeting in Caracas. After his election to the ICJ, Guyana's attorney general and minister of state, Shridath S. Ramphal, became secretary-general of the Commonwealth Secretariat.

It was difficult to recruit and hold members from countries under military rule. Alberto Ramón Real of Uruguay resigned to avoid military retribution for the ICJ's attack on his government. Former vice president Osvaldo Illanes Benitez resigned and protested that MacDermot's negative reports on Chile were inaccurate. Chilean professor Alfredo Etcheberry was elected in his place and joined the Executive Committee.

THE NORTH

The well-advanced ICJ network in the North produced a growing pool of national section activists and prospective leaders. European Executive Committee members included P. J. G. Kapteyn, councilor of state for the Netherlands; Rudolf Machacek, member of Austria's Constitutional Court; Louis Joxe, ambassador of France and minister of state; Christian Tomuschat, professor of International Law, Bonn; and Gerald Gardiner, former Lord Chancellor of England. Paul Sieghart of "Justice" frequently attended committee meetings as an alternate but was never elected to the ICJ. Two members of the European Human Rights Commission were elected: Michael A. Triantafyllides, president of the Supreme Court of Cyprus, and Norwegian professor Torkel Opsahl. Former prime minister of France Edgar Faure was unanimously elected in 1971. Former Secretaries-General Marsh and Lalive were named Honorary Members.

In 1987 and 1988 three women succeeded such elder statesmen as John Humphrey, former director of the U.N. Human Rights Division. Claire L'Heureux-Dube was a Canadian Supreme Court judge. Nicole Questiaux was a member of the Council of State of France, former minister of state, and an expert on the U.N. Sub-Commission on Prevention of Discrimination and Protection of Minorities. Ireland's feminist senator Mary Robinson complained at the triennial meeting in Caracas about the under representation of women. She suspended her membership when elected as Ireland's president.

The European sections conducted extensive activities at both the national and regional level without assistance from Geneva. Section representatives regularly attended triennial ICJ meetings and renewed requests for closer collaboration. MacDermot and Butler both resisted staff and membership pressures for closer integration of local affiliates and the Geneva Secretariat. They did not seek their financial support and did not want responsibility for settling local problems. Section leaders elected to the Commission or hired as staff qualified on their individual merits and did not represent national groups. New sections might organize with a minimal start-up grant, but then MacDermot insisted on full autonomy.

Independent ICJ sections thus had less difficulty organizing under local law than did new AI groups, which registered as branches of the international secretariat in London.

In the late 1970s ICJ executive secretary Hans Thoolen, of the Netherlands, urged MacDermot to seize a unique opportunity for growth resulting from unprecedented public support for human rights. As new NGOs grew dramatically, Britain's former secretary to the treasurer cautiously kept the ICJ from bankruptcy with a modest staff and budget. In the United States, Bill Butler did not recruit new AAICJ members or encourage new lawyers' groups to affiliate. Former ICJ interns joined the new International Human Rights Law Group in Washington, the New York Lawyers Committee for Human Rights, and the Minnesota Lawyers International Human Rights Committee.

All sought grants from the same U.S. foundations and appealed to the same bar constituency. Amnesty International USA organized a legal support network with urban chapters throughout the country. If the growing human rights bar in the United States had affiliated with the ICJ, Americans would undoubtedly have resumed their domination of the organization. In Europe, MacDermot helped launch several new organizations. Thoolen served on a planning committee that followed the ICJ model in establishing the International Commission of Health Professionals for Health and Human Rights based in Geneva.

Lawyers organized new national sections in the new democracies, first in Spain and Portugal, then in South Africa, Hungary, and Poland. Spain's former ombudsman, Professor Don Joaquin Ruiz-Gimenez was elected as an ICJ member and Vice President. Young activist lawyers in the Netherlands organized a new section, Nederlands Juristen Comité vor den Mensenrechten (NJCM), which took major initiatives on European issues. Thoolen helped initiate the Human Rights International Documentation System (HURIDOCS) to assist NGOs in handling and exchanging information. He also campaigned at the Council of Europe, which awarded the ICJ its first Human Rights Prize in 1981. In the Netherlands the ICJ received the Wateler Peace Prize and the Erasmus Prize.

Thirty years after beginning its war on socialist legality, the ICJ welcomed opportunities for dialogue with Soviet jurists. The Nixon-Brezhnev experiment with détente encouraged people-to-people and professional-to-professional exchanges, including lawyers. In 1972 fifty members of the Washington, D.C. Bar Association visited Moscow, and seven observed a civil trial.

The USSR honored former ICJ Secretary-General MacBride with the Lenin Peace Prize, and MacDermot made valuable official contacts during a 1974 holiday in Moscow. The Austrian section arranged for joint meetings with Eastern European counterparts. A conference on children's rights in Poland, cosponsored with the IADL, was the ICJ's first friendly appearance behind the Iron Curtain.

In 1984 the Association of Soviet Lawyers (ASL) initiated formal exchange arrangements with both the ICJ and the American Bar Association (ABA). The ASL hosted twenty ICJ representatives in Moscow for a discussion on nuclear weapons, human rights internal legislation, and judicial procedure. Practicing attorneys constituted about half of the ICJ representatives, while academics dominated the Soviet delegation. ICJ members unsuccessfully sought permission to observe prosecutions involving slander against the state, to visit psychiatric hospitals, and to obtain statistics on trials.

In October 1986 the ICJ reciprocated by hosting a session for the ASL in Madrid that took up free expression, economic rights, and human rights and peace. The participants did not mention specific violations or seek relief for particular individuals. Law as a means for securing international peace remained a paramount concern for the Soviet participants.

The Soviets eschewed rhetoric about bourgeois imperialism and requested that the summary report not refer to "socialist" legality or "socialist" justice. By the time the ASL-ICJ representatives met for the last time in 1989,

Gorbachev's constitutional revolution had brought about pravovoye gosudarstvo-a state based on law. The rule of law had still not arrived, but the communist empire soon crumbled. By 1990, new entrepreneurs and patrons were needed to mobilize advocates for development in Northern Asia and Eastern Europe.

During the two decades when human rights activism mushroomed, the ICJ switched government patrons, recruited leading Southern jurists, launched new affiliates, and revitalized its membership. Amendments to the Statute enlarged the Executive Committee from five to seven and reduced the length of members' terms. Early members with more than twenty years' service were given honorary status; new members were elected to five-year renewable terms up to fifteen years.

ICJ tactics for spreading human rights values included seminars, conferences, lectures, publications, and local organizing. In regional seminars the ICJ proclaimed development as a basic right, recruited third world lawyers, and launched new groups. In conferences with jurists from Islamic countries, African one-party states, and the Soviet Union, the [C] proselytized among non-Western elites. ICJ experts preached rule of law gospel in lectures to professional groups, at U.N. human rights seminars and NGO conferences, in publications, and in private meetings with public officials. Sweden's development agency funded technical assistance through ICJ training seminars on legal services in rural areas. A practitioner's manual was developed to help paralegals represent third world peasants. ICJ studies on asylum, privacy, and states of emergency promoted international protection for basic civil liberties.

The ICJ launched new NGOs of local advocates for universal human rights and also recruited elite members who were or who became leaders of international organizations.

Remarkably, the NGO honored for challenging state sovereignty elected public officials as members and depended heavily on government support. Other NGOs may confirm social movement theories about grass-roots protest. The ICJ developed as a political interest group with state patrons, following a corporatist approach. Why did Northern governments fund, and Southern governments allow, ICJ programs that advocated subversive political and economic ideas? Industrialized states with multinational corporations funded development experts who bit the hand providing grants. Community activists in totalitarian states organized national and regional groups to change unjust systems. At a Swedish-funded seminar in Indonesia, for example, the ICJ might inveigh against European arms sales and organize local activists to demand land reform.

A major study of North Atlantic foreign aid found that governments collaborated with seemingly hostile private organizations because the benefits outweighed the costs. Northern donors want cost-effective aid programs that circumvent corrupt public officials.

Direct foreign aid to local organizations would violate national sovereignty. NGOs such as the ICJ can reduce bureaucratic overhead, avoid legal obstacles, and directly promote local self-help. For their part, third world governments too poor to provide rural legal aid prefer NGO technical assistance over government grants that have more strings attached. Radical community activists may organize as a result, but such reform groups might harness passions that would otherwise ignite revolutionary movements.

With its reputable cadre of establishment figures, the ICJ enjoyed a special entrée with many governments, churches, and foundations. The secretary for human rights of EKD, a church foundation, was a member of the German national section. To an extent, the ICJ's individualist human rights doctrine offered ideological support for both North and South. The third world had a right to development and the North a duty to assist, as long as modernizing states allowed popular participation and respected human rights. Economic growth must be accompanied by political development.

That ICJ prescription for development enticed Western donors and some third world elites, even though the correlation between democratic institutions and economic growth has been uncertain at best.

Totalitarian South Korea developed more wealth per capita and much higher literacy than democratic Portugal. Undemocratic ASEAN countries that violated human rights-Malaysia, Thailand, and Indonesia-had twice the per capita growth rates of countries in other regions; they enjoyed 7 to 9 percent real economic growth in 1991. A growing middle class in Southeast Asia has now demanded the democratic reforms the ICJ proclaimed as prerequisites of development.

SOCIALIZATION

The time for powerful democratic ideas appeared to arrive around 1990, and the ICJ was a small agent of transnational socialization. The organization took several hundred third world lawyers, judges, scholars, public officials, and community activists outside their own countries for meetings with people from other states.

They received working papers, heard speakers, met U.N. and foundation officials, discussed human rights, and were urged to organize for action. ICJ staff conducted follow-up meetings and secured start-up funds for selected groups. Middle-class activists inspired by Western democratic ideals were exposed to radical economic demands by more populist groups in the movement.

That cross-fertilization has had little impact on Western views of civil society and the state. MacDermot viewed ICJ promotional activities as "bread upon the waters." The scattered particles spawned minimal commitments to universal values, but could nurture future links across cultural fault lines. Alternately, fundamentalist religious movements in the third world could frustrate global integration by challenging human rights NGOs as alien agents of Westernization.

By educating members and staff, the ICJ socialized human rights advocates for democracy, modernization, and world citizenship. The organization enhanced idealists' commitment to service but also attracted opportunists seeking personal gain. Attendance at ICJ promotional activities and leadership in the organization were no guarantees of principled commitment to human rights. Conflicts of interest were unavoidable given the ICJ preference for established jurists with high government experience. On balance, the celebrated heroes far outnumber the few fallen angels.

RECRUITMENT

After retirement, MacDermot reflected that his ICJ career had been far more rewarding than the limited experience of his bar-association and party colleagues in Britain. His sympathetic understanding of non-Western political and economic conditions attracted to Geneva capable Secretariat staff from Uruguay, Senegal, India, and Indonesia. They left their third world homes to serve a transnational cause that transcended partisan or personal interests. Their enthusiasm influenced young interns from Argentina, Chile, Hong Kong, Bangladesh, and Sri Lanka. Underpaid staff made the greatest economic sacrifices and developed the strongest loyalty to transnational ideals.

Few third world lawyers in Africa and Asia could sustain effective local organizations without Northern patrons. Christians educated in Western institutions became active recruits. Affiliates in South America and the Occupied Territories became highly respected independent organizations with staff, publications, and extensive programs. The ICJ's prestige attracted well-known jurists to accept membership and propelled lesser known recruits into international leadership positions.

Three third world members won election to the International Court of Justice, two members served on the European Commission of Human Rights, and one member each served on the Inter-American Commission, the U.N. Commission on Human Rights, its Working Group on Disappearances, and as U.N. Rapporteur on Summary and Arbitrary Executions.

Other members and staff took leadership positions in the U.N. and Commonwealth Secretariats, the ILO, and the U.N. High Commissioner for Refugees. The activists enlisted by the ICJ joined a global human rights network. With limited resources, the ICJ reached comparatively few individuals, and some of its own leaders have not always practiced what they preached. Its profound influence on others reveals why idealists conclude that a new transnational consciousness could result from the cumulative impact of many such groups mobilizing advocates for human rights.

5

New Directions in the Nineties

Almost every leading commentator on current international developments assumes that recent momentous changes at the international and national levels will produce profound but often unpredictable outcomes. Certain changes from the mid-1980s to the early 1990s are, in many ways, "sea-changes." They include developments that are global in impact and previously almost unimaginable in scale and scope. Taken together they drastically alter the balance of ideas as well as more conventional elements of power that shape such fields as employment and human rights. Such developments include the collapse of Marxism-Leninism as an ideological weapon and the consequent loss of will and motive to contest dominant Western perspectives concerning many employment and human rights issues. As a result, debates in these subject areas increasingly reflect other alignments, including struggles between North and South and within the widened Western sphere.

The global and regional changes that will determine how we think and act regarding employment in the final years of this millennium is a mixture of the political, economic, social, cultural, and military. In many cases the connections between these forces and aspects of employment are indirect and less than obvious. Yet they provide, individually and collectively, an international context for policies that greatly determine our welfare and well-being now and in the foreseeable future.

This book has chronicled the impact of a definable Soviet bloc on the international politics of employment and human rights. This bloc, consisting primarily of the nation-states associated with the Warsaw Treaty Organization and the Council for Mutual Economic Assistance, utilized internationally, and benefited domestically, from proclaimed constitutional guarantees of employment. Each of these states built into their economies and legal systems a variety of policies that kept overt unemployment to a minimum - including onerous requirements before certain kinds of dismissals could proceed and incentives that led enterprising managers to maximize persons on payrolls by under employing and featherbedding.

The members of this bloc, perceiving that the provision of employment and job security constituted an area of major ideological and political advantage over many capitalist systems, took advantage of various opportunities to use this perceived favorable dimension of their domestic policies at international forums. Although such efforts were usually politically clumsy, they constituted for bloc spokespersons an issue that seemed to confirm Marxist-Leninist ideology and sometimes caused visible squirming in the ranks of Western adversaries.

Subsequently, there began the era of East European political transformation, privatization, uneven transition toward market economies, and negotiations for debt relief and Western economic assistance. This period also brought wide-ranging East-West cooperation in the very intergovernmental organization forums that had provided significant battlegrounds in the recent history of the right to employment. The politics of ideas and systems shifted drastically as Soviet, successor state, and East-Central European leadership increasingly competed for Western favour and support.

Yet this shift in the rhetorical struggle and the blurring of East-West social and economic systems constitutes only one part of the sea change regarding Eastern Europe. Another is the advent or threat of horrific levels of unemployment in the aftermath of the collapse of Communist rule. This has perhaps been most dramatic thus far in the territory of the former German Democratic Republic, which registered a jobless rate of 14.6 percent in mid-1992, for which the term "employment catastrophe" is being used. Even this high level of unemployment, credited with leading to massive suicides and political disaffection, may have less long-term impact than the ongoing economic freefall of the early 1990s in most post-Soviet republics.

Various repercussions of the East-Central European experience can be expected to reinforce regional and global consciousness of the powerful negative impacts of mass unemployment. Together with recent political developments in France, the United States, and elsewhere they also can be expected to challenge assumptions made in the 1980s concerning the lack of substantial impact of unemployment on the political vulnerability of particular government administrations and on national political systems.

It was one thing to have "unacceptable" levels of unemployment in stable democracies facing, at worst, slight declines in overall GDP. Evidence is building to demonstrate that the impact on political stability is much greater in regimes facing sharply rising expectations, few established political leaders or parties, and rapidly changing constitutional orders. Political trends in the united Germany of 1991-92 and in several East-Central European countries indicate that this backlash is already affecting the direction of politics in and out of the former Soviet bloc, increasing support for radical rightist, ultra nationalist, xenophobic, and even Communist elements.

A second geographic area experiencing sea-change affecting employment and related human rights policies is the European Community. The essence of the consensus favoring the Single European Act of 1987 and its plan for the completion of the internal European market was a neo-liberal one. The Cecchini Report, sponsored by the European Commission, promised that "a new competitive environment" fostered by the elimination of remaining national and market barriers was to result in "major reductions in chronic European unemployment after a short-term adjustment period." The completed internal market would add 1.8 million jobs Community-wide, reducing the overall unemployment rate by some 1.5 percentage points.

However, the Single European Act set off tremors in European labor circles as well as among other advocates of social causes. Fears centered on potential efforts by less affluent Community member states to compete for new investment through such measures as reduced social security obligations for firms, less social protection in such areas as working conditions, health, and safety, and the encouragement of lower wages and weaker trade unions. The expected short-term surge in mergers, acquisitions, and joint ventures, posing threats of marked increases in plant closings and large-scale redundancies, also threatened to generate greater labor market instability.

The leap of faith and action into a Europe in which barriers to free movement across national barriers were to be markedly reduced for goods, services, workers, and money was part of a search for a larger consensus about the future of Europe involving such issues as monetary and fiscal policy, the restructuring of national and Community political power, and defence cooperation. It also prompted renewed efforts to meet the social challenges posed by the new economic order.

One of the major considerations for the future direction of the Community on employment and related issues is the pressure to admit new member states. In several cases this is a matter of when rather than whether particular states will be included. New members will presumably come first from European Free Trade Association (EFTA) members, and may come later from states of the former Soviet bloc, Turkey, and other applicants. The consequences of such expansion will be enormous and will take various forms. The problems of relative industrial backwardness and societies in transition to free markets characterize the former Communist East, with Germany's Eastern leader offering an early trial run for the expansion of the geographic scope of subsidies, regional policy, and other methods of adjustment and equalization.

The remainder of Scandinavia, Austria and Switzerland offer fewer problems together with prospects of increased interest in the Community in some of their approaches to active labor market programs. Throughout most of 1991 the EC and the seven EFTA states struggled to shape a new provisional economic and political relationship, which bore fruit in a treaty signed in October of that year. The implications of that agreement are discussed below.

One of the major problems of further Community expansion is the prospect of diversion of structural fund, investment bank, and other financial resources away from weaker regions of present member states to accommodate new states. Unless total resources available for redistribution and social programs are increased well beyond present levels, income inequality and regional disparities within and among the present member states will be difficult to reduce when the internal market advances. This prospect led to new agreements on augmentation and reallocation of Community budget obligations at the December 1991 Maastricht Summit that was signed by the participants in February 1992.

Perhaps the potential sea-change with the least predictable result is the prospective North American common market initiated by the establishment of the Canada-U.S. Free Trade Agreement that entered into force in 1989. The authorization of "fast track" treatment of U.S. Mexican-Canadian free trade negotiations in 1991 by the U.S. Congress led to the signing of the North American Free Trade Agreement in 1992. Similar "fast track" treatment was promised in 1991 in regard to GATT's Uruguay Round. These decisions were stimulated by North American fears about Europe's proposed completion of its common market by the end of 1992 as well as Japanese and other East Asian competition. A vision of an enlarged European Community viewed as capable of creating major new barriers to external trade spurred free trade developments.

Many U.S. labor and environmental spokespersons, together with their allies in the Clinton Administration, the Ross Perot camp, Congress, and elsewhere, perceive the expansion of free trade to Mexico as threatening the wholesale exportation of U.S. jobs as well as the creation of major environmental risks. Although the employment outcomes of the North American developments cannot yet be predicted confidently, certain warning signals are apparent.

The European Community demonstrated how countries with unequal levels of industrialization and technology can succeed in moving toward a free trade area. This, however, required substantial transfers of resources to backward countries and regions, other political and financial payoffs, and the stimulation of increased efforts to train and retrain workers in the various participating countries. Although the U.S. government has responded rhetorically to such concerns on this side of the Rio Grande, there is ample reason to doubt that the U.S. federal government has the commitment or financial ability to match existing European programs. In any event, no foreseeable North American free trade community is likely to have political or financial strengths comparable to that of the European Community, and therefore will face greater risks of collapse in the face of major and prolonged losses of jobs and national income in any of its three parts. Economic and political strains in Canada in 1992-93 illustrate those risks.

The forces of change noted above distort the reader's vision insofar as they stress trends in the OECD and post-Communist lands rather than in the developing countries that house most of the world's population. No single recent event, or combination of developments, has substantially shifted attention to the social and economic problems of the Third World, and it is unlikely that any soon will. For many of these countries the many ominous economic developments of the 1980s forecast continuing socioeconomic difficulties in the 1990s, especially the sharp fall in aggregate net financial transfers to developing countries from 1982 onwards.

Most intergovernmental and national lending, granting, and technical assistance organizations continue to downplay the significance of unemployment in most developing countries -even after receiving massive criticism of painful Third World experiences with structural adjustment and debt repayment demands imposed in the 1980s. Unfortunately, labor force growth in many regions of Asia, Africa, and Latin America will continue to outstrip the ability of most countries on those continents to create jobs. Although the anticipated slowing of labor force increases in various developing countries can be expected to improve prospects on the unemployment front in the coming decade, an average of some 35 million new members are expected to join the labor force in developing countries annually for the remainder of the 1990s.

East-Central Europe and the former Soviet republics remind us that political and economic stability count as much as labor force trends in predicting unemployment and underemployment. The trends of the first years of the 1990s point to some possible improvement in overall political stability and democratization in Africa and Latin America combined with growing risks of instability in parts of the Arab world, China and India. China, the world's most populous country, is at this writing continuing repression of human rights even as it continues with highly beneficial economic reforms and rapid growth in foreign investment, production, and exports.

Its highly profitable trade relations with the United States are increasingly at risk due to both human rights abuses and bilateral trade imbalances. The pro-democracy movement that set the stage for Tiananmen derived in part from patterns of labor force growth and mobility that shattered China's full employment commitments even as Communist political discipline wavered.

India's 850 million people face the combined effects of high levels of political corruption and violence, much of the latter driven by nationalistic and religious separatism and chauvinism. Yet it is the underlying weaknesses of an economy that until recently won much credit for stability and moderate growth that will have the greatest effect on the employment situation. In 1992 India was struggling to avoid default on its foreign loans. One journalist notes that this is accompanied by "a spiral of 17 percent inflation, a strangling bureaucracy, poverty, illiteracy, overpopulation and huge environmental problems."

The Economist recently viewed India as a country in which development has gone tragically wrong, one that "has achieved less than virtually any comparable third-world country." While solid progress on unemployment and underemployment remain out of reach, it is clear that competition for jobs by workers at all levels of educational attainment continues to be a volatile element of India's political situation.

Several trends in the international political economy deriving from the fall of Communism in East-Central Europe and the former Soviet Union have had major impacts on national and regional employment patterns. These include the accelerating tendencies to reduce arms budgets and dismantle certain weapons, the pressures to make Western economic assistance available to the former Warsaw Pact countries, the economic costs of violence in the former Yugoslavia and elsewhere, and the increasing threats of large-scale Westward migration. Each of these trends are probably in their early stages, assuming that the continuing radical transformation of the economies of the former Soviet republics proceeds.

Such interrelated developments will offer opportunities as well as problems of short- to medium-term adjustment for East and West alike. Outcomes depend on the ability of the new regimes to adapt their economies and labor forces without shattering domestic political support. For leading Western powers, new demands for bilateral and multilateral grants and credits create extraordinarily difficult decisions relating to quantity, form, and timing in the context of other large foreign economic obligations and, in several cases, exceptionally large national budget deficits.

A highly influential area of international political economy affecting labor markets is the trade arena. An era of evolving trade liberalization, begun with Bretton Woods nearly fifty years ago, has become one of emerging regional trading groups, renewed national and regional protectionism, and increasingly aggressive competition for high-value markets. Fears of being fully or partially shut out by regional trading blocs mount in much of the world even as hope is focused on the professed liberal goals of the Uruguay Round. Key trade issues of the early 1990s include agricultural subsidies and trade in services. In the minds of many experts the politics of trade and foreign investment are the principal politics of profits and employment. No one can deny its relevance. "Fair trade" is a rallying cry of those who fail to see equity or optimum employment outcomes from competing against and in protected markets.

Closely connected with trade developments in their current and future impacts on employment are issues of foreign direct investment and international debt. The 1990s began with a strong rush of transnational corporate investment in the Europe of 1992 and beyond, with increased emphasis by these firms on establishing privileged access to the Community's internal trade. This, however, is threatened by the contention in some European circles that certain foreign-owned assets should not be given such equal access - especially in the automobile industry. Robert Reich declared a death knell for the very idea of nationally based multinationals - positing "the coming irrelevance of corporate nationality."

The already existing realities of international political economy include the ignoring of home country national interests by many multinationals. They also include a conflicting intensification of national government efforts to exert influence, and in some cases direction, over multinationals in various industries and issue areas. Japan may be one of the leaders in this continued nationalist concentration of effort, but it is not alone. U.S. and European industrial policy may be less obvious than Japan's but these countries are also increasingly proactive in such policy areas as competition/antitrust, subsidization, and the encouragement of meaningful efforts to meet the challenges of cutting edge technology.

In the present decade the increasingly subtle neo-mercantilist, authoritarian corporatism practiced in much of East Asia probably exerts more influence than the fading efforts to shape increasingly hyper liberal states in the United States and Britain. As to the situation of ordinary workers, they face the increasing ability of firms and industries to dictate terms of employment. Although valuable research and managerial talent is benefiting from a seller's market for their labor, the bargaining power of various strata of workers below those levels is declining in an era of global production-sharing, markedly weakened trade unions, and "lean and mean" workforces.

Although some progress has been made since the mid-1980s to reduce the overhanging impact of massive global debt especially that in Latin America and East-Central Europe, on the world economy, the combined impacts of debts engendered by national budget imbalances and trade deficits continue to constrain economic growth. The impacts of debt are felt by lenders and borrowers alike, as leading Western countries lose potential markets in states forced to curtail imports.

The impacts of this debt on employment are also felt through real interest rates that are much higher than normal at comparable stages of previous economic cycles. The world is being significantly affected by the growing budget deficits as well as trade imbalances experienced by the United States and many European countries. Kevin Phillips recently compared the U.S. situation with that of the Gilded Age of the 1920s. The consequences for world employment from the excesses of that period were, of course, truly grave.

In most Western economies the ordinary worker is functioning in a global environment that is both forcing increasing migration of workers and engendering sharply increased resentment against this phenomenon. This environment also typically includes the levelling off or contraction of indigenous labor force growth, an obvious enlargement of clandestine sectors of many national economies, and the ability of many industries to produce more goods and services with fewer workers. Although each of these trends significantly affects both international and national responses to employment, the negative and positive effects vary considerably from country to country.

At present, factors presumably favorable to employment prospects include the slowing of the growth in the labor force in many developing countries, the creation of regional free trade areas, and the flexibility inherent in the expansion of clandestine economic sectors. The more obvious negative factors include, at least in the short run, the need to readjust from peak levels of military production in the United States and Russia, the poorer prospects for further major trade liberalization across regional lines, and the inability of large numbers of production workers to secure their jobs in the face of the increasingly flexible global division of labor.

The continuing power of internationally generated monetary discipline should be noted. Countries contemplating major efforts to stimulate employment and their economies as a whole through looser monetary and fiscal policies are faced with withdrawals of banked funds from abroad and competitive pressures to devalue national currencies. Efforts to maintain considerable stability in many European currency values accentuated this macroeconomic discipline until the European monetary system began to shatter in the fall of 1992. Such a linkage of currencies was crucial to the virtual collapse in 1992 of Sweden's ability to use its model labor market policy to hold unemployment well below most European Community states.

Recession had compounded a loss of Swedish competitiveness in international trade, and rather dramatic fiscal and monetary measures became necessary by September 1992. By late 1992 Sweden's open unemployment was rising rapidly toward Western European norms. In sum, the global political economy has experienced extraordinary turbulence in its structure and processes that has been described by James N. Rosenau and others as unprecedented.

All of the major sea changes involve enormous implications for workers on all continents. Some of these implications are great opportunities, as in the case of poorer countries set to benefit from some aspects of freer internal markets as well as liberalized foreign trade and direct foreign investment. Many others are mixtures of long-term opportunities and shorter-term dangers, risks that are faced most directly by elements in the labor force that are least educated or adaptable, inadequately trained, and in need of social protection.

FULL EMPLOYMENT AND THE RIGHT TO EMPLOYMENT

The major forces and sea-changes noted in this book are closely associated with a continuing evolution (and some recycling) of ideas about employment. The combined impacts of events and ideas have shaped public policy and thoughts about employment, related rights, and governmental obligations. An effort will be made here to review recent relevant academic and official writings about employment, and related issues intended for various national, regional, and global audiences.

Our task includes the separating of the wheat from the chaff in various writings about employment. One criterion for doing this is the inherent quality of particular proposals and analyses. Another is their expected and actual impact on policy. We have already noted the influence of a wide variety of intellectual contributions to the international consideration of employment issues, some written by and for national governments or international organizations, others primarily for academic or general audiences. Some presentations, including those of Beveridge and Keynes, had substantial impact at the national and international levels within a few years of publication. Others, including early contributions of Hayek and Milton Friedman, had major impacts only decades after the ideas were first presented.

On the subject of employment a disproportionate share of articles, books, chapters, and pamphlets continue to have a utopian character, apparently lacking the potential to gain substantial political or intellectual support. Some of it constitutes a literature of protest or an isolated call to arms against technological, bureaucratic, corporate, or "imperialist" targets or realities. The ideological orientation of recent writings on employment continues to lean toward the neoclassical. There are good reasons to expect continued dominance of neoclassical liberal views. The collapse of the Soviet bloc in East-Central Europe has left those countries in search of Western advice about transition to market economies. Many though, not all providing that advice reflect neo-classical tendencies.

The transition of these economies as well as many developing states provide great opportunities for economists and others who can help guide the way to privatization and unsubsidized production, prices, and employment. At least in the short term, this seems to have given neoclassical economics a new lease on life despite the strained aftermaths of the Thatcher and Reagan eras. Yet criticism of its tenets has also been mounting both in the East and in the West.

Post-Soviet and East-Central European economic, social, and political transitions involve major economic and political risks that neoclassical approaches may well fail to adequately anticipate. This has already begun to bring more balanced advice from diverse directions. For example, the highly influential 1991 analysis of the Soviet economy prepared by the leading economic IGOs endorsed "exceptional programs" to deal with employment in the transition period, including diverse ameliorative programs developed in Western Europe and North America. Although these proposals prominently feature neoclassical suggestions concerning self-employment, qualified support is also given to public works, a broadened approach to retraining, and a "carefully formulated" system of income support for the unemployed.

Despite a widespread inclination in East-Central Europe and in the West to reject the full employment traditions of former Communist ruled countries, it has proved impossible to do that in every case. The continuing legacy of the constitutionally guaranteed right to employment in such countries is demonstrated even in the strongly neoclassical writing of János Kornai, a leading Hungarian economist. Kornai concedes that "one of the greatest achievements of the socially planned economies in Hungary and many other socialist countries was full employment."

Yet he adds that this was achieved before 1990 not by incorporating the right to work in their constitutions but by specific strategies of economic growth designed to sop up the labor supply. Kornai consciously echoes Hayek's title, The Road to Serfdom, in his review of what he conceives to be the reverse kind of voyage. In effect, only the idea of full employment as a long-range goal and area of government responsibility remain in his formulation, the objective being "the establishment of a lasting, long-run relationship between the labor market and job rights."

Yet few Eastern European writers dismiss the relevance of labor market stability as completely as do certain Western neoclassical theorists. Soviet government officials and politicians and their Russian successors felt the need to soothe fears of mass unemployment. One agency called in 1990 for a "new conception of social protection for the population during the changeover to market relations." A draft position paper from the USSR State Committee on Labor and Social Questions was designed to elicit broad public discussions on social protection under market conditions.

Notably, this transitional Soviet conceptualization retained the idea that every able-bodied person should be guaranteed the right to work, this incorporating "the freedom to earn money and, consequently, the opportunity to improve his circumstances and raise his standard of living without any restrictions." This was presented as part of an effort to contrast proposed state policy with the "shock therapy" suggested by others. Yet even with an approach that minimized the dangers of massive unemployment, the spokesman for the draft, Vladimir Shcherbakov, acknowledged the need to devise "new approaches to a definition of the 'right to work.'"

Unemployment would not be legitimized, and the unemployed would not be left to "the mercy of fate."

There would be state assistance for training and "a system of legislatively codified social guarantees representing the minimal obligations of the owner and giving him the right to use the employee's labor." Experts from international organizations and various Soviet scholars reportedly participated in the development of this document, which constitutes a potentially important step toward a market oriented, post-Soviet conception of full employment policies. It does not, of course, answer all the questions asked by workers and others in a country and era in which the pace and extent of the transition were still being actively contested.

Growing unemployment encouraged political forces termed conservative to challenge the more radical Yeltsin administration from their base in the Russian parliament in 1992-93. The president was forced to grant major concessions to those forces, slowing economic reforms, until his significant victory in several referenda in April 1993.

Current neoclassical prescriptions for Central and Eastern Europe and for much of the developing world often rely on the willingness of these societies to accept delayed gratification. Such conceptions must contend with the reality that delayed gratification was also basic to Communist and various previous Third World economic strategies and that there is now insufficient public patience in many cases. The challenge for the West is to encourage social, economic, and political strategies that factor in an understanding of the many decades of frustration endured by the majority of the citizens whose economies are now to be restructured. Although such understanding is not altogether lacking in such works as A Study of the Soviet Economy, it needs to be more tangible and responsive. It must include the encouragement of social protection for pensioners, others on fixed income or dependent, and the unemployed.

Many countries in Asia, Africa, and Latin America have had even longer experience with the politics and economics of structural adjustment than have the post-Communist regimes. No overview of thought in such diverse countries can do justice to the existing range of views. Reports published in the New York Times in mid-1991 claimed to have detected a coalescing of elite opinion in a large number of developing countries on behalf of liberal economic reforms and fundamental structural adjustment.

That newspaper indicated that it was able to confirm World Bank optimism about the broadening of the base of countries with leaderships prepared to abandon protectionist foreign investment policies, to deregulate and privatize industry and finance, and to reduce subsidies and price controls. Related to this alleged consensus was a further weakening of commitments to employment security, especially as reflected in a resolve to reduce public payrolls and to allow companies greater flexibility regarding layoffs. The Times series indicated a growing sense that protectionist business as usual was increasingly seen as foreclosed by international carrots and sticks. As in Eastern Europe, the perceived collapse of sectors of various national economies also made new outlooks and policies inevitable.

Although these positive orientations toward neoclassical policies are seen as increasingly influential, the post Cold War climate has not eliminated contrary orientations in the developing world. One set of at least partially contrary viewpoints results from the strong industrial policy orientations of leading East Asian countries, including South Korea and Japan. In the Japanese case the idea of employment security, at least in the larger firms, helps underlie strategies for redeployment of the labor force and the replacement of fading industrial sectors by more advanced ones.

The South Commission, formed in 1987, represents an effort on the part of intellectuals and officials from various developing countries to respond to neoclassical pressures from the West. It follows a path set by the United Nations Conference on Trade and Development (UNCTAD), the Brandt Commission, and other official and unofficial groups created for research and advocacy. This commission's work, spearheaded by former Tanzanian President Julius Nyerere, then Prime Minister Mahathir Mohamad of Malaysia, and Manmohan Singh of India, offers a further cooling off of the New International Economic Order rhetoric. Instead it emphasizes economic cooperation among Third World states and the need to focus on developing human resources in the South.

The report is notable in the context of the present book for its insistence that social questions are as important as economic dimensions in the development process, its call for development strategies that emphasize employment policy, and its protest against the increased levels of unemployment resulting from externally forced fiscal retrenchment. It strongly emphasizes technology related education and training - thereby rejecting the idea that the problems of employment and development need be approached in fundamentally different ways in the North and South.

Although recent Third World perspectives on employment and related human rights issues have received some overdue attention, writing on these subjects continues to emphasize the context of particular Western countries and regions. Such publications reflect the enormous socioeconomic and political changes noted above but also involve an ongoing reassessment of public policies carried out by the leading Western countries.

To what extent is there a residue of opinion in support of full employment policies and the right to employment at this juncture? On the whole not very much emphasis is being placed on either concept, and strong right to employment advocates continues to be rather isolated in various forums. Even many negative assessments of Reagan-Bush-Thatcher policies have tended to stress outcomes other than disquieting overall employment levels, targeting instead such issues as growing income and asset inequality as well as unfairness in tax systems.

A 1989 report that rallies support for full employment from Socialist and Social Democratic perspectives itself confirms the collapse of broader support for this concept in

Western Europe. The report of the Commission on Employment Issues in Europe, formed in 1986 and known as the Kreisky Commission combines some worthy updating of thinking about economic stimulation and active labor market policy with the rallying of political forces that had been forced on the defensive throughout the 1980s. It presumes that, in Western Europe, fighting unemployment then had relatively little political support and that a kind of depoliticization of the issue had taken place.

It also argues that few European politicians or governments remained wedded to the principle of full employment and that "a new orthodoxy" encouraged governments to concentrate on improved functioning of markets. From their somewhat narrow ideological base, which they view as gaining increased support in the wake of the absence of progress against unemployment in the 1980s, the Commission's authors frame a new call for full employment and the right to employment. Yet even they limit their conception of full employment to the restoration of the 5 percent unemployment level of the late 1970s, this to be achieved in a half decade. Further, the right to work is now phrased as labor market and not job security, a personal right to employment opportunity but not necessarily a right to be maintained in the same job. This conception is based on Scandinavian models of rights to training and increased employment opportunity for all.

Perhaps the most notable theme in the Kreisky Report is the full recognition that the best answers to mass unemployment need be developed through highly developed international coordination and harmonization, most particularly efforts to stimulate economic expansion. The report consciously builds on the European Commission's conceptions of social protection and job creation through the completion of the Community's internal market. It agrees with John Kenneth Galbraith's rejection of "the pursuit of full employment in one country," recognizing the power of other major economies to frustrate national macroeconomic policies in the absence of appropriate coordination.

A major barometer of official opinion about those rights and state duties is the ongoing flow of papal encyclicals on this subject. The one hundredth anniversary of Pope Leo XIII's Rerum Novarum was observed in 1991, providing an opportunity for Pope John Paul II to provide a current perspective on the Catholic social thought advanced by that work. It has been argued here that papal perspectives on labor issues have often been underestimated as influences on social policy in many Catholic and other countries.

With the current trends toward democratization in Central Europe, Catholic social thought has some new opportunities to help shape public and elite opinion. This weight, most evident in the close relationship of the church with Poland's Solidarity Movement, can be exercised through the expanding role of official church bodies and organizations as well as through Christian Democratic and other party and trade union organizations.

Centesimus Annus (The 100th Year) is limited in terms of new ground because the Polish pope had expounded on Rerum Novarum a decade earlier. The newer concerns include a stronger criticism of the treatment of much of the Third World by leading capitalist powers as well as its focus on the needs of transitional East-Central Europe. On the whole the guidance offered is consistent with previous recent interpretations of Catholic social thought, with no evident curtailment of earlier themes about the materialism, consumerism, and bureaucratization of capitalist states and societies. In one memorable passage the pope refers to a risk "that a radical capitalistic ideology could spread which refuses even to consider such problems as global exploitation and human alienation."

The concept of a right to employment is advanced further in the latest encyclical only in its insistence that the church's engagement with social questions must focus on work as an essential part of its task of preaching the Gospel. As in the 1981 Laborem Exercens (On Human Work), John Paul II seeks to be more explicit than his predecessors on this subject. The explicitness is, however, both positive and negative. On the positive side the 1991 statement embraces various aspects of what might be termed "active labor market policy," insisting that the state has a duty to create economic conditions that ensure job opportunities, especially in time of crisis. On the other hand the several references to a right to work are undercut by his argument that "the state could not directly ensure the right to work for all its citizens unless it controlled every aspect of economic life and restricted the free initiative of individuals." The net result is a church position that can be utilized by Catholic-oriented and other politicians holding a wide range of positions on state obligations to workers.

If the dominant character of official and quasi-official writing on employment and workers' rights was defensive between 1987 and 1991, writings by academicians in that period moved the debate both back to themes worked over decades before and forward to ideas stimulated by a new internationalism. Motivated by evidence of decline in the quality of employment in such regions as East-Central Europe and the United States, Norway's Jon Elster challenges continuing emphasis on the proportion of the population that is working for pay. He contends that in a capitalist economy "full employment can only be achieved at the expense of creating a second-rate work force that is paid lower wages than private-sector workers performing the same tasks."

In the United States both Kevin Phillips and Robert Reich agree that the increase in the number of American jobs in the 1980s constituted something other than a net achievement given the growth in low-paying service employment. They both raise the question of job quality in ways that force the recognition that guaranteed minimum- and low-wage employment accomplishes little for the individual and even less for the country.

Reich, a liberal Democrat who became the Clinton Administration's Secretary of Labor in 1993, reciprocates Phillips's ideological iconoclasm when he directs attention away from the redistribution of benefits, including work, and stresses instead enhanced skills and capacities for the population as a whole. Reich argued in 1991 that "unemployment is now less of a problem" and that the "the more important issue over the longer term is the quality of jobs, not the number."

The decline of ideologically based support for full employment was remarked on by Robert W. Cox in his 1987 tour d'horizon of the global political economy. This neo-Marxist and neo-Gramscian writer with former ties to the ILO notes, "It is remarkable, in the light of scholarly stress on the 'legitimacy' function of the welfare states, how little opposition there has been to the tendency to sacrifice employment in the fight against inflation and how little of that has been clearly grounded in alternative ideology."

Cox provides a penetrating analysis of why this lack of full employment policies occurred, stressing the roles of international non-governmental organizations (e.g., the Trilateral Commission) and intergovernmental organizations in preparing the demise of the conception of the state as the ensurer of high employment levels. He points to the OECD's McCracken Committee Report of 1977 as a negative turning point and stresses the role of the IMF in supervising a global order that set limits on national efforts to reduce unemployment in the short term. Cox emphasizes the role of what he terms "the international financial network" as "the principal external constraint" on such national policies as increased state expenditures in support of welfare state and full employment objectives.

The recent academic debate on the future of employment continues the discussion, begun in 1946, concerning governmental responsibility for full employment and the possibility of a right to employment. Some new wrinkles have been added, but the student of these issues will note frequent allusions to ideas and arguments offered decades and even centuries ago.

By and large the issue of a right to employment in academic discourse has long been less an interest of economists and more one of other social scientists as well as philosophers, historians, and legal scholars. Yet few who are not economists or political economists are fully comfortable writing in practical terms about the economic requisites of full employment. As a result many discussions of the crucial concepts of this book remain amorphous or contain unconvincing prescriptions.

The calls of late twentieth century scholars for a right to work differ in important respects from those rooted in the desperation of nineteenth century French workers or of Americans and others caught up in the Great Depression of the 1930s. Even the very high Western unemployment rates of the early to mid-1980s and 1990-93 failed to generate well-articulated demands that reflected the anguish of the long-term unemployed and others receiving diminished real social benefits.

A large part of the recent Western academic discussion had an air of unreality and lacked an element of serious intent to transform public policy at the national or international level. Instead of established economic theorists debating the feasibility of a universal right to employment in the nineties, the discussion is characterized by philosophical argument that fails to achieve great urgency. The current discussion sometimes retreats from proclaimed universal rights, shifting back to arguments for the right to employment as a dimension of national citizenship. Such an approach, mapped out by American political theorist Judith Shklar in 1991, can be viewed as setting back the clock by returning to the line of thought about citizen (and not human) rights developed by William Beveridge and T. H. Marshall, among others.

Shklar discovers some impressive centuries old American roots for the right to work and argues for the essentiality of employment as a dimension of full American citizenship. However, even as a right of citizenship it is advocated as a presumption that should guide U.S. policy rather than a constitutional or legal right, a right because it is viewed as implicit in American citizenship. This "right to earn," as Shklar wisely phrases it, is "a right not to be deprived of one's standing as a citizen."

In her view the minimal political obligation of the state must include the creation of paying jobs that are geographically close to the unemployed and that offer them a legally set minimum wage and the chance for advancement. Such a view may well advance the present excessively limited American conception of citizenship. Yet it is not framed to project such a conception of citizenship into the international discussion of the scope of human rights.

Of course, even in the 1940s and 1950s philosophical and legal arguments for and against a right to employment were far more common than economic ones. Such themes as self-esteem, basic human needs, and distributive justice continue to be related to employment rights in the writings of Richard Arneson, British political scientist Raymond Plant, and others. Such contemporary views are characteristically offered in direct reply to neoclassical opponents who have collectively succeeded in inhibiting the advancement of redistributive conceptions of rights. The political barriers to advancing a right to employment are emphasized both in the highly supportive book published in 1989 by Philip Harvey and in a strongly negative contribution by Jon Elster.

Harvey argues that in the United States "groups opposed to the idea exercise substantial political power and benefit from a well articulated ideology supporting their position." He adds that even their more interventionist counterparts are less inclined than before to promote measures that extend beyond macroeconomic manipulation. The Democratic Party's belated and exceptionally limited responses to the 1991-92 U.S. recessions support this judgment. Elster emphasizes that no Western democratic country has chosen to create a legal right to employment in the wake of growing doubts about its economic and legal feasibility.

England's Michael Rustin asserted in 1983 that, with no British political party currently advocating a program to restore full employment and the right to work, there is "little prospect of these being restored." Given the subsequent non-socialist trends in Labor Party positions there is little reason to believe that Rustin would have a different judgment a decade later.

Yet support for the right to employment persists, often consciously or unconsciously echoing prior arguments. Elster acknowledged in 1988 that, "in the past ten or fifteen years, in particular, the proposal to create a legal right to work has been put forward and discussed in most Western countries." One can still find a presentation of "a practical program to secure the right to employment," a term used by Harvey that could well have been taken directly from seventeenth century English tracts.

Harvey's proposal builds on the same foundation that Gösta Rehn stood on twenty years earlier - that such countries as Sweden and Japan already represented virtual full employment states and that the best lessons from such systems could be transferred flexibly and with cultural sensitivity to other strong economies. Michael Rustin's proposal centering on labor boards with overall responsibility for subsidies to employers and a mandate to create jobs has even closer links than Harvey's to the three hundred year tradition of English practical and utopian proposals.

The idea of a right to employment is defined by Harvey as "the obligation of society to ensure adequate employment opportunities for all job-seekers." Rustin calls for a similar "universal access to work at a fair income." Arneson, concerned with devising a right that meets his standards of equality, self-esteem, and dignity, proposes a moderately high standard for the quality of state-guaranteed employment offered as a matter of right. Less evident in the current proposals is the idea of an enforceable individual legal right to obtain a job. The consensus clearly supports a qualified state obligation to promote full employment rather than an individual legal right to a job.

Summing up this review of recent comments relating to employment issues, it is evident that advocates of both full employment obligations of government and the right to employment are on the defensive but are still active in the arenas of academic and public debate. This debate is marked by cyclical tendencies that peaked in the early to mid-1980s in the direction of downplaying concern for even mass unemployment. In that political climate advocates for social protection generally, and the right to employment and full employment obligations of governments in particular, often conceded in advance that their support was too thin to successfully advance such ideas at the national or international level in the short run.

Some of this reluctance also derived from perceived structural changes relating to technology and the globalization of the corporation. It was argued that such forces were now too powerful to accommodate full employment obligations. As more people agreed with Dahrendorf that fewer workers would be able to produce the needed goods, public optimism tended to focus on the employment creation potential of political and economic integration and liberalized trade as well as more flexible labor markets more than on state obligations to the unemployed.

Nonetheless, it is evident that voices favoring public responsibility for the unemployed, many feeling a need to provide decent jobs as a human right, would not be stilled. Part of this relates to the opportunity provided by the passage of time for neoclassical or radical conservative approaches to political economy to alienate many left behind. Those appalled by associated income inequality, imposed austerity, and unfair tax practices again grew stronger.

At this writing, in June 1993, it is too early to read definitively the inconsistent and rapidly changing ideological trends in countries having or soon to have national elections. Neglect of mass unemployment ultimately brings very real demands for policies more consistent with societal needs for national solidarity and economic security. In several important countries pressures are building for new and recycled employment measures that are consistent with prevailing national budget constraints.

While many of the serious discussions of employment, the welfare state, and socioeconomic rights discussed above incorporate awareness of the impacts of international forces, few systematically addressed the roles of international organizations and regimes. Exceptions to this include the South Commission's emphases on structural adjustment and conditionality policies of the IMF and the World Bank and the Kreisky Commission's effort to integrate its proposals with developments in the European Community.

INTERNATIONAL REGIMES AND EMPLOYMENT

The dramatic changes in global and regional politics in the late 1980s and early 1990s markedly transformed many of the specialized international regimes that had been partially shaped by Cold War politics. While this has been most evident in areas of international security and finance, such other issue areas as employment and human rights have also been greatly affected by the ending of the Cold War and related realignments in international relations.

The transformation of international regimes has involved both the universalization of membership in international organizations and the intensification of regional integration. Universalization was greatly facilitated by the ending of the Cold War, which made possible the admission of some divided and new states as well as Communist and post-Communist regimes to such organizations as the United Nations, the IMF, and the World Bank. This process had already been underway by 1989, but new impetus came as economic aid for East Central Europe, the Soviet Union, and its successors became an important interest of the Western leaders. Economic interdependence was viewed as bolstering domestic political prospects for new regimes as well as regional peace. In this new climate neutral Western states also felt freer to make or explore new organizational ties.

Universalization of critical economic regimes has augmented the power of leading intergovernmental organizations as, for example, their stabilization and development loans flowed to a wider range of countries. Also, in the current climate new forms of cooperation have emerged between global and regional agencies, as exemplified by the association of two global (IMF, World Bank) and three Western regional organizations (OECD, the European Community, and the European Bank for Reconstruction and Development) in recent official efforts to promote the adaptation of the economies of Russia and East Central Europe.

Such globalization already has had positive impacts on employment, providing new sources of funding, research, and advice in support of such aspects of active labor market policy as training, public works, and placement services. The pre-existing reliance on the ILO for global assistance for such programs is now being supplemented by more involvement by the OECD, IMF, and World Bank staffs in such regions as South Asia and Eastern Europe. On the whole, Western economic organizations and political leaders have demonstrated somewhat greater concern for "the harsh by-products of reform" in East-Central Europe than in most of the rest of the world, presumably because of enhanced awareness of the political consequences of unmitigated economic shock treatments.

In the short run this globalization will advance approaches to structural adjustment favored by the staffs of several of these organizations as well as by the consensus of leading Western governments. An example of this is the accelerated liberalization of markets and government regulatory and tax practices in India in 1991 in anticipation of IMF loan conditionality. However, these organizations and their principal donor countries should anticipate that full globalization may well eventually lead to new constraints on conditionality as the recipients of unwelcome pressures are encouraged to coalesce and resist various measures that increase unemployment and political disaffection.

Such inclinations to resist build in part on recognition that the highly successful East Asian models for growth featured strong national government intervention. They are also stimulated by consciousness that even the present level of $30 billion annually in combined IMF / World Bank/ UN Development Program financing does not match the continuing reverse flow of funds from the South to the North resulting from the debt crisis built up a decade earlier. Pressures from within these organizations to markedly increase international liquidity were building in 1993.

In an array of available forums, including UNCTAD, the ILO, and the United Nations itself, Third World spokespersons of various ideological persuasions have continued to challenge conditionality agreements and their implications. The ILO Director-General noted in 1990 that the International Labor Office "continued to present an alternative approach to adjustment policy in which equity and participation considerations figure prominently." Yet no breakthrough in power has been achieved by developing countries working through friendly forums.

The International Labor Office has apparently had to restrain its inclinations to challenge structural adjustment, and instead often facilitates it. This has been balanced in part by increased attention to the negative employment and poverty impacts of forced restructuring in U.N. organs, including the General Assembly, the Economic and Social Council (ECOSOC), the Commission on Human Rights, and the Commission's Sub-Commission on Prevention of Discrimination and Protection of Minorities.

These activities have opened up channels through which human rights standards and implementing agencies are increasingly being turned to in order to challenge the raw political and economic power of the sometimes callous champions of restructuring. Human rights implementation devices such as special rapporteurs and official reports have been introduced into the politics of economic restructuring to express the preferred approach of the United Nations to implementing socioeconomic rights in the context of enforced austerity. However, the ability of such U.N. organs to alter the policies of the leading lending agencies through such pressures does not seem great.

The central question for international global policy and regimes regarding employment is the potential for fundamental transformation in the wake of momentous political and economic developments. The international employment regime reflected limited organizational development as well as a consensus that employment was still essentially and primarily a domestic issue. It also involved reluctance to utilize global or regional agencies to promulgate or implement authoritative international rules or policy mandates except in such limited areas as social security and where certain human rights principles were implicated.

Questions remain as to how such factors as widening European Community policy and geographic scope will affect these tendencies, how the universalization of the principal financial organizations will affect employment at a global level, and what new roles such long-committed organizations as the ILO and the OECD will take on in the near and medium terms.

The international employment regime is still marked by ambivalence and compromise regarding the setting and enforcement of standards that touch directly on the right to employment as well as state duties to promote full employment. Although leadership in the enforcement of labor standards, including those connected to human rights, remains in the ILO, only dim echoes remain of the previous efforts of its Committee of Experts on the Application of Conventions and Recommendations to sharply criticize various national regimes for neglect of mass unemployment. My review of the 1989 and 1990 reports of the ILO's Expert Committee found a rather benign approach to the responsibility of most states for employment, with moderate criticism of selected Western European states (including Ireland, Italy, and France) standing as exceptions to this pattern.

The Committee has been inclined to accept imposed structural adjustment as a sufficient excuse for Third World failures to deal with unemployment and give the East-Central European countries a substantial grace period. Such leniency was even extended to the absence of meaningful estimates of national unemployment and underemployment by many governments, an approach that seems unduly generous in some cases and a clear retreat from the Committee's posture less than a decade earlier.

A typical example of recent standard-setting regarding unemployment was the ILO's drafting of a Convention Concerning Employment Promotion and Protection Against Unemployment, adopted in 1988. It broke very little new ground regarding a right to employment or active labor market policy and focused on unemployment insurance. One workers' representative noted that the "essential standards - at least as regards the industrialized countries - do not even surpass those levels which had clearly become standard practice at the end of the 1920s" in leading Western European countries, referring here primarily to unemployment insurance.

New options to allow any ratifying state to suspend standards temporarily were accepted. Among the few gains since the previous ILO effort to deal with employment was the fact that a binding convention was adopted, a course that was not taken in 1984, and the decision to stress the need to find "suitable" employment when denying insurance benefits. The weakening of the ILO supervisory role is being partially balanced by a determined effort to enhance the processes and roles of the relatively new U.N. committee responsible for implementing the International Covenant on Economic, Social, and Cultural Rights.

While the committee, under the leadership of Philip Alston and others, has not yet attempted to seek remediation of deficient national efforts, it has made substantial progress in just a few years to improve state reporting on Covenant provisions and to elaborate the meaning of that covenant constructively and authoritatively. Although a strong admirer of the committee indicated in 1991 that "no one would dispute that economic, social, and cultural rights remain de facto second class rights," he added that it is increasingly becoming a body in which people can vest hope for change.

Perhaps an avenue for further breakthroughs in the implementation of economic and social rights will be the 1993 World Conference on Human Rights to be held in Vienna.

Some of its ninety sponsors in the United Nations view further development of implementation, at national, regional, and global levels, to be a ripe diplomatic issue. However, at this writing the prospects for a constructive effort to set a new agenda for human rights are not promising.

The current politics of international standard-setting and enforcement also reflects changing political and economic trends. The absence of various Communist spokespersons left the lines of contention in the ILO operating primarily along worker-employee as well as North South lines. The major change in East-Central European rhetoric was epitomized by then Polish Prime Minister Mazowiecki's comment to the 1990 International Labor Conference: "Full employment - at the price of waste and economic stagnation - is no longer the ideal situation for us. Unemployment is not ideal either, but it is a necessity that we have to learn to live with, just as the other market economies."

The Soviet government's representative endorsed both the 1988 ILO convention and the unorthodox and conservative-oriented conciliation process that shaped the final product. A few years later a delegate to the International Labor Conference referred to that organization's "first post-Cold War programme and budget." Clearly the East-West dimension of the international politics of employment was being rapidly and profoundly transformed in various intergovernmental forums.

While a political struggle between worker's and employers' organizations was played out in the watering down of the 1988 ILO employment convention, it is the North-South division that has become distinctly more salient in an array of organizations shaping global approaches to employment and human rights issues. Although no single Third World position can be distinguished, frequently stated views include reluctance to codify additional labor standards or to be judged on public policy outcomes that are viewed as decisively influenced by external forces.

Additionally, a broadened southern coalition has sought to use ILO and U.N. forums that can potentially be dominated by Third World spokespersons to challenge the dominance of structural adjustment advocates in the leading economic and financial organizations. Various Third World governments have also resisted making ILO technical assistance to particular member states contingent on that organization's assessment of previous compliance with certain ILO standards.

Having traced some specific changes in intergovernmental agency activities involving employment, we need to explore the potential for fundamental changes in the international order affecting unemployment, underemployment, and the conditions of workers. One reason to do so is the emerging evidence that international cooperation in a variety of issue areas is being fundamentally transformed in the 1990s in the wake of monumental global and regional changes.

Sometimes with clear U.S. government leadership, as in the 1990-91 Gulf War and other times as a result of broad coalitions mobilized by other states, the potential for breakthroughs in various global policy issues seems greater than before. From the August 1991 attempted Soviet coup to the postwar attempts to control Iraq's nuclear efforts, from attempts to dismantle South African apartheid to the environmental politics of ozone and rain forests, the willingness of the international community to respect national sovereignty seems to have lessened. This provides some hope for constructive international involvement with such issue areas as employment that have been viewed as essentially national responsibilities for so long.

The arena for which promising international policy responses are most possible is the European Community and its potential areas of expansion and influence. Other possible sources of augmented regional and global involvements affecting employment include the G-7 governments' efforts to improve international coordination of monetary and fiscal policies, old and new intergovernmental lending agencies with expanded financial resources, and the evolution of Britain and the United States away from radical conservative (or hyper liberal) policies.

Further, there is a possibility that the employment problems of the Third World will gain greater saliency as they become increasingly linked with such issues as trade and environmental protection. None of these factors assures a major transformation of the politics of employment even in Europe, much less globally. Yet together they offer hope of greater than incremental change through such mechanisms as regional redistribution of funds, promotion of social learning in new contexts, and new rule-making.

The lack of substantial growth in financial resources experienced by most major IGOs in recent years will certainly limit the opportunities for transformation. And in several cases available additional funds are being competed for by governments as never before. In the principal new sphere of large-scale funding, the flow of Western monies to Russia and East-Central Europe, fiscal and monetary policy conditions have not always been met by receiving countries, delivery on commitments has been slow, intergovernmental coordination has been frustrated, and the role of employment promotion and safety net issues have not been as prominent as might have been hoped.

Many of the paradoxes noted in this book are rooted in European Community ideas and experiences. One central idea associated with the completion of the internal market is a liberal commitment to the efficiency of markets freed from barriers impeding the production and movement of goods, services, capital, and labor. One of the central initial promises of the Single European Act of 1987 was very substantial job creation, specifically 1.8 million additional jobs and the reduction of the EC-wide unemployment rate by some 1.5 percentage points.

Yet another principal goal of the post-1985 transformation of the Community was to markedly increase the international trade competitiveness of its member states. As is evident in the large scale corporate reductions in force on both sides of the Atlantic in the early 1990s, competitiveness is not necessarily viewed as compatible with employment security

- especially in the short run. It will be interesting to see how Europe will play out the built-in tensions between the social market pressures for employment and income security on the one hand and the increasingly difficult competitive pressures from North America, East Asia, and elsewhere on the other.

To a far greater extent than ever before the European Community of the 1990s is in a position to lead international efforts to minimize unemployment and promote active labor market policies. These results primarily from the nature of the negotiations associated with the Single European Act of 1987 that will double the Community's structural fund resources to about 14 billion ECU by 1993. It also involves the important role of the Community in aiding and guiding post-Communist East-Central Europe as well as the new opportunities for social legislation in the new era of completion of the internal market. Social learning has at least temporarily shifted from the boundaries of the Community and OECD to a broader external sphere of influence, and the intensity of Community and OECD cooperation with each other and with other intergovernmental agencies has grown markedly.

The year 1991 turned out to be one of the most significant for the European Community members and aspiring members. In December eyes were on Maastricht, Netherlands, where the twelve member states worked to negotiate a new Community order that would go beyond the Single European Act in a wide array of policy areas and also transform Community decision-making. Strikingly, this Community Summit functioned simultaneously with the first efforts to restructure relations among the emerging post-Soviet republics at the Brest Summit, and followed by only a few months the apparently successful negotiation of a new European Economic Area (EEA) that would take the EFTA states far beyond EC associate status. Although the structure, powers, and decision-making processes of the future European order were not settled by these summits and agreements, the outlines of a new European order seemed generally clearer in their aftermath.

The treaty creating the EEA potentially extends European Community social policy, together with many other areas of Community policy later expanded at Maastricht, to the EFTA nations. If allowed to become operative it will inaugurate free movement of workers among the nineteen associated states (with Switzerland granted five extra years to comply). Most observers view the treaty as a transitional step toward amalgamating the twelve with all or most of the EFTA states, and are impressed by the extent that the EFTA states agreed to be governed by EC rules without receiving major interim power in Community decision-making.

At the opening of the December 1991 Maastricht Summit it was not clear whether the Community would poise itself for further major political transformation that would allow it to go well beyond the 1987 Single European act. At the Summit the situation in such areas as monetary union and defence cooperation clearly advanced but the social policy issues relating to employment were partial victims of the compromises and creative diplomacy forced largely by British intransigence. Before Maastricht the Community had put itself further into the forefront on employment and related social issues through such means as the implementation of the Single European Act's commitment to double its structural fund resources and its assumption of a leading role in the coordination of aid and guidance to East-Central Europe. Additionally, many plans were being floated to redistribute power on social issues, still viewed primarily as employee-management matters.

At the close of Maastricht the monetary union appeared to have been given critical impetus, with agreement on the goals of a European central bank and a common European currency before the end of the 1990s. This process was tied to criteria on interim member state economic performance aimed at promoting low common levels of inflation and fiscal discipline. In the context of the ongoing widespread recession such measures did not bode well for further efforts to stimulate European economies. However, long-term prospects for a more competitive community seemed to have advanced. It is much less clear whether democratization was advanced at Maastricht, with the European Parliament gaining only incrementally even as national parliaments were to be asked to cede very important policy turf. Maastricht again confirmed the point that "at the core, the community has always been a mechanism for governments to bargain."

Building on the catch-word "cohesion," the principle that poorer countries should pay less into the EC's budget was placed in a legally binding protocol and a cohesion fund was to be set up by 1994 to help pay for environmental and transport projects. Additionally, qualified majority voting was agreed to in new treaty chapters applying to socio-cultural issues ranging from consumer protection to education. Maastricht built on the redistributive approach of the Single European Act compromise, which had already committed, in its most generous case, EC structural fund aid to Greece equal to 5 percent of that country's GNP by 1993.

On an array of issues at the core of the present study politics at Maastricht was strained but the outcomes seemed moderately hopeful. At stake was the viability of potential new community legislation in an array of social policy areas linked to a social market approach to political economy. This policy has been embodied as a set of principles and standards in the EC Charter on Basic Social Rights (henceforth Social Charter), signed by eleven heads of government in December 1989, and was subsequently developed into a forty-seven-point Social Action Programme and a set of proposed European Commission directives. This process has already demonstrated an ability to achieve effective advances through further standardization of the practices and approaches to labor issues of the most corporatist and socially protective member states.

Yet its scope and strength have always been limited by the bargaining power of community employer groups, the British government, and other less enthusiastic forces. Both the Action Programme and the provision at Maastricht for a separate Agreement on Social Policy are little more than statements of intent. However, it is now clear that if the Maastricht initiative for a Treaty on European Union can be ratified in a coherent version, the Social Europe initiatives in such areas as the labor market, freedom of movement, social protection, equal treatment of men and women, and health and safety in the workplace can advance, at least in each member state other than Britain. Regarding employment policy per se, the Commission summarized the situation in 1988 as follows:

> Although this remains the responsibility of Member States and is still therefore outside the scope of the Community, a start has been made on concerting national policies. There have been exchanges of information and experiences and resolutions have been adopted, dealing in particular with flexibility of retirement age, fighting long-term unemployment, the contribution of local employment-creation initiatives to the struggle against unemployment, and an action programme for increased employment.

In 1989 Paul Teague and John Grahl suggested that the contemporary Community debate included the issue of "whether the Community should adopt interventionist legislation and policies to regulate the European labour market." After Maastricht such an interventionist approach remains possible, but had not been explicitly endorsed. The principle of subsidiarity, involving deference to national solutions to commonly perceived problems, was affirmed at Maastricht while explicit reference to a federal European future was negotiated out of the final language.

The eleven-nation Agreement on Social Policy signed at Maastricht affirmed in its Article I the objectives of "the promotion of employment, improved living, and working conditions, proper social protection, dialogue between management and labour, [and] the development of human resources with a view to lasting high employment and the combating of exclusion." Maastricht was primarily the voice of the governments that will continue to dominate the

Community through Council meetings and subsequent summits. Even more hopeful are the European Parliament's and Commission's commitments in the period leading up to Maastricht to emphasize labor legislation relating to such major issues as paid leave for training, children's work, gender equality, and the rights of refugees and guest workers. In 1988 various Nordic spokespersons contrasted their own positive record on employment policies with that of the Community.

Perhaps this perception can be altered before the end of the century in the wake of the initiatives of Francois Mitterand, Jacques Delors, Helmut Kohl and others from the mid-1980s to the aftermath of Maastricht. Many of the developments relating to Maastricht are subject to further delay and compromise at this writing as a result of the close defeat of the Maastricht proposals in a 1992 Danish referendum (reversed in 1993), the severe monetary crisis in the fall of 1992, and continuing strong British opposition.

Such developments can be welcomed if they result in subsequent adjustments that promote broader participation in European decision-making, raise new social concerns to the fore, and prevent present and future monetary integration and discipline from strangling national efforts to stimulate recessionary economies. The key requirements of European monetary union outlined at Maastricht appear to be on a collision course with existing monetary and fiscal policies in most Community states as well as in various countries seeking early admission to the EC.

Whereas the European Community is in the process of major transformations that will affect aspects of policy ranging from employment training to treatment of foreign workers, the OECD has changed much less quickly or fundamentally. Some OECD leaders would like the organization to become a vehicle for effective policy collaboration for a broader range of countries that would include the former Soviet republics and bloc as well as what it terms the "dynamic Asian economies" of East and Southeast Asia. It already serves to link Japan and Australasia with its expanding European area of attention. Yet at this point its influence in new geographical areas will be largely through data and policy-monitoring as well as consultation. The OECD sees a likely growth in its involvement with "multilateral surveillance" as well as with legally binding international agreements. The former will involve the strengthening of its "structural surveillance programme," relating to the basic elements of liberal structural adjustment, as well as somewhat increased attention to national programs needed to expand and upgrade labor forces. While a new round of OECD policy statements regarding the labor market emerged in 1990, these fell short of being legally binding agreements and failed to advance its policy advice much beyond that in the 1964 and 1976 OECD Council instruments.

Those documents added a new focus on broadened labor force participation and the upgrading of human resources, using the rubric of the "Active Society." Economic liberalization continued to hold a firmer and less conflicted hegemony in the OECD than in the Community in the early 1990s despite the OECD Secretary General's 1991 statement that "it would be a shame if the OECD was characterized at the end of the century as an economic success and a social failure." It has been rarer for social market or social democratic approaches to employment to be effectively promoted in the OECD context as compared with the Community. OECD publications continued to support the reduction of industrial subsidies and social security taxes rather than their harmonization and to emphasize the pitfalls of interventionist industrial policies.

The Organization's emphasis on labor participation and upgrading has in recent years been juxtaposed with statements that appear to devalue the need for regular, long-term, and full-time employment. A recent returning visitor to OECD headquarters would find some significant changes made in the past decade. The Organization is much more likely than before to be working in formal cooperation with one or more of a half dozen regional and global economic and social policy IGOs, including the IMF, World Bank, European Community,

Conference on Security and Cooperation in Europe, and ILO. Further, its leadership, like that of other major economic IGOs, takes credit for a somewhat greater staff capability in social science analysis outside of economics. This has facilitated improved and expanded research and monitoring of such topics as migration of workers and families as well as the relationship between technology and economic growth.

Yet the same visitor would also note that the work of the dominant Economic Policy Committee and Directorate continued to emphasize values and goals other than full employment even as the 1990-93 recessions dragged on. The increasingly perceptive work of the Manpower and Social Affairs Committee on negative employment trends failed to be strongly reflected in the Secretary-General's Annual Report in 1990, which tended to stress the Economic Policy Committee's emphasis on control of inflation as the key to continued economic expansion. The OECD seemed quite slow to alert its member states to the risk of serious recession that began in 1990 and intensified in 1992 and 1993 in much of Europe, though the Manpower and Social Affairs Directorate and Committee did sound alarms about both the growing political crisis in Europe concerning worker migration and a sharp rise in unemployment in most of the members states in 1991. The central questions of this book revolve around the meaningfulness of regional and global influences on national employment policy and the potential for considering employment as an internationally recognized human right. Has employment been considered a distinct policy area meriting a global or regional policy response? Did an employment policy regime emerge, and to what extent did it overlap with international human rights regimes?

The 1985-92 periods was one of great opportunity for those seeking to advance an employment regime as well as global and regional policy? It was a time of such momentous global and regional developments as the ending of the Cold War and the decisions of the European Community to move further toward political and economic union. Unemployment was increasingly perceived as a global policy issue, and not merely a problem of developed market economies. In many developing countries debt obligations, lending agency conditionality and impacts of structural adjustment exacerbated national and regional employment trends while necessary actions were taken to promote market liberalization.

Third World unemployment grew in the second half of the 1980s in the midst of what most of the First World experienced as a major economic expansion. Even in many favored developed countries the boom of the 1980s ended with unemployment at a higher level than at the end of the previous cyclical expansion. And the recession of 1990-93 brought unemployment levels to politically dangerous levels in such countries as Britain, France, Spain, Germany, and Italy.

Despite these and other forces for transformation the global and regional employment regimes remained limited in structural development, resources, powers, and functions, and failed to more fully develop identities separate from those of extant economic and human rights regimes. Employment remained a recognized regional policy issue of considerable urgency only in some parts of Europe. It developed further as a human rights issue only in a few international forums oriented to socioeconomic rights. For the most powerful global IGOs and Western governments employment was not so much a distinct global policy issue as a socioeconomic concern secondary to such regime-defining concepts as development and economic growth.

The structure of a global regime concerned with employment advanced with the emergence of an assertive United Nations Committee on Economic, Social, and Cultural Rights. Yet this step forward only seemed to balance out a loss of momentum for ILO supervision of standards in areas ranging from active labor market policy to social insurance. The OECD, a critical actor in the embryonic employment regime of the 1970s, spread its geographic reach but failed to intensify its activities in the most affluent countries on behalf of full employment policies. No highly influential rights-oriented or policy-based international rules or standards were produced in the most recent period.

Notably, no broad-based rebirth occurred for the most positive concepts underlying national and international commitment to protect against mass unemployment, these being full employment goals and the right to employment or paid work. The most powerfully phrased endorsement of the full employment concept, the 1989 Kreisky Commission Program, resulted from the work of an independent Social Democratic and labor-oriented body, and not from a mainstream intergovernmental organization or conference. Contemporaneously, ideological support for these concepts declined greatly in the emergent independent republics of the former Soviet Union as well as in the politically liberated East-Central European states. Intellectual support for the core concepts continued to be expressed in academic circles, but this did not generate a groundswell at any national or international level for a new effort to prevent mass unemployment.

The failure to advance an employment regime was strikingly reflected in economic data for the 1980s. Goals of an employment regime based on international social learning and technical assistance, combined with significant financial redistribution and standard-setting in parts of Europe, were largely unmet. The OECD reported in a recent summary of the issue area that, "by historical, post-war standards, the 1980s were a decade of particularly high unemployment." For the OECD countries as a whole, the average unemployment rate for 198089 was 7.3 percent, compared to a figure of 5 percent or less for the period from 1960-79.

The share of unemployment that was long-term also grew markedly, and no overall progress could be reported for the facilitation of geographic mobility of employees within their own country. Such a positive trend as the improved ratio of female to male earnings also leveled off in the 1980s. Finally, the dramatic differences in standardized unemployment rates among the leading market economies remained largely untouched by efforts to influence the outcomes in such laggard countries as Spain and Ireland. The gaps between, for example, Northern and Southern Europe and between North America and Southern Europe grew markedly from the 1970s to the 1980s. The comparative unemployment situation of women and youth improved somewhat, but that of foreign workers deteriorated.

Perhaps even clearer evidence of the limited impact of an employment regime was the failure to influence greater harmonization of national policies in such areas as active labor market policies. For example, the following percentages of GDP expended on public labor market programs were reported for major OECD countries in 1985 and 1990. Overall, national expenditures showed no major trend to increase or decrease. Unemployment insurance declined markedly in relative terms in the large majority of OECD countries, even in countries without proportional declines in unemployment.

Official concerns communicated through the OECD and other forums about the loss of labor market flexibility from overly generous unemployment programs may have been influential. Growing national budget deficits and more conservative national leadership also contributed. Although no OECD-wide trend appeared for spending on active labor market measures, there was an interesting tendency for European Community member states to partially catch up to the Nordic states. On the whole the Nordic states leveled off, with Sweden - the global leader - showing a significant drop.

In the Community the states that rose closest to the Nordic level for active measures were Italy, Germany, Ireland, and Spain. With Belgium and the Netherlands already spending over one percent of GDP on active measures in 1985, the overall trend was one of considerable EFTA-EC convergence. Countries left out of the trend to more substantial active public programs included the United States, an earlier pioneer in this domain, as well as Australia, Austria, Canada, Greece, Japan, Great Britain, Luxembourg, Portugal, Switzerland, and Turkey. This produced a strong dichotomy between the European and non-European membership, with several exceptions evident in the European group. A further regime impact was to reinforce the inclination of political leaders not to engage in major public direct job creation programs. In 1989-90 only Belgium and Finland, among the 23 reporting OECD states, spent more than 0.25 percent of their GDP for this purpose.

A somewhat greater degree of convergence could be observed in the sphere of legal job security for those already employed. To a limited but important extent access to the courts for job protection grew in the United States while it declined somewhat in much of Western Europe. "Fire at will" was weakened at the federal, and especially at the state, level in the United States, as various public policy and other criteria were successfully raised in order to restrain American employers. Western European employees lost some of their administrative protection but remained substantially better protected than their American counterparts against both mass and individual termination.

The impact of the employment regime was limited in part by the absence of any one intergovernmental organization with a commitment to deal with unemployment and job growth from an integrated perspective that combined policy and rights. Full employment policy clearly requires far more than the strategies identified as active labor market policy. It must integrate the following strategies and approaches.

HUMAN RIGHTS AND ETHICS

A full employment strategy should incorporate a rights-based approach. Such an approach facilitates and builds on a spirit of national socioeconomic solidarity as well as on ethical concerns for social justice. Although the extension of such an approach from rights of citizens to human rights can be difficult to put into effect, the case for socioeconomic justice and at least minimal entitlements for all can be justified philosophically and morally. The rights that need to be assured in principle include equal employment opportunity, free association, and security against arbitrary and sudden termination of employment. These should be combined with a reinforced duty of all states to use all available policy instruments to prevent high levels of unemployment.

Many of the lessons of the history of advocacy of a right to employment are clearly negative, and have provided historical evidence of pitfalls and unanswered questions. Implementing such a right is not feasible without full integration of the establishment of such a right with broad panoply of effective employment-oriented social and economic policies. If such a right is to exist it must be based on the duties of each state and a more effective international regime for implementation of full employment.

This regime should effectively utilize the best of international social learning about employment related policies and seek to elevate socioeconomic rights to the level that political and civil rights are held in the leading constitutional democracies. Without an effective rights dimension full employment has been repeatedly sacrificed to concerns and interests relating to inflation and trade competitiveness that may or may not have been valid. The right that must be championed must be more than an entitlement to mere subsistence or income maintenance. Rather, it should be recognized that the opportunity to receive pay for work is understood by a very large part of every society as an indication of full citizenship and even full humanity.

Many of the critical remaining questions about socioeconomic rights are presently being answered by organs of the ILO and United Nations as well as by scholars. Obligations of states must be effective immediately and must grow with their resources and capabilities. States must not be permitted to trade mass unemployment or its exacerbation for other political or economic interests. Intergovernmental organs and forums can define responsibilities of national governments as well as their own obligations. Potential workers or the long-term unemployed may never be able to win lawsuits to gain particular jobs or the right to any employment, but they should have recourse to complain to international organizations when states ignore the interests of workers.

National, regional, and global agencies should be held fully accountable on a frequent and timely basis regarding their efforts to promote full employment and to avoid mass unemployment. Rapporteurs and on-site visiting delegations must reinforce existing reporting and hearing processes, adapting methods already employed to guard against such violations as genocide and disappearances.

This is an era in which "down-sizing" and "lean-and-mean" corporate strategies are emphasized throughout much of the world, and job security and corporate responsibility for employee welfare lie far down the list of priorities. Pressures for international competitiveness and the opportunities provided by technological breakthroughs allow and encourage such "flexibility," and recent recessions have provided an environment enabling firms in and out of financial difficulties to reduce workforces drastically or to move large-scale operations to countries with cheaper and less protected labor without engendering substantial public criticism. Weakened labor unions are less and less able to contend with these pressures and actions, instead concentrating on such issues as required procedures associated with redundancies as well as the protection of pension and other assets owed to employees.

Another major manifestation of the ethical and moral gap is the relative lack of concern for Third World unemployment and underemployment by many governments of those countries as well as the greater part of the international community. It is as if this issue is moot in the absence of fully acceptable national data and massive civil unrest. Economic development and structural adjustment strategies are evaluated and advocated without appropriate concern for predictable transitional or long-term mass unemployment.

At the root of full employment policy should be concern for individual victims of mass unemployment as well as for the potential social and political risks in affected societies. Without a sense of solidarity for all members of a society, no strategies involving policy or rights will be fully effective. Some of the core ethical and moral dilemmas about welfare rights from prior decades and centuries have been partly overcome. We no longer blame the victims of mass unemployment as much as we once did, recognizing now that personal motivation cannot overcome all adversity.

Policy incentives and disincentives can motivate many unemployed workers to find and accept less desired work in some circumstances, and intentional overstaffing and most job creation schemes do not offer a sound long-term strategy for firms or government units. Yet the root of all full employment policy must be concern for the workers who are already victims or are vulnerable to economic cycles, technological change, and negative trade impacts. Workers need a trump card in the form of national and international commitments to full employment that have legislative, regulative, and financial teeth and meaningful methods for monitoring and implementation.

MACROECONOMIC POLICY

Employment is necessarily only one of the concerns that national and supranational agencies must consider when steering national economies with fiscal, monetary, and other economic policies. Productivity, competitiveness, and price and wage stability are clearly also vital to the short- and long-term welfare of national and regional economies. The central issue is one of priorities and the weight that full employment plays in macroeconomic policies that dominate national economic policy.

The critical British and American Employment Acts of the 1940s recognized the centrality of macroeconomic policy for full employment, and were initiated with confidence that Keynesian macroeconomic policies would successfully avoid mass unemployment. No rights-based or policy-based full employment strategy can succeed without a solid basis in macroeconomic policy dedicated to avoiding large-scale unemployment. Such fiscal and monetary policies of the various major states must be coordinated, with full employment as a major goal of such efforts. Coordination must not be allowed to choke off necessary stimulation of faltering or recessionary national or global economies.

Much of the failure to deal effectively with unemployment since the 1960s results from the frequent ineptness of national macroeconomic policies as well as intergovernmental efforts to seek financial stability together with growth. The priorities of most finance ministries and central banks and their counterparts in the OECD and IMF are quite different than those of many Labor and Social ministries and such of their counterparts as the ILO. The dominance of agencies controlling fiscal and monetary policy in national, regional and global economic policymaking is evident in the present study. Labor and Social ministries and the ILO are relegated to the promotion of microeconomic and social policies that cannot compete in total impact with macroeconomic policy unless they are funded at the level of the Swedish active labor market program.

The thrust of the present book is not to favour consistently accommodative fiscal and monetary policies. The responsibility for the prolonged recession of the early 1990s is substantially due to excessive fiscal pump-priming by some national governments amidst the long-term economic expansion of the 1980s. In contrast, more responsible fiscal and monetary policies fostered by steps toward economic and monetary union have helped several European Community countries to set their financial houses in better order and to be in a better position to participate in a European resurgence. Efforts at accommodation need be coordinated or harmonized at the global and regional levels in order to prevent the frustration of necessary national efforts.

Yet there is a glaring absence of concern for unemployment trends in many of the most important reports and statements from the IMF, the OECD, and their counterparts in major Western governments. Monetary policy is periodically allowed to tighten abruptly and severely - effectively planning and implementing higher levels of unemployment. Although accommodative monetary and fiscal policies cannot alone assure a strong climate for economic growth, profits, and employment, an overly restrictive approach to monetary and/or fiscal policies can certainly negate strategies that include commitments to rights and to active labor market policies.

Macroeconomic policies embodied in the financial stabilization and conditionality efforts of the IMF and other agencies and banks involved with the extension of credit to many Third World and other governments often have a severe negative impact on employment, especially in the short term. Further, the negative effect on employment of a global debt problem that peaked several years ago at approximately one trillion U.S. dollars has been and continues to be enormous.

While some significant momentum for partial write-offs of debt has accelerated in the more realistic political and economic environment of recent years, Japan and other lending states continue to place limits on the amelioration of this central problem. Debt has helped throw much of East-Central Europe and Africa into depression, and it continues to threaten economic and political progress in Latin America. It also constrains export opportunities to each of those region, and thus limits economic growth in even the strongest export-oriented economies. Lending for financial stabilization as well as debt reduction strategies must be influenced much more than they presently are by considerations of employment stability and growth.

INDUSTRIAL, INVESTMENT AND TRADE POLICY

Industrial, foreign investment, competition, and trade policies raise difficult problems from an employment perspective insofar as the maximization of advantage for national industries may well result in beggar-thy-neighbor results. Yet each of these policy areas needs to be pursued in the interest of growth and full employment at the national, regional, and global levels.

A full recognition of the realities of global interdependence requires a global approach to both industrial and trade policy that maximizes employment growth and stability. Appropriate industrial policies can steer countries and regions toward more competitive export postures and can help assure rising living standards for the average worker. Combined with progressive human resource development they can stimulate viable home-grown industries and attract the most appropriate direct multinational investment. The European Community offers a model of how substantial human resource and regional development funds can be channeled through international authorities. Bargaining by national governments at critical political junctures facilitated both substantial augmentation of such resources and increased hopes for future competitiveness in weaker member states and their most vulnerable or underdeveloped regions.

In the aftermath of the Cold War an effective global employment regime will have to incorporate similar ideas in order to prevent the renewed transformation of national economic conflicts into political and even military ones. The most positive scenarios for a more viable global economic community also depend on some constraints on the existing efforts of major exporting countries to compete to displace each other in particular national and regional markets.

A closely related source of economic conflict is the increasingly costly competition to use public resources for export stimulation and to promote research and development breakthroughs by home-based firms. With the end of the overarching Cold War it is possible to anticipate a transition from such unrestrained economic competition to new political and military conflicts. At the root of such conflict may be a grave concern for employment security in the three existing centers of economic power as well as in other regions.

EMPLOYMENT AND THE WELFARE STATE

William Beveridge and Richard Titmuss are among the most prominent of the writers who focused on the reciprocal impacts of social welfare and employment policies. Among the most penetrating recent analysis of this relationship is Gösta

Esping-Andersen's The Three Worlds of Welfare Capitalism. In this and other works Esping-Andersen portrays three models through which "welfare regimes" have integrated or failed to integrate employment and welfare policies and goals. He distinguishes a cluster of welfare states as liberal, another as corporatist-statist, and a third as social democratic.

Virtually every advanced welfare state is viewed as sharing attributes of more than one approach but fitting primarily into one or the other. Esping-Andersen finds that "Of the many social institutions that are likely to be directly shaped and ordered by the welfare state, working life, employment, and the labor market are perhaps the most important." The welfare state is traced as a major employer, as a facilitator of labor turnover and rationalization, and as a device for negotiating deferred compensation through the social wage. He concludes with the view that the contemporary welfare state is a powerful societal mechanism that decisively shapes the future in terms of the structure of employment as well as other critical aspects of societal change.

With this impressive book as context, it is possible to conceive of changes in welfare states that can maximize human resources and promote full employment. Especially given the recent difficulties even in Swedish welfare and labor market policies, no one country can serve as a clear model. The real need is to examine all aspects of the welfare state mix with minimal ideological blinders.

The utility of such programs often depends on fine tuning and planning. Early retirement measures that connect the labor market and pension systems may or may not prove productive to governments and firms, depending on such factors as whether resulting vacant positions are refilled. National health care delivery systems (or non-systems) may save jobs through controlled government and firm outlays. Bad health insurance systems prevent desired mobility among workers whose insurance is tied to a particular employer. International interest in such issues has increased our knowledge of such larger and smaller consequences as well as the menu of social welfare and labor market measures that work in particular social, cultural, and political contexts.

ACTIVE LABOUR MARKET AND EDUCATION POLICIES

Active labor market policies are among the most important measures developed directly in response to the fear or actuality of high unemployment. They are often discussed separately from education policies but should be understood as needing to be integrally linked to educational efforts from preschool to adult. No country that seeks to compete for multinational investment and shares of markets for sophisticated technology can afford not to effectively prepare its children for each level of education; maintain high expectations and standards at all levels and in all educational tracks; provide the large proportion of secondary school graduates who do not advance to higher education with communication skills and flexible knowledge of technology; ensure a smooth transition from school to employment; establish lifelong opportunities for necessary further education and retraining; assure the full commitments of various levels of government, as well as employers and labor unions; target those groups with the least relevant skills and the least opportunities in the present and future labor market; and provide innovative higher education that gives full due to science, technology, and the communication and human relations skills of the liberal arts.

Critical knowledge about education and active labor market policy must be learned from diverse societies and needs to be adapted to each particular country with concern for its cultural, social, economic, and political distinctiveness. The purpose of a given country's program may well be served by a very different structure in another society. As such, certain imperative goals need be accepted while methods are experimented with. The structure for effective training can be an American community college, a German apprenticeship program, or a training center of the Swedish Labor Market

Board. Whether from public, trade union, or corporate contributions of funding and training, programs need be developed that enable the changing labor force to meet the challenges determined by international competition.

Appropriate models and ideas are not in short supply. The Kreisky Commission Report embodies but one excellent blueprint. While perhaps demonstrating over attachment to such labor-supported solutions as work hour reductions, it is anything but parochial in its endorsement of broad education together with lifelong retraining, its focus on the need to further stimulate investment and employment in such areas as environmental protection, infrastructure, and information technologies, and its call to target backward regions as well as such groups as the long-term unemployed, foreign workers, racial minorities, women, and the disabled.

In this last theme it merges with the "Active Society" emphasis of the OECD. Clearly, countries with low birth rates and rapidly aging populations can hardly afford to concentrate on measures that reduce the size of their labor force. As the new U.S. Clinton administration reviews its options for labor market policy it will have as much international experience to review as exists in the health care field. It may also benefit from extensive national and IGO efforts to evaluate particular measures. This is a policy area that will profit from a highly pragmatic orientation, stressing proven experience with such measures as apprenticeships for youths, required corporate investments in training, and tax incentives for the employment and retention of targeted groups. Better labor market policy requires the careful study of past weaknesses and failures as successful national programs are selectively adapted to national and regional cultures and needs.

DEVELOPMENT POLICY

There is a need to greatly augment the role that employment plays in national and intergovernmental development policies. The contributions of the ILO in technical assistance related to labor markets have always been marginal, and the major lending IGOs have not yet developed a sufficient emphasis on human resource development. There is no question that vast opportunities exist to remove impediments to economic growth through structural liberalization, including privatization and removal of barriers to direct investment and to importation of various goods.

Yet the painful transitions that are being experienced are exacerbated by the lack of adequate social protection for the unemployed and for the poor, who lose direct or indirect subsidies for basic goods. More attention needs to be given, as has been explicit in the current East-Central European transitions, to developing critical national and regional systems and structures that can sustain trade, monetary stability, and labor markets.

The overall need is for regime and global policy development that incorporates and integrates each of these policy areas in order to overcome the fragmentation of IGO roles and ensure the necessary social learning, development of norms and rules, resource redistribution, and technical assistance. The result needs to be a social and human rights regime as well as one for economic policy.

Global policy needs to reach well beyond the present politics of comparative disadvantage in order to maximize a far greater degree of social justice and to modify the inevitable pain that results from unrestrained and unequal economic power. This can be accomplished best with a largely new approach to intergovernmental activity affecting employment, one that looks at the global needs of the 1990s and beyond, much as Western Europe looked hard at its needs in the late 1980s and early 1990s.

Industrialization and affluence created the possibilities for realizing the long-advocated ideal of a guarantee of paid work as a human right. The impact and memory of the global depression of the 1930s, combined with World War II, made this goal popular and timely. Then the faltering of dreams of much greater affluence beginning in the 1970s weakened the power and feasibility of the idea. Declining labor movements, forced to shift from proactive to defensive and protective measures, weakened the base of support. Market-based ideologies were restored to prominence and power, and shifted the ground on which the struggle was fought. Association of full employment and the right to employment with the Soviet system in an era of intensified Cold War further eroded the base of support.

Yet the ideas of full employment and the right to paid work remain part of the political language of our times, partly because they have been endorsed in international declarations, conventions, and recommendations. They also gain from new experience with post-Communist mass unemployment, persistent high levels of unemployment in many OECD countries, and increasing awareness of unemployment as an aspect of Third World poverty. Fortunately, the knowledge needed to formulate measures that can help countries and regions to approach full employment continues to be discovered and disseminated, much of this through international processes. The national, regional, and global programmes that have been designed to promote employment constitute a wealth of experience to be adapted and integrated with a wide array of other social and economic policy initiatives.

6

Beyond the Covenants

Although Susan Moller Okin may not be quite correct in stating that the Universal Declaration "started the controversy" about the legitimacy of economic and social rights as human rights, it is evident that a debate on this subject was greatly stimulated by that document as well as by the subsequent U.N. Covenant on such rights. Failure to achieve greater consensus concerning various particular rights in debates and votes on the Declaration and covenants limited the legitimacy of those prescribed rights. Contemporary and subsequent academic and media criticisms often focused on the right to employment itself, but also targeted ancillary employment rights, other particular socioeconomic rights, and socioeconomic rights in general.

Much as the idea of a right to employment gained from such social and economic events as the Great Depression and World War II, other great forces and events tended to revive competing classical liberal themes during and subsequent to that period. In circumstances of mass unemployment and later wartime mobilization, many intellectual and governmental leaders in leading Western democracies supported such measures as industrial cooperation, corporatism, increased governmental planning, and expanded social security.

This was true despite the existence of negative as well as positive models of each of these phenomena. Although it could be argued that the ends of national solidarity and socioeconomic stability required movement in the direction of social democracy, others set different priorities based on their own intense mid-century experiences. Revival of crucial elements of classical liberal social and economic policies was accelerated even before the U.N. debates of the late 1940s by the writings of Friedrich Hayek and others.

As William Beveridge advanced a new welfare state era in the 1940s, Hayek contemporaneously drew a line between the traditional role of the welfare state as provider of a floor of benefits for the truly needy and a concept of distributional justice that included a state obligation to assure employment to all. His challenge was not only to the methods of Keynes and others but also to the ends themselves. By 1944 Hayek had framed a broad attack on efforts to promote security of employment through state planning and controls, asserting, "There can be little doubt that it is largely a consequence of the striving for security by these means in the last decades that unemployment and thus insecurity for large sections of the population has so much increased."

He anticipated that "the fascination of vague but popular phrases like 'full employment' would lead to extremely shortsighted measures and even desperate expedients." The preferred alternative, one that was to be fleshed out by his disciples in the 1970s and 1980s, was a strategy focused on the adaptation of workers and technologies in national and international economies prepared to sustain substantial transitional pain.

Hayek's free market economic prescriptions were linked to his identification of the right to work with Soviet-style and fascist coercion. He emphasized individual freedom to choose and change employment rather than to be assured of a state-chosen job, asserting that "the able worker" who is prepared to "sacrifice" could achieve his employment goal.

Although Hayek's writings were viewed by many contemporaries as the last gasp of nineteenth-century free market liberalism, they turned out to be more of a new beginning for a slowly reviving classical liberal policy tradition. Thirty years later Robert Nozick cited Hayek approvingly while asserting that "no end-state principle or distributional patterned principle of justice can be continuously realized without continuous interference with people's lives." From Hayek and Nozick to George Gilder, a renewed thrust was given to Western social thought that fundamentally challenged an apparently strong consensus supporting social and economic human rights dependent on positive state action and obligations.

Various Hayek arguments regarding the inadvisability of committing nation-states to full employment and the right to work were refined by others. Employment as a human right was closely linked to the confidence of such figures as Keynes, Beveridge, Frances Perkins, and Gösta Rehn in the availability of policies and programs adequate to assure full employment. In most of Western Europe confidence in the availability of the necessary economic tools to achieve full employment was rarely flatly rejected during the three decades following World War II. Instead, belief in the possibility of shaping full employment economies has been countered most often by arguments concerning alleged unacceptable trade-offs, especially higher inflation and the promotion of a duty to work, expected to result from programs and policies that accept full employment as the major priority.

Nonetheless, a strong undercurrent of criticism has centered on the claim that the right to work is impractical and unworkable. One aspect of these concerns the difficulties involved in defining the right. Certainly the aimlessness of the United Nations effort to provide a definition helped suggest to Dutch jurist J. J. M. van der Ven that "the right to work must be more sharply defined to become workable." Dahrendorf carries forward a version of the impracticality argument from the vantage point of 1988, viewing full employment as necessarily resulting from the creation of peripheral or dispensable jobs in inefficient economies.

A variation on the impracticability argument is the non-enforceability theme. One version of this argument held that the Covenant on Economic, Social and Cultural Rights was vulnerable insofar as it pointed to goals as much as existing conditions, and also initially involved weaker implementation mechanisms than those provided for in the Covenant on Civil and Political Rights. The former covenant was challenged by some who asserted that rights could not be termed human rights if they needed to be achieved progressively and could not be prescribed in terms that involved effective national or international guarantees or implementation processes. Dahrendorf argued recently that the term "right" was being misused in regard to work because "no judge can force employers to hire unemployed people." For philosopher Joel Feinberg, the failure of most socioeconomic rights to be treated as "grounds of any other people's duties" leaves them as "manifesto" rights that are merely "permanent possibilities of rights."

Another major line of Western criticism focuses on the theme that employment is at most a citizenship right in certain states, and is not a universal right of all persons. Such a view links the positions of D. D. Raphael, Maurice Cranston, and Ernst Haas. Raphael emphasized the distinction between "rights as a member of a particular society" and the human rights each person has "simply as a member of the human race." While Raphael endorsed the inclusion of such "rights of citizenship" as employment in international declarations of rights, he insisted that there is "a difference of principle" between "the rights of liberty" and all others. (It may be recalled that T. H. Marshall had not acknowledged any such difference of principle among the various rights that he combined under the heading of rights of citizens.)

Haas contended that advocacy of such welfare rights as employment is tantamount to suggesting that "the Scandinavian welfare state is to be the model for the world," insisting that this is clearly beyond the economic and administrative capacity of most states. Cranston expanded on this theme by insisting that human rights need enjoy universal moral standing and also be "of paramount importance." He observed that such rights as social security and holidays with pay "belong to a totally different moral dimension" from such others as freedom of movement or life itself. It seems clear that he placed employment rights in the category of such "inferior" rights.

Sociologist John Boli-Bennett builds on Hayek's effort to associate the advocacy of such rights as employment with a kind of conspiracy to aggrandize the modern state at the expense of the liberty of the citizen. Attacking the welfare state itself, Boli-Bennett condemns socioeconomic rights and their guarantee by the state as incorporating the citizen into the state's programs, thereby further legitimizing the state's control over society. As such, socioeconomic rights are not merely lesser rights; they are seen as means by which true human rights are subverted. Dahrendorf picks up this theme when he suggests, "In terms of liberty, it is more important to establish the right not to work, so that governments cannot force people into a dependence which they want to escape."

The arguments of these and other critics challenge the legitimacy of the right to employment together with or separately from other socioeconomic or welfare rights. In the following section we review how the legitimacy of the idea of employment as a human right has been defended and evaluate its prospects for increased acceptance as a right of all.

NEW SUPPORT FOR A HUMAN RIGHT TO EMPLOYMENT

Broad acceptance of a human right to employment requires an adequate rationale as well as supporting developments in positive law and public policy. Various elements of the needed justification have sometimes developed in direct response to such criticisms as those noted above. As such, the case for the human right to employment is partly a refutation of objections offered on natural rights and other grounds. However, creative cases for the standing of employment as a human right have also emerged, some of these based on frontier concepts of philosophy, law, and related fields.

It was noted earlier in this study that the intellectual grounding for the right to employment was relatively undeveloped before and during the United Nations debates on that subject. Various advocates based their views more on their sense of the value or attainability of such a right than on theoretical conceptions of how employment related to any broad conception of human rights. Yet usefulness or achievability are not adequate foundations in themselves for a basic human right. Acceptance of something such as a right requires linkage to the great tradition of natural rights, to another historical source of human rights, or to respected emerging conceptions of the sources of such rights. The development of each of these possible sources for the right to employment is reviewed below.

THE NATURAL RIGHTS CASE

For many Western-educated scholars the concept of natural rights provides the only true basis for a human right. To concede that employment cannot meet the tests of natural rights would be to concede a great deal in terms of legitimacy and standing for the right to employment. As the debate unfolded, various advocates of the human right to employment made no such concession. Instead, they rejected the host of objections leveled against employment and other socioeconomic rights on natural rights grounds, including the charges that such a right lacks practicality, enforceability, universality, fundamental importance, ability to generate duties, and moral dimension.

The proponents of the natural right status of employment rights generally seek to establish it as co-equal to major political and civil human rights, and as part of the panoply of basic rights. This is evident in the natural-rights-oriented defences of the human right to employment offered by Carl Friedrich and Jack Donnelly. However, James W. Nickel goes beyond this to identify employment as "the central means to many of the essential goals of life." Proponents appeal to the readers' own presumed notions about the enormous value of employment and the prerequisites of natural rights. Some reject excessively comprehensive criteria for the existence of a natural right, explicitly objecting to the proposition that such a right need be immediately practicable or enforceable.

Somed challenges to those who reject employment as a natural right have been very direct. Okin asserts that Cranston, in rejecting the fundamental importance and moral dimension of socioeconomic rights, has slanted his own argument "by comparing the most essential liberty rights with the least essential economic rights." Further, by reminding her audience of Locke's concern for protection of rights against private persons in the state of nature, Okin seeks to refute the idea that natural rights are limited to spheres of governmental obligation to the individual.

What is the major significance of the natural rights case for a right to employment? First, it provides support that is based on the most traditional, and probably most legitimate, Western frame of reference concerning rights. To the extent that the right to employment can be related to classical authorities and various great historical documents listing natural rights, it is less necessary to rely on newer and less widely accepted bases for such a claim.

Secondly, the identity of the contemporary supporters of the natural right to employment is significant. They include the late Carl Friedrich, a patriarch of political science with a strong reputation for concern with the "liberty" rights that he saw destroyed by "totalitarianism," as well as various scholars who are helping to set the agenda for current research in this field. Notably, the inclusion of employment as a natural right is supported in the highly influential Pacem in Terris of Pope John XXIII and the Laborem Exercens of John Paul II.

As was true in the last quarter of the nineteenth century, Rome was responding to increasing concerns transmitted by national churches about employment and related social issues. In the 1980s the Canadian and U.S. Catholic bishops led the way with impassioned and detailed calls for full employment, linking this to such values as human dignity, increased social solidarity, and self-reliance. Such significant authorities bolster the legitimacy of a claimed natural right to employment and can be invoked in debates inside and outside of international organizations. At the least, ridicule of the idea of a natural rights claim to employment has been blunted by authorities who share the same intellectual traditions as some of their challengers. Western voices have thereby helped to establish a natural rights justification of the right to employment, one that can stand alone or be combined with other rationales that have emerged.

POSITIVE LAW BASIS

Increasing support for the right to employment and other socioeconomic rights appears in the varied sources of international law accepted by legal positivists. This is an age of proliferating sources of international and national law affecting human rights and employment, though much of the new international law is quite weak in terms of the sanctions that are central to positivist legal theory. Of course, the Universal Declaration and covenants themselves fit into the positive law framework and are intended to be anchors for further development of sources ranging from multilateral treaties to national statutes. Yet the positivists can also point to other international legal instruments that more plainly embody rules, not just principles, and incorporate sanctions and compliance mechanisms that seek to meet tests of effectiveness.

A continuing array of resolutions, conventions, recommendations, and other intergovernmental instruments have proclaimed the right to work and the necessity of commitments to full employment.

Most chroniclers of international labor law have accorded human rights standing to only some of the developments in their fields. This reflects a refusal to extend the use of the term human rights beyond such civil liberties and civil rights issues as forced labor, non-discrimination and free trade union association. However, the conscious effort of Myres S. McDougal, Harold D. Lasswell, and Lung-chu Chen to integrate positivism with several other perspectives on human rights suggests the possible future acceptance of other contributions of international labor law as socioeconomic human rights, including the right to work.

The importance of developments in international positive law is greatly augmented by its ability to promise a degree of compliance and sanctions. Certain recent developments within the European Community and the Council of Europe regarding the legal protection of socioeconomic rights represent institutional breakthroughs in this regard. These include the provision of effective recourse by individuals and other non-government actors to agency organs, the adoption of authoritative international legislation, active enforcement efforts by organization officials, and enforceable rulings by international courts.

This is not to paint a picture of accelerating or rampant supranationalism. The Council of Europe brings relatively few complaints to its European Court of Human Rights. The European Community has faced periodical member state defiance of its legal judgments and successful efforts to reduce the supranational and federal pretensions of its administrative arm. Further, neither of these European organizations was created primarily to champion the human rights of workers; their efforts in this regard have been secondary to other organizational objectives. Nonetheless, additional forms of international authority have been developed, especially in the area of equal protection.

McDougal and his colleagues emphasize advancement of the right to employment through international promotion of equal protection and non-discrimination. The significant advances in the prescription of global and European rights of equal opportunity and treatment regarding employment are developed in sections of their work focusing on "claims for freedom from discrimination" on the basis of race, gender, and religion, political opinion, and language, age and alien status.

However, their presentation of the considerable progress in prescribing equal protection rights is combined with the concession in 1980 that "the contemporary provisions for implementation and application of the vast body of transnational prescriptions designed to secure equality of women with men is even more primitive than that designed to minimize racial discrimination."

McDougal-Lasswell-Chen perspective to call attention to the contribution that international law based on the concept of equal protection has played and probably will continue to play in the development of the human right to employment. Equal protection and non-discrimination are among the most widely accepted and certainly among the most frequently prescribed human rights principles in the world today. Note the emphasis on opposition to discrimination in many U.N.-initiated human rights instruments of the past two decades and the somewhat special treatment given to racial discrimination complaints in U.N. human rights review processes.

Employment rights play a central role in international law aimed at discrimination, with legal efforts seeking to reach such basic aspects of that right as opportunity and remuneration. The employment rights of women have been given special attention by the ILO and European Community. Although no society has been cleansed of widespread employment discrimination based on gender, many European and North American women, at least, have obtained meaningful rights of access to training and non-traditional employment, as well as greater equality of pay and working conditions.

Many aliens in European Community states have been able to enjoy individual rights to job retention despite great pressures to resolve a major part of Europe's prolonged post 1973 economic crises at their expense. And international efforts have begun to focus on the employment rights of persons disabled by HIV and other diseases and injuries.

A second major area in which positive international law contributes to the right to employment is that of termination of employment in the face of arbitrary individual firings, large-scale plant closings, mergers, and dissolution of firms. Due process and other issues raised in these situations go to the heart of the job security dimension of the right to employment. Such catastrophic situations became increasingly serious public policy issues during the deep global recession of the early 1980s.

These pressures led to a plethora of proposed and enacted protective legislation at the local, national, and international levels. The force behind such legislation is the political view that, in times of shrinking employment opportunity, governments need to emphasize the avoidance of unnecessary job losses and the provision of appropriate re-training and other assistance for those affected by necessary economic adjustments.

With prodding from trade unions and other labor-oriented organizations various national governments and international organizations have cautiously but meaningfully challenged such basic concepts of managerial prerogative as "employment at will" during the past three decades. Steps have included ILO and OECD "codes of conduct" for multinational enterprises and the European Community directives on transfers of business units and "collective redundancies."

In 1982 the ILO completed its review of its 1963 recommendation on termination of employment and developed its first convention on individual and collective terminations. Several studies indicated that the 1963 recommendations stimulated related national legislation. The latter convention at least initially enjoyed substantial support from employers' organizations as well as from trade unions, and has had significant impacts even in states with relatively advanced approaches to such matters as notice, information, and consultation.

International acceptance of the ideas that workers have rights to their jobs, individually and collectively, largely depends on support for such an idea in various influential countries. Although the United States has acted strongly against numerous terminations resulting from discrimination, its national and state governments have been reluctant to develop protective legislation in relation to more typical individual dismissals or collective redundancies. This has reflected both the relative weakness of U.S. trade unions and their historical preference for employing collective bargaining to deal with such problems.

Even the United States has recently begun to approve various state and federal statutory proposals for protection of workers in the face of large-scale closings and mergers, stressing the concept of notice. Such measures, however, come decades after more comprehensive protective measures were adopted in various Western European states as well as in Canada.

More characteristic of the 1980s were modest roll-backs of such employment protection measures, these reflecting Thatcher-Reagan orientations to free enterprise. This is evident in the German Federal Republic's 1985 Employment Protection Law, which that country's trade unions charged "encroached on the established protection rights of employees." Martin Vranken noted in 1986 a distinct trend toward deregulation in the social domain in Western Europe, involving "government efforts to reform or even to abolish major parts of basic social legislation mold employment relationships."

Employment security in the industrialized world is being undercut both by the efforts of various national governments and intergovernmental organizations to promote "structural adjustment" globally and by the collapse of Marxist-Leninist regimes in Eastern Europe. The politics of the structural adjustment effort in such organizations as the OECD and International Monetary Fund in the 1980s, targeted at real as well as possibly dubious rigidities in labor markets, is traced in subsequent parts of this book.

In the Soviet Union and the East Central European countries, the sources of severe strains on employment security even before the political collapse of 1989-91 included unsustainable international debt and the loss of guaranteed markets for inferior industrial goods. After 1989 some new regimes have proceeded with radical economic restructuring marked by "shock" methods that accept very high levels of unemployment and prices as a necessary short- or intermediate-term price to be paid for eventual recovery.

A third area of relevant positive law development relates to formal national commitments to the right to employment. This includes national constitutional guarantees and statutes as well as the continuing efforts to prescribe and advocate the right to employment through intergovernmental organizations. The number and type of nation states that have declared a right to employment in their constitutions have increased, albeit only incrementally.

Nonetheless, it is probable that the strength of efforts to promulgate the right to work continues to decline at the national level. A very disappointing turning point occurred during the 1975-78 U.S. debate over the proposed Humphrey-Hawkins Full Employment Act. Various drafts of the bill proposed a right to a job and a general statement calling for employment opportunity for all. However, its history mirrored that of the 1946 Employment Act in fundamental ways, and the final statute fell far short of its sponsors' hopes despite strong testimony from such advocates as Leon Keyserling, Lester Thurow, Sar Levitan, and Eli Ginzberg.

The passage of a statute that lacked specific provisions for job creation was followed by the Reagan administration's replacement of the Comprehensive Employment and Training Act (CETA) with a far less ambitious approach to employment training and governmentally sponsored employment. The collapse of Marxist-Leninist regimes in Eastern and Central Europe has produced both a practical and ideological retreat from full employment and the right to employment. It was argued in Pravda in March 1988 that "Looking back at the false 'welfare' notions of social protections and full employment that prevailed in the period of stagnation and leveling, and that allowed a fair number of people to take life easy, will carry us backward to stagnation, shortages and hard times."

The efforts of the past several decades to continue to prescribe a right to work or employment through intergovernmental organizations are discussed. This effort has not progressed significantly beyond the statements in the

U.N. Covenants and may well have been effectively blunted by challenges made in the ILO arena in 1983-84. Nonetheless, the effort to codify in international legal and policy instruments such a right as well as the goal of full employment is quite likely to be revived in other times and circumstances given the history of persistent support for these causes.

Such developments reflect the various ways in which positive law addresses the employment rights agendas set by contemporary conditions and social forces. Such agendas are usually first dealt with experimentally and partially at the national level and then promoted at the international level in order to broaden and harmonize national trends. Necessary employment rights have been defined through political compromise and judicial edict. In some instances the system has helped to eliminate outrageous patterns of discrimination and arbitrary exercises of managerial prerogatives that are no longer generally accepted in most Western and certain other societies.

However, the greatest parts of such problems as discrimination, job insecurity, and mass unemployment are not being resolved through such international positive law prescriptions. Most intergovernmental formulations are marked by diplomatic vagueness and compromises that reflect the least common denominators of national law and international debates, even as critical employment rights issues are being addressed and some new flesh is being put on the previously skeletal right to work.

FRONTIER CONCEPTS

The assertion of natural rights and the development of numerous positive law protections have promoted recognition and respect for the right to employment. However, these developments alone have not been sufficient to create a consensus for the idea that the right of all men and women to employment is worthy of effective national and international protection.

Additional conceptual underpinning is clearly needed to convince a greater proportion of intellectual leaders, governmental and intergovernmental administrators, and politicians that a human right to employment is more than a luxury relevant only to rich industrialized states or a right that can appropriately be ignored when nations face serious economic problems. Such a right can obtain greater weight through association with emerging conceptions of human rights that complement natural and positive rights and affirm new perspectives on social and economic justice. Such concepts that have been linked in recent decades to the right to employment include distributive justice, basic needs, the right to development, and new interpretations of the values of human dignity and self-respect.

Louis Henkin has written of the fusion of democratic-libertarian and socialist conceptions during the formative post-1945 stage of the prescription of universal rights. Such a synthesis is already proceeding through another stage in an era in which the formulation of new concepts of international law and global reform are increasingly shaped by Third World advocates who recognize that unemployment and underemployment are among the most serious problems in developing as well as developed countries.

As expressed in the Declaration of Principles of the 1976 ILO-sponsored Tripartite World Conference on Employment, Income Distribution and Social Progress, "Unemployment, underemployment and marginality are a universal concern and affect at least one-third of humanity at the present time." This new emphasis on Third World unemployment has been reinforced by reports from the Brandt Commission on International Development Issues and other authoritative observers of the plight of developing countries.

Such perceptions have given considerable impetus to human rights theorists who emphasize basic needs. The 1976 ILO Employment Conference Declaration asserted, "In all countries, freely chosen employment enters into basic-needs policy both as a means and an end." Basic needs were elevated to a major category of human rights by numerous international resolutions and were even recognized authoritatively by the U.S. Carter administration. Its standing has also been strengthened by the philosophical defence of the human right to "subsistence" developed by American philosopher Henry Shue and others.

Before 1976 employment had generally not been included among the primary elements of the basic needs concept. Rather, the focus had been on such commodities and services needed for human physical survival as food, shelter, and health care. As such, the later inclusion of employment as a "basic need" involved broadening that concept, a step justified by the contribution made by employment to the obtaining of the means of subsistence as well as the direct role played by employment in human physical and psychological well-being.

The latter perspective seems increasingly justified in the light of growing evidence that unemployment contributes significantly to levels of physical and mental illness and disability even in societies that provide substantial income maintenance. The International Labor Office has built its position regarding employment and basic needs on the connection between employment and poverty, stressing that hundreds of millions of unemployed or underemployed in the developing world constitute a very large part of the global poverty problem.

The right to employment has also been linked in the past decade to an emerging right to development. It has been difficult to sell the idea of a right to development in the First World, in part because such a claimed right has been hard to define, has tended to be viewed as the right of nations rather than one enjoyed by individuals, and has few explicit links to various formulations of human rights adopted between 1945 and 1966.

Yet such criticisms offered by certain Western scholars have not deterred the linkage of employment rights to the right to development in major international instruments and statements. This has been most consistently evident in positions developed under ILO and U.N. auspices. The Declaration on the Right to Development adopted by the U.N. General Assembly in December 1986, the most authoritative statement of the right to development thus far, links it to socioeconomic rights in general and to equal employment opportunity in particular.

It cannot, however, be clearly demonstrated that employment and other socioeconomic rights have been assisted by the recent contentious debates on the right to development. The primary thrust of the Third World effort to promote a right to development has been to broaden the human rights agenda to include "third generation" issues ranging from disarmament to the creation of a new international economic order.

References to greater responsibility of developing states to their own destitute and unemployed people are sometimes placed in such documents as a tradeoff for language asserting the need for greater responsibility of leading industrial countries for the welfare of Third World peoples. The right to development debate emerged from efforts to explore and promote the realization of economic, social, and cultural rights in the developing countries. Some important new directions for human rights and policy have emerged from this debate, including a stress on broader public participation in national decision-making regarding development. Yet efforts to connect the right to development explicitly to socioeconomic as well as to civil political rights have yet to achieve a clear international consensus.

The 1976 ILO Declaration noted above also suggested that unemployment offends human dignity, a concept that has taken on new meaning in association with human rights scholarship concerning such values as self-respect, wealth, and skill. Many studies have stressed the great importance of work to the psychological well-being of individuals. The central role played by work and its variations (labor, callings, workmanship) in expressing ourselves as humans has been articulated by writers from Marx to Arendt.

Other significant frontier efforts to bolster the legitimacy of the right to employment have been greatly influenced by John Rawls's A Theory of Justice, a work that emphasizes the value of self-respect and the provision of at least minimum standards while placing primary emphasis on the value of liberty while Shue and others find Rawls's perspective inadequate as a framework for a general entitlement to socioeconomic rights. Nickel utilizes Rawls's core proposition to help bolster the right to employment by arguing:

> The justification for a universal right to employment would lie, in this view, in the fact that because of class interests and various group prejudices any non-universal distribution of employment opportunities will be unfair to the disadvantaged classes and minorities. Hence the only fair distribution available is one that guarantees each person a job.

Nickel also stresses the Rawlsian conception of the centrality of dignity and self-respect in his effort to promote a right to employment. An even broader Rawlsian case is made by Charles R. Beitz, who explicitly cites the Rawlsian social justice model and recalls the social justice arguments for socioeconomic rights proposed in 1945 by the Inter American Judicial Committee.

The development of frontier concepts and the reinterpretation of some older perspectives may have marginally broadened the base of support for a human right to employment. Employment has been a central issue in the discourse on global distributive justice and a New International Economic Order. The integration of employment with conceptions of basic needs and development represents a potentially important development.

The present section reviewed the development of new sources of the right to employment by contemporary intellectuals, policy-makers, and diplomats. It was suggested that this right has been given greater breadth by subsuming into it such issues as employment security, basic needs, and equal opportunity, and that such efforts may have enhanced its legitimacy. Yet from the perspective of the early 1990s the future of the right to employment seems highly problematical due to ideological, geopolitical, and economic developments that have blunted efforts to establish this right more firmly at the national and international levels. The concept of a right to work has remained highly controversial and difficult to formulate.

THE 1984 ILO EMPLOYMENT POLICY RECOMMENDATIONS: A CASE STUDY

In the quarter century since the adoption of the 1964 ILO Employment Policy Convention and Recommendation, many countries made formal commitments to full employment goals and instituted various unprecedented national programs designed to promote employment and develop human resources. Further, a growing international commitment to the concept of a right to work could be inferred from such steps as the ratification of the International Covenant on Economic, Social and Cultural Rights and the explicit references to that right in various U.N. General Assembly resolutions.

These steps pointed toward a breakthrough in ILO acceptance of the right to work in a new convention or recommendation on employment policy scheduled for adoption in 1984. However, various political factors determined that such an instrument would include only a formalistic acceptance of the right to work. The pattern of steeply rising unemployment in developed and developing countries alike in the decade following the 1973-74 oil crisis sharply increased concern about the issue.

Yet these developments also made the goals associated with full employment and the right to work seems more elusive than ever. Further, growing inflation, concerns about unstable export markets, and other economic concerns led many countries to target their macro - and microeconomic policies on other objectives. Several forces and trends undercutting international and national commitments to the right to work are discussed below.

THE FOCUS OF THIRD WORLD SUPPORT

While evidence could be assembled to demonstrate both growing support and loss of momentum for the right to work in the 1980s, debate in the ILO primarily reflected the limited nature of the gains made to that point. The search for new linkages connecting this right to basic needs and a New International Economic Order did bolster Third World support somewhat in the 1970s.

Yet these themes faded in the 1980s, replaced by efforts to secure more immediate and practical concessions from the industrialized countries in such areas as debt relief and trade preferences. Third World support for a right to development and the New International Economic Order emphasized the shifting of responsibility for economic development from developing to industrialized states. One result was to reduce the possibility of any ILO convention or recommendation that would stress additional obligations of Third World governments to their own unemployed.

Further, the governments of various Western industrialized states became demonstrably hostile to new international prescriptions of the right to work during the 1980s. This opposition derived from several sources. One was their declining confidence in the capability of Keynesian or other macroeconomic policies to return advanced economies to the favorable unemployment rates of the 1960s without contributing to unacceptably negative impacts on inflation and other critical national economic outcomes. In the 1940s and 1950s powerful elements in many Western states came to accept full employment as a feasible national objective and a paramount national priority.

Support for the right to employment and full employment in Western industrialized countries grew out of favorable economic conditions, the perceived potency of Keynesian demand-management and other economic policies, and ideological attachments to full employment as a basic goal of the welfare state.

These preconditions of full employment policies faded or were shattered in the wake of the oil shocks and stagflation of the 1970s. In the face of such forces, major international organizations (including the European Community, the International Monetary Fund, and the OECD) and the most influential Western governments increasingly supported deflationary economic policies, especially tighter monetary policies, that were virtually certain to increase rather than decrease unemployment in the short and medium term.

Such goals as stable currencies, control of inflation, and the repayment of international debt acquired vastly greater weight relative to full employment in an environment that appeared to force choices and trade-offs. Further, no single economic medicine or known combination of prescriptions offered real hope to large numbers of developing and developed states affected by economic upheavals.

Although a wide variety of economic policy packages were formulated and implemented in the early and mid-1980s, international pressures often mandated relatively tight monetary policies and the slowing of the rate of government expenditure increases. Periodic OECD and European Community calls for marginally more expansionary economic policies for the majority of their member states often met with limited national responses due to continuing concerns about inflation and pressures on national currencies. Even greater pressures to create austerity affected much of the developing world and Eastern Europe as structural adjustment became a condition for new loans and debt rescheduling for countries ranging from Poland to Brazil.

By the early 1980s an increasing majority of informed observers concluded that even a strong and widespread economic recovery would not recreate labor market conditions approaching full employment. Even many European trade union leaders increasingly shifted emphasis from the promotion of expansionary macroeconomic policies that could create new jobs to the protection of the jobs of those still employed.

GLOBAL POLITICS

From 1948 to 1966 the ebbs and flows of East-West and North-South conflicts did much to shape intergovernmental prescriptions of the right to employment. One of the worst of those ebbs came between 1979 and 1984, precisely the time that the ILO formulated and adopted updated policies on employment. The negative consequences of that political environment on the ILO consideration of what became the

Employment Policy (Supplementary Provisions) Recommendation of 1984 is reviewed below in order to indicate aspects of continuity over a forty year period and to provide a baseline for review of potential changes in the subsequent era of perestroika and post-Cold War politics.

The political environment for the ILO deliberations included the causes and effects of the U.S. government's departure from that organization in 1977 and its return in 1980. This extraordinary action was part of a concerted effort on the part of the United States and some of its allies to pressure certain member states of various intergovernmental organizations to be less defiant of Western political interests. It was followed in the Reagan years by U.S. withdrawal from UNESCO and the withholding of dues owed to the United Nations and other organizations. These policies responded to the perceived politicization of such organizations by Third World and Communist-ruled states, particularly the positions taken by them on such issues as Israeli-Palestinian relations.

In retrospect the assertive position taken in the 1983-84 ILO debate by the Soviet Union and most of its close allies and clients was a poorly chosen strategy. States facing decline and imminent crisis proceeded on the basis of ideological reflex that still seemed appropriate to their leaders in the years before perestroika and New Thinking, and their principal Western adversaries were more than pleased to reply in kind.

ORGANIZATIONAL AND BUREAUCRATIC POLITICS

The formulation between 1979 and 1984 of a new ILO policy instrument on employment policy revealed the balance of forces regarding the prescription of the right to work that existed just prior to the Gorbachev era. That this right would be a major issue in the debates and votes concerning a new ILO convention or recommendation on employment was assured by the attention given the concept by the 1979 Session of the International Labor Conference. Subsequently, the Soviet Union and its allies decided to make the prominent treatment of this concept in a new ILO convention a principal political objective. Other ILO participants, particularly certain Western governments, formulated contrasting objectives involving more limited or alternative formulations of the right to work. They also opposed altogether any new legally binding convention on employment, especially one that advocated a right to employment.

The ensuing deliberations took place within the unique tripartite structure of the ILO, involving voting participation by representatives of employers and workers as well as governments. With a global approach to membership, the organization developed by the 1960s a built-in Third World majority, at least when these countries were not sharply divided. However, the cross-cutting impacts of the employers' and workers' caucuses complicated the maintenance of government based coalitions.

It is also pertinent that the ILO was created and has been maintained as an organization concentrating on social policy, with its primary constituents in national governments being Labor, Employment, and Social ministries. Even affiliated employers' organizations generally understand and often accept most ILO social priorities and usually avoid stating positions based wholly on cold economic calculations or laissez faire ideology. It is assumed by most observers that the International Labor Office, the ILO's secretariat, will actively promote actions by national governments that advance the interests of workers at the expense of some employers. In this sense the Office resembles a progressive International Labor Ministry.

The Office developed an initial draft of an Employment Policy instrument in response to the replies of member states to a questionnaire. One is impressed with the considerable leeway left to the Office at various stages of policy development. Meetings with various Office officials and reviews of its published materials suggest to me that ILO adoption of the right to work concept was never an Office priority. This is consistent with the general Office preference for what it considers to be tangible and achievable objectives rather than what one prominent official referred to as "big statements."

The Office's important introductory report on law and practice emphasized that interest in the right to work in the ILO arena was late to emerge and that only a minority of member states recognized the right in their constitutions. However, the Office also recognized that the degree of emphasis to be placed on this concept would be a political decision that it could influence but not control.

As to the appropriate meaning of the concept, both the Office and the ILO's Committee of Experts on the Application of Conventions and Recommendations consistently viewed it as excluding guaranteed employment. They considered it to involve such ingredients of international labor standards as active labor market policy, rejection of forced labor, non-discrimination, and protection against arbitrary termination of employment. This perspective was consistent with the incremental development of organizational ideology that included only a few areas of human rights as "fundamental human rights."

The Office was reluctant to accept the positive obligation of governments to develop policies and programs to maximize employment as the basis of a fundamental human right equivalent to non-discrimination, freedom of association, and the absence of forced labor. However, the right to work concept was viewed as useful for tying together seemingly separate ILO priorities and for increasing acceptance of government programs designed to promote full employment.

Although the ILO's provisional resolution of the right to work issue in 1983 was greatly influenced by the Office and by the views of government and employers' representatives, it was largely decided by the representatives of non-Communist trade unions. The immediate questions at issue included:

1. Would endorsement of the right to work be limited to a reference to the existence of the relevant article in the International Covenant on Economic, Social and Cultural

Rights, or would the concept be endorsed independently in an ILO instrument?

2. Would the ILO support an interpretation of the concept different from that in the Covenant, particularly in regard to guaranteed employment?
3. Would reference to this right be restricted to the new instrument's preamble, or would it also appear in the main body of the text?
4. Would the concept be incorporated into a convention or in a less-binding recommendation?

The objectives of the U.S. government regarding such right to work issues reflected the deepening of the chasm between East and West in the wake of strained international developments and the highly ideological and often confrontational approach of the Reagan administration in its first term. Some of its views were echoed by the Thatcher administration as well as by certain other Western governments.

The strong Reagan administration counter-attack to the Soviet initiative on the right to work was intensified by the strong input of business-oriented and highly ideological Department of Commerce officials. A position paper on employment policy prepared by Commerce for the U.S. delegation (USDEL) to the 1983 ILO Conference dealt with most of the issues introduced by the International Labor Office that had survived the initial member state questionnaire. That paper presented the right to work as a vehicle for Communist propaganda and as a Communist euphemism for denial of "such basic human rights as freedom to choose their jobs or career paths, to participate in the determination of their wages, or to emigrate."

The idea of a governmental guarantee of employment was challenged directly, the concept deemed "dangerous because the only way it can be implemented is by restricting imports and/or artificially depressing wages, thereby exporting unemployment to other nations." As such, older human rights complaints are joined with some economic arguments that I had not encountered earlier in the right to work saga.

The major goals of the U.S. delegation regarding the right to work were set as follows:

USDEL [the U.S. delegation] may support reference to the 1966 International Covenant on Economic, Social and Cultural Rights (Article 6), but should propose that the "right to work" be elaborated in either: (a) its positive form (e.g., policies that maximize individual opportunities to find freely chosen and productive work); or (b) that it be qualified to express what it does not mean (e.g., that an individual is obliged to work at a specified job which he has not chosen and for wages which are determined without his consent). USDEL should support amendments to delegate this provision if the suggested changes noted above are rejected.

In June 1983 a tripartite ILO Committee on Employment considered a draft document that included numerous issues that had become more salient in the years after the 1964 Employment Policy Convention and Recommendation. These included the relationships of employment to policy developments in the areas of population, technology, regional development, international economic cooperation, and migration. The debate also provided opportunities to raise issues that many, especially Western representatives, considered to be more appropriate for other instruments or for other organizations, these topics including disarmament and multinational investment.

At the 1983 ILO Conference the Workers' Group tentatively supported (subject to review in 1984) a supplementary recommendation in preference to a convention and also endorsed major limitations on references to the right to work in that recommendation. As a result, the Communist-ruled states were largely isolated in their efforts to have the Committee endorse their conception of that right and expand upon the language in the International Covenant on Economic, Social and Cultural Rights. The Employment Committee endorsed the idea that "The promotion of full, productive and freely chosen employment provided for in the Employment Policy Convention and Recommendation, 1964, should be regarded as the means of achieving in practice the realization of the right to work." This formulation, endorsed years earlier by various ILO organs, seemed designed to credit the previous work of the ILO without breaking new conceptual ground or acceding to the political agenda of the Soviet Union and its supporters.

Some of the major choices made during the struggle over the International Covenant's article on the right to work were revisited in the 1983-84 ILO arenas. A proposed mandate that the "full recognition by member states of the right to work" be included in domestic legislation was defeated handily despite Workers' Group support. Proposed Socialist state amendments relating the right to work to other social values (e.g., human dignity, the development of the personality, and social justice) were also rejected, often by crushing margins. Despite the continued stress by Communist representatives on the concept of a state guarantee of employment, this proposition had no chance of acceptance.

The Soviet delegation had to take solace from the references to the right to work included in an accompanying ILO resolution concerning employment. This less-binding action of the 1983 Conference affirmed "the leading role that the ILO should play within the United Nations system in the promotion of that right," and closely linked the right to work theme to the ILO's evolving World Employment Program.

Despite efforts by the Soviet and like-minded delegations to reverse the major decisions taken in 1983, the 1984 Conference incorporated the right to work in the Employment Policy (Supplementary Provisions) Recommendation essentially along the lines decided the previous year. Although it could be argued that the right was kept alive by the 1984 Recommendation's references to the International Covenant and by the 1983 Resolution, it would be more accurate to view the process as one of diminution of support for this right, both as a symbolic objective and as an element of a strategy for promoting full employment. Major Third World governments and Western trade union representatives again turned down numerous proposals advanced by the Soviet Union and its allies to further develop a rights approach to employment.

Conclusions about the ILO and U.N. formulations of the right to work must be stated cautiously. Socioeconomic context, organizational processes, intellectual thought, and global political relations contributed to the outcomes in each case. As compared to the earlier United Nations considerations, the role of intellectual thought was somewhat smaller in the later ILO forum and the contribution of political considerations manifestly greater. The ILO proceedings were so highly politicized partly because ILO prescriptions often directly affect the allocation of staff time and other organizational resources. Further, tripartite politics is often more complex than policy-making that is more completely controlled by government representatives.

It remains to be seen whether the 1979-84 ILO process represents turning away from a human rights approach to the horrendous problems of unemployment and underemployment in the long-term. In the ILO debate it seemed evident that larger ideological and organizational considerations dominated. The strongly ideological Reagan and Thatcher administration representatives had persuaded a sufficient number of governmental and non-governmental representatives to perceive the right to work as an ideological issue of the renewed Cold War and to vote accordingly. In the wake of the U.S. withdrawal and return to the ILO, these Western governments marshaled increased political weight in such matters.

The processes through which the right to work or employment has been incorporated into significant international legal instruments and the factors that have determined the nature of those formulations were analyzed in this chapter. As these developments involved the history of ideas, socioeconomic trends, international politics, and organizational processes, the conclusions cannot be tidy ones.

Major divisions persist among scholars, trade unionists, and officials of national governments and international organizations concerning the legitimacy and utility of a human right to work. Only a limited consensus has emerged concerning the philosophical and legal sources of such a right.

Despite the mostly negative positions taken by ILO delegates in 1984, the process of prescribing a right to work, formulating its meaning, and associating it with tangible international and domestic programs continues. The most influential historical experiences that advanced this right in the present century were the Great Depression and World War II. Additional support has come from the growing recognition of the seriousness of recent mass unemployment and underemployment in Europe and the Third World.

As a result, the right to work has repeatedly been placed on the agenda of international organizations. Although the endorsement of this right in some form by such organizations has rarely been in doubt, the form of the endorsement and the definition of the right have invited debate and struggle. In the 1940s and 1950s there was little or no scholarly consensus and minimal official interest in providing a comprehensive justification for a right to work. However, broad agreement existed then concerning the desirability and feasibility of full employment even as proponents differed about the means to achieve that goal. The right to work seems to have thrived on a sense of the achievability of full employment, at least in industrialized countries, and to have faltered when full employment again appeared to be a distant or impossible dream after 1973.

It is not certain whether academic and political supporters of the right to work will seek to further legitimize this concept through future international instruments. Scholars from various regions and political orientations continue to reinforce as well as challenge efforts to associate the right to work with such perspectives as basic needs and the right to development. The goal of full employment has lost ground even as an element of Marxism-Leninism while it has gained from wide-ranging critiques of internationally supported austerity measures in Eastern Europe and the developing world.

Efforts to advance a positive definition of the right to work have been marked by the defeat of a guaranteed employment focus, except perhaps in relation to youth programs. However, the foundation of a meaningful right to work has been partially built on the elements of equal opportunity, free movement of labor, attention to job security, and commitments to active labor market policies. A right to work must be built on a foundation of principles, goals, and rules. The principles include equal opportunity, free choice, and state and international responsibility. The stated goals relate to full employment and the achievement of a decent standard of living for all. The rules can be explicit, at least in regard to equality of treatment and limited aspects of employment security, and should also mandate that no state may consciously disregard responsibility to maintain high rates of productive employment as a principal policy objective.

The power of the idea of human rights elevates such principles, goals, and rules even in the absence of effective sanctions or compliance mechanisms. Indeed, it is not the weaknesses regarding sanctions or compliance that most clearly separates the international protection of the right to work from that for certain precious political and civil rights. Rather, it is the lack of consensus about the nature of state responsibilities and the appropriate tradeoffs with other socioeconomic objectives that makes the right to work exceptionally problematical even as a goal. This became increasingly clear when the international community sought to implement certain of its elements during the past forty years.

Bibliography

Alfred M. de Zayas, *The Follow-Up Procedure of the UN Human Rights Committee,* 1991 *Int'l. Commission Jurists Rev.* 28 (1991).

Amnesty International USA, *The Universal Declaration of Human Rights, 1948-1988: Human Rights,* The United Nations, and Amnesty International, New York: Amnesty International USA, 1988.

Ann Marie Clark, *Strong Principles, Strengthening Practices: Amnesty International and Three Cases of Change in International Human Rights Standards,* 1995 (unpublished Ph.D. thesis, University of Minnesota).

Asbjorn Eide, *Pocket Guide to the Development of Human Rights Institutions and Mechanisms,* Strasbourg: Council of Europe, 1989.

Conference on Security and Cooperation in Europe: An Overview of the CSCE Process, Recent Meetings and Institutional Development, Washington, D.C.: Commission on Security and Cooperation in Europe, 1992.

Diana Vincent-Daviss, *Human Rights Law: A Research Guide to the Literature—Part I: International Law and the United Nations,* 14 N.Y.U.J. *Int'l L. & Pol.* 209-319 (1981).

Diana Vincent-Daviss, *Human Rights Law: A Research Guide to the Literature—Part II: International Protection of Refugees and Humanitarian Law,* 14 N.Y.U.J. *Int'l L. & Pol.* 487-573 (1982).

Dominic McGoldrick, *The Human Rights Committee,* Oxford: Clarendon; New York: Oxford University Press, 1991.

Economic, Social, and Cultural Rights: A Textbook, Dordrecht; Boston: Martinus Nijhoff Pub., 1995.

Glenn A. Mower, *International Cooperation for Social Justice: Global and Regional Protection of Economic/Social Rights*, Westport, Conn: Greenwood Pr., 1985.

Gregory J. Walters, Human Rights in Theory and Practice: A Selected and Annotated Bibliography, Metuchen, NJ: The Scarecrow Press, 1995.

Ian Martin, *The New World Order: Opportunity or Threat for Human Rights*, Cambridge, MA: Harvard Law School Human Rights Program, 1993.

Jack Tobin and Jennifer Green, *Guide to Human Rights Research*, Cambridge, MA: Human Rights Program, Harvard Law School, 1994.

Louis B. Sohn, *The Human Rights Movement: From Roosevelt's Four Freedoms to the interdependence of Peace, Development and Human Rights*, Cambridge, MA: Harvard Law School Human Rights Program, 1995.

Matthew C.R. Craven, *The International Covenant on Economic, Social, and Cultural Rights: A Perspective on its Development*, Oxford: Clarendon Press; NY: Oxford University Press, 1995.

Nadine Strossen, *United States Ratification of the International Bill of Rights: A Fitting Celebration of the Bicentennial of the U.S. Bill of Rights*, 24 U. *Tol. L. Rev.* 203 (1992).

Philip Alston, *Making and Breaking Human Rights: the UN's Specialized Agencies and Implementation of the International Covenant on Economic, Social and Cultural Rights*, London: Anti-Slavery Society; La Crosse, Wis: National Association of Interdisciplinary Ethnic Studies, (1979).

Rosalyn Higgins, *Admissibility Under the Optional Protocol to the International Covenant on Civil and Political Rights*, 1991 *Can. Hum. Rts. Y.B.* 57 (1991).

Scott Davidson, *The Inter-American Court of Human Rights*, Aldershot, England; Brookfield, VT: Dartmouth Pub. Co. Ltd., 1992.

Scott Leckie, *Towards an International Convention on Housing Rights: Options at Habitat II*, Washington, DC: American Society of International Law, 1994.

Scott Leckie, *When Push Comes to Shove: Forced Evictions and Human Rights*, Mexico; Utrecht, Netherlands: Habitat International Coalition, 1995.

Thomas Buergenthal & Harold G. Maier, *Public International Law in a Nutshell*, St. Paul, MN: West Publishing Co., 1990.

Thomas Buergenthal, *International Human Rights in a Nutshell*, St. Paul, MN: West Publishing Co., 1995.

Thomas D. Young, *International Human Rights: A Selected Bibliography*, Los Angeles, CA: Center for the Study of Armament & Disarmament, California State University Los Angeles, 1978.

Torkel Opsahl, *The Coexistence Between Geneva and Strasbourg Inter-Relationship of the International Covenant on Civil and Political Rights and the European Convention on Human Rights and Their Respective Organs of Implementation*, 1991 *Can. Hum. Rts. Y.B.* 151 (1991).

Ved P. Nanda, *The United States Reservation to the Ban on the Death Penalty for Juvenile Offenders: An Appraisal Under the International Covenant on Civil and Political Rights* (Symposium: The Ratification of the International Covenant on Civil and Political Rights), 42 DePaul L. Rev. 1311 (1993).

Walter S. Tarnolpolsky, *The Canadian Experience with the International Covenant on Civil and Political Rights Seen from the Perspective of a Former Member of the Human Rights Committee*, 20 *Akron L. Rev.* 611 (1987).

Index

Index

S

T

U

W